THE ARCHAEOLOGY OF AMERICAN MINING

The American Experience in Archaeological Perspective

UNIVERSITY PRESS OF FLORIDA

Florida A&M University, Tallahassee
Florida Atlantic University, Boca Raton
Florida Gulf Coast University, Ft. Myers
Florida International University, Miami
Florida State University, Tallahassee
New College of Florida, Sarasota
University of Central Florida, Orlando
University of Florida, Gainesville
University of North Florida, Jacksonville
University of South Florida, Tampa
University of West Florida, Pensacola

THE ARCHAEOLOGY

OF

AMERICAN MINING

PAUL J. WHITE

Foreword by Michael S. Nassaney

University Press of Florida
Gainesville · Tallahassee · Tampa · Boca Raton
Pensacola · Orlando · Miami · Jacksonville · Ft. Myers · Sarasota

This book may be available in an electronic edition.

22 21 20 19 18 17   6 5 4 3 2 1

Library of Congress Cataloging-in-Publication Data
Names: White, Paul J., author. | Nassaney, Michael S., author of foreword.
Title: The archaeology of American mining / Paul J. White ; foreword by
    Michael S. Nassaney.
Other titles: American experience in archaeological perspective.
Description: Gainesville : University Press of Florida, 2017. | Series: The
    American experience in archaeological perspective | Includes
    bibliographical references and index.
Identifiers: LCCN 2017016664 | ISBN 9780813054551 (cloth)
Subjects: LCSH: Mines and mineral resources—United States—History. |
    Mineral industries—United States—History.
Classification: LCC TN23 .W55 2017 | DDC 622.0973/09009—dc23
LC record available at https://lccn.loc.gov/2017016664

The University Press of Florida is the scholarly publishing agency for the State University System
of Florida, comprising Florida A&M University, Florida Atlantic University, Florida Gulf Coast
University, Florida International University, Florida State University, New College of Florida,
University of Central Florida, University of Florida, University of North Florida, University of
South Florida, and University of West Florida.

University Press of Florida
15 Northwest 15th Street
Gainesville, FL 32611-2079
http://upress.ufl.edu

To Pat, Pat, and Pat
(Martin, Malone, and Rubertone)

CONTENTS

FIGURES

FOREWORD

As young adolescents exploring the boundaries of our universe on warm summer days, my friends and I would ride our bikes to a distant swimming hole formed by the abandonment of a quarry pit in the village of Lime Rock in northern Rhode Island. Watching older boys jump off the cliffs into deep, dark waters, I heeded my mother's admonitions against swimming in such restricted and unmonitored areas. Proof of their danger was an occasional report of drowned or missing persons who could not resist the lure of this foreboding place. The bright, white dolomitic marble that surrounded this old pit had attracted English settlers to this source as early as the 1660s to procure materials to produce mortar, plaster, and stone blocks for stone-enders—a distinctive Rhode Island architectural form. The Conklin Limestone Company stopped working their last quarry there in 2004, thus ending over three centuries of operation.

People of all backgrounds have extracted useful raw materials from the ground in North America for as long as the continent has been occupied, arguably conducting one of the most basic human activities that contributed to the formation of the archaeological record. While the limestone quarries were daunting to me in my youth, traces of mining activities elsewhere are subtler and much more sublime. Less than ten miles south of Lime Rock is an equally unusual and important geological formation that Native Americans discovered over three thousand years ago. In the 1940s archaeologists identified and documented evidence for the production of stone bowls at the Oaklawn Quarry in Cranston, part of a talc belt that extends across the Northeast. Amid the outcrops at the Ochee Springs Quarry in nearby Johnston lie numerous abandoned incomplete bowls resembling mushroom caps still perched on steatite stems, suggesting that the early stage in the production process involved pecking to shape the exterior-inverted form before it was undercut and snapped at the base. The blanks were then hollowed out with smaller tools. Most evidence of these aborted bowls was obliterated by later twentieth-century developments.

Of course, modern mining activities—those associated with labor formations and technologies that derive from professional, mechanized, capital-intensive, and scientific procedures—have left and continue to leave transcendent traces that bear testimony to their scope and extent. As miners depleted high-grade ores and deposits, they were forced to move on to materials in lower concentrations necessitating massive movement of earth and the production of increasingly larger quantities of spoil. Witness the Berkeley Pit, a former open-pit copper mine in Butte, Montana, which measures a mile long by half a mile wide and approximately 1,780 feet (540 meters) deep. Water that has seeped into the mine is laden with toxic chemicals, though this does not dissuade tourists from paying to view this monstrosity from an access platform. While tourists are voluntary visitors, often people of low socioeconomic status are permanently relegated to degraded environments caused by mining and other industrial processes as victims of environmental racism.

Mining has invariably left an imprint on the American landscape—one that is amenable to archaeological analysis. In *The Archaeology of American Mining*, Paul White surveys the extant literature on the history of mining in America, how archaeologists have turned their attention to its study, and the lessons that emerge from a close examination of the prospecting, development, and extraction of the material legacy that miners produced.

Mining is a long-standing and ubiquitous if somewhat controversial practice intricately chiseled into the American experience. Archaeology can help to expose the range of mining activities that occurred over the past four centuries (and earlier) in every nook and cranny where successful prospecting impacted the landscape, as well as to challenge our stereotypes about mining. While mining looms large in the enduring mythology of the American western frontier, it was by no means confined to the gold rush era. Americans extracted a broad array of subterranean minerals and resources leading to a variety of responses from the miners themselves and the people who were dispossessed and displaced in this exploitative process.

In an effort to evaluate the place of mining archaeology in contemporary thinking and its future, White examines the ways in which the materiality of this legacy has changed since the colonial era. Because miners left few records (and those that did were prone to concealment or exaggeration), an archaeological approach invites us to engage with the detritus of daily life by exposing the worlds miners built and the materials they abandoned, lost, and discarded in their working and living spaces at multiple scales of analysis. White's summation contributes to an important body of historical archaeological scholarship and provides a critical synthesis of the extant literature pertaining to the history of mining and its potential for challenging unfounded beliefs about this massive industry that many take for granted. He shows that historical archaeologists have investigated sites of American mining for nearly a century, while an increase in the number of mining-related theses and dissertations demonstrates a recent rise in interest.

White discusses mining at three historical moments to highlight colonial efforts (1600s), the gold rush era of the nineteenth century, and the mechanized industry beginning in the 1950s. His overview demonstrates that mining has required greater economies of scale with varying consequences including environmental degradation (such as deforestation), increased occupational hazards (such as black lung among coal miners), air and water pollution, the creation of multinational corporations in search of offshore resources, and the formation of labor unions seeking to redress low wages, long hours, and unsafe working conditions.

Despite general trends observable in the mining industry, archaeology can reveal variability in local practice indicative of the ways people experience mining in their everyday lives. While early studies focused on technological aspects of mining, more-recent work aims to disclose the social and political-economic aspects of the industry, including the role of mining in global capitalism, consumer culture, and frontier processes. Miners negotiated their identities in complex dynamic relationships with miners different from themselves and capitalists whose aim was to realize a profit. The outcome was a contestation between managerial ideals (for example, corporate paternalism) and worker autonomy expressed materially in the structure of settlements, access to consumer goods, dietary practices, health care, technological innovation, and the ethnic-, gender-, and class-based associations that formed in and outside of the workplace. Archaeology demonstrates that distant goods and fashionable styles were quickly adopted in mining communities. Miners self-medicated to ward off disease and infection attendant to harsh work conditions, poor hygiene, and inadequate sanitation. And foreign-born workers of different ethnicities (particularly the Chinese) along with Native Americans were segregated and pitted against each other to ensure low wages and labor deskilling.

Yet miners were not passive victims; evidence of their responses can be gleaned from the material remains of everyday life, despite the implementation of standardized practices that were adopted in the early twentieth century in tandem with the American system of manufacture to reduce dependence on labor. White reminds us that trade manuals promoted the latest technological developments, but some technologies persisted long after many considered them outmoded. The archaeology of mining sheds light on the actual variations in application and reveals creative strategies, ingenuity, pragmatism, and improvisation that miners used to keep equipment in working order to get the job done. In short, archaeology reveals the dichotomy between the real and the ideal.

These insights into our mining past evoke very different sorts of legacies than the messages perpetuated in re-created mining towns, theme parks, monuments, and other places where mining is commemorated. Archaeology challenges us to consider how legacies have been mythologized and the ways in which representations are politically charged. White rightly notes that archaeology can counter dominant narratives, expose the hidden histories of the oppressed, and redress social injustices, even as we ask why we might want to preserve places of such abomination. He reminds us that archaeologists are, after all, in the memory business and archaeology has made substantive inroads into assessing the material legacies of mining. We would be remiss if we were to ignore the giant piles of tailings, abandoned mine shafts, broken machinery, and rusty tin cans that litter and define the mining landscape, insofar as they represent important building blocks in the foundations of the American experience.

Michael S. Nassaney
Series Editor

PREFACE

The first mining site that I worked on as an archaeologist drove home just how little I knew. I was a graduate student at the time and still learning the literal and figurative nuts and bolts about how to document the industrial past. While I had gained some familiarity with the range of written sources available, the immediate concern was that I needed in short order to make sense of a sprawling mine complex that included not only bunkhouses and a multistory processing mill edging onto a glacial moraine but also, 4,000 feet farther up, four distinct mines connected to the mill by wagon roads and aerial tramways. It was an expansive site, and one liberally scattered with artifacts ranging from discarded bottles and tobacco tins to items with names that I could not specify and functions to puzzle over. I desired to know what I was looking at and *how* to look at it. I wanted to learn more about how to connect the discarded items before me with the experiences of those who had labored in this setting and sought to make a go of it. I was struck also by the incongruity of intensive activity in this remote spot. One thing without question was that I had been hooked.

As I reflect now upon this early experience, the specific site seems less significant than the realization that all mining sites present a combination of challenge, intrigue, and opportunity for archaeological inquiry. This book sets out to make this case, and it does so by drawing together a range of archaeological findings that have accumulated over several decades and by positing directions in which archaeologists have yet to explore. The most fundamental contention, however, and the governing impetus for writing this book, is that attention to the material evidence of mining offers new and needed insights into an industry that is intimately connected to the American experience. At times, these can be very personal histories, for the material record commonly refocuses our attention to the scale of lived experiences. Artifacts can allow us greater insight into who the American miner historically was, as well as the cultural value systems influencing arrangements of workplaces and domestic spaces. We also acquire new perspectives into themes with continuing resonance in the present, including conflicts between capital and labor, legal battles over land and resource rights, and environmental costs. Archaeological analyses underscore ways that grand narratives connect to even the most isolated of mining places, and they also provide a means for subjecting our historical understandings of this industry to closer inspection. This book takes stock of archaeological findings to the present, with an eye to encouraging continuing engagement.

Any synthesis owes a significant debt to prior labors, and it has been a privilege to comb through the works of so many dedicated professionals. Thanks first to the steadfast efforts of interlibrary loan staff at both Michigan Technological University and the University of Alaska Anchorage for working through hundreds of requests, and to John Foster, Karl Gurcke, Heather Hall, Ron James, Patrick Martin, and Aaron Woods for assistance in tracking down hard-to-find reports and manuscripts. The scope of this book changed over time, and I benefited early from conversations with Patrick Martin, Bode Morin, Erik Nordberg, and Scott See. Susan Martin, with her matchless combination of encouragement and acumen, pointed to areas in need of greater coverage. My colleagues Margan Grover and Ryan Harrod listened patiently as I worried over various sections, and I am grateful to Don Hardesty, Logan Hovis, Ron James, Patrick Martin, Robin Mills, Michael Nassaney, and an anonymous reviewer for their constructive critique of manuscript drafts. Thanks to Michael Nassaney and Meredith Babb for their assistance throughout and to Marthe Walters and Sally Boyington for helping the manuscript through its final stages.

I dedicate this book to three people who have shaped my interests in historical archaeology in pivotal ways. Patrick Martin has long championed the value of fieldwork, and his enthusiasm and curiosity for what can be learned from the detritus of industrial sites set a gold standard. Patrick Malone's dedication to—and adeptness at—integrating written sources with the material evidence of industry is likewise a wonderful reminder of the benefit and necessity of sweating the details. Patricia Rubertone motivated me to broaden the frames of reference by which industrial sites could be examined, and she also provided me with another persuasive model of diligent scholarship made manifest. It is with no small debt to these three that I have come to see that issue of how to look at material evidence not as a problem but as a touchstone for inspiration.

Introduction

Today the products of mining filter into nearly every aspect of our lives. The plastic and metal components in alarm clocks, cars, iPhones, and pens; the clay, temper, and glaze of our coffee mugs; and the phosphates in fertilizers, the aggregate in concrete, and the fuel required at coal and nuclear power plants to generate electricity all share this mineralogical common denominator. The spread of mineral products is so complete that frankly we think little about it. Comparatively few Americans encounter active mines on a daily basis, and even fewer find work in one. Thus, it may come as surprising that the United States mines more coal today than ever before, that the amount of gold needed for a typical ring now leaves tons of mining waste in its wake, and that despite major shifts to a service economy, the North American continent remains an important supplier of gold, silver, lead, copper, titanium, nickel, and phosphates to global markets.

Mining seems to invite paradox. The industry is celebrated for economic contributions and vilified for environmental consequences that include pits and waste piles more than a mile wide and watersheds compromised by contamination. Historical contradictions and ironies abound. The expansion of mining in the mid-nineteenth century fueled an enduring mythology of the American West as a land of opportunity, and yet mining is also associated with histories of racial exclusion, ethnic segregation, and colonial appropriation. American mining came to be shaped by lengthy and violent disputes between capital and labor, but the mineral rushes also served to promote laissez-faire individualism. Histories of mineral exploration have come to be celebrated in towns and cities that began life as mining supply centers but are observed with less cheer in communities struggling to find an economic base after the mines closed.

Such juxtapositions hint at the complex and contested issues surrounding the legacies of American mining, and yet tallies of industry successes and failures all too easily bury the human story. We talk shockingly little about who the American miner was and is and the working conditions they labored under. We gloss over considerations of the rich historical depth of mining on the continent, in which organizational and technical arrangements varied significantly over the centuries as well as contemporaneously. We overlook ways that mining shaped the built environment and contributed to a high but unevenly distributed standard of living in the present. In so doing, we ultimately forgo a richer understanding of how the historical trajectories of mining came to shape facets of our own lives, be they desired aspects or not. In short, there is need for a closer engagement with mining history.

This volume examines ways that historical archaeologists have taken up the call to investigate the American experience of mining, and it places special emphasis on the understandings resulting from the analysis of material culture. Archaeologists have gained significant insights into the livelihoods, backgrounds, and aspirations of the historic American miner by examining what miners and their families threw away. Material evidence provides a fuller reckoning of how the hardships of the mining life became expressed variously through class identities and miners' bodies. Mining workplaces have, under examination, revealed cultural preferences shaping technological change and spotlighted significant variations in local practice. Beneath the surface uniformity of company towns, archaeological analyses have exposed fault lines of resistance to the ideals of social engineering. Threaded through such disparate findings is how the archaeological analysis of American mining sites draws consistent attention to the lived experience.

Historical archaeologists have purposely investigated mining sites for upwards of five decades, but the results accumulating through these efforts have to date largely escaped synthesis. This book seeks to remedy this gap. The following pages cast a wide net over archaeological endeavors for the purpose of identifying major research directions and areas with promising potential, and from which also to seize upon the most significant findings. The objective is to present what archaeologists have had to say about America's historical experiences with this vital but troubled industry. The contention is that material residues offer historical correctives and valuable viewpoints for better understanding the polarized caricatures that have become dominant in the presentation of American mining. A necessary first step is to define what mining entails more precisely and to provide a better sense of the evidentiary materials that historical archaeologists set to work.

The Varied Signatures of Mining

By its simplest definition, mining is the act of removing useful material from the ground. Mining is associated most often with underground excavation, but it also entails the digging of surface deposits by a wide range of techniques and the processing of all this material into usable raw products. The minerals of interest include those useful more or less in the state that they are found (such as salts, clays, gravels, and granite), as well as "ores" that contain metals seldom in pure state but in concentrations high enough to warrant excavation. Ores are encountered in primary rock deposits called *lodes* or as secondary deposits of eroded gravels termed *placers*. For precious metals especially, lode mines typically added a milling facility on-site to refine ores down to valued products and concentrates. Mining, then, is the business of conducting all this work. While the goal is straightforward, the methods for excavating and recovering minerals, the ways of organizing labor and other resources, and the laws and customs governing how tasks are accomplished have varied enormously over time and space.

There can be little doubt that mining has been practiced widely over a long time depth in North America. Archaeologically, the durable products of quarrying (that is, stone flakes and projectile points) are what first alert us to an early human presence in the Americas (Goebel et al. 2008; Meltzer 2009). The full extent of mining nevertheless remains difficult to quantify—and this includes for the historic period, about which this book is specifically concerned. The core of the problem lies with definitions. The term *mine* can apply equally to a single feature such as a shaft or to an entire mining complex, and this slippage of scale makes it difficult to calculate the number of mines with confidence. Even so, a database of current and abandoned mines managed by the U.S. Geological Survey (USGS) provides at least a starting point. According to this source, United States gold mines total 57,980 sites, sand and gravel 45,032, copper 13,659, iron 12,524, lead 10,515, clay 5,702, and uranium 10,114—the grand total standing at 267,072 mines (USGS 2005).

Displaying all these data at once leaves just a few sections of the contiguous United States comparatively neglected. Mining occurs practically everywhere, and yet the database remains incomplete. Not all mines are known, and several minerals are grossly underrepresented. Only three records relate to petroleum sites, for example, and the database also lists just three dozen coal mines (an earlier version of the database listed more than 10,000). Problems of representation abound. Mines are listed according to the primary mineral extracted, but mines often recover more than one mineral in the course of business. The classification of approximately 120,000 mines as "past producers" falls short of the Environmental Protection Agency's conservative estimate that the United States contains at least 200,000 abandoned mines, and the figure may exceed a half million in the western states alone (Lyon et al. 1993; US EPA 2004: 13). It is striking to consider that practically all of the mines under consideration in these wide-ranging estimates operated within the past two hundred years, and largely under the guiding framework of industrial capitalism—an economic system associated with a profusion of technological developments, labor deskilling, intensifying class disparities, and the rise of labor unions.

The residues of historic mining activity encompass a wide array of features. Archaeologists encounter mining settlements most often as collections of tent pads, cellar holes, privies, wells, and artifact scatters (Noble and Spude 1997: 9). The structures preserved at mining camps can range from canvas wall tents and bunkhouses to entire streetscapes. At mining workplaces, the forms of material evidence are directly influenced by the nature of the deposit. Historic work at lode mines might include shafts and adits (respectively, vertical and horizontal mine entrances), as well as open pits and quarries, employed wherever valued materials are found close to the surface. Placer workplaces are more difficult to separate into discrete sites, but work areas can be identified by the arrangement of waste materials; remnants of water control devices such as ditches, dams, and pipelines; and the escarpments created when pressurized water was directed against gravel banks. Mining sites extend also to the property markers staked at the corners of mining claims, the aerial tramway systems moving materials and men between mine locations, and the pits, trenches, and surface scrapings formed by prospecting efforts. Mining equipment in various states of disrepair may be present at any and all of these sites.

The most conspicuous archaeological feature of mining sites, however, is the waste dumped beside mine workings. "Mining waste" is the generalized term, but there are important technical distinctions. *Overburden* refers to the nonmineralized material overlying a deposit, *waste rock* to the barren rock mined but not processed, and *tailings* to the material discarded after ore treatment. In lode mining, this constitutes finely ground material ejected from processing facilities. At placer mines, tailings include gravels and cobbles discarded after passing through a sorting device such as a sluice (a trough fitted with screens or bars). As one has probably gathered, the recording of mining sites necessitates facility with a specialized terminology that the industry happens to excel at generating. A dictionary of mining and mining-related terms published by the U.S. Bureau of Mines (Thrush et al. 1968) exceeds 1,250 pages.

An impressive range of documentary evidence complements the vast numbers of abandoned mines. Prior to the mid-nineteenth century, information about mining operations might survive in patents, tax assessment records, censuses, diaries and correspondence, and ethnohistorical accounts. Source materials expanded notably after the 1850s: primary records from that point forward came to include claim filings, water appropriations, and proof of labor forms bound in weighty volumes at county courthouses. State and federal agencies (including the USGS and the U.S. Bureau of Mines) published accounts of mining districts with regularity, discussing geology as well as the activities of specific companies. Historical records also include an extensive array of newspapers, professional journals, and treatises on mining practice. The expansion of capitalist enterprise additionally encouraged mine managers to adopt new forms of accounting. By the mid-twentieth century, customized expense ledgers, forms for tallying the value of mill runs, cards detailing characteristics of each employee, and spreadsheets for calculating the amount of rock excavated during each shift for each mine level could filter into the day-to-day business of even small-scale operations. Topping off the set of potentially available research materials are collections of historical photographs, maps, film reels, and oral accounts.

"Potentially" remains the necessary qualifier when considering all of these forms of archival and archaeological evidence. Despite seemingly immense numbers of mines, preservation varies greatly across both the material and documentary records. The unfortunate truth is that few primary documents survive for the majority of historic mining endeavors.

To be sure, archives and private collections across the country include invaluable assortments of company records, photographs, and oral histories, but the selection is fortuitous. Historical collections sometimes have been rescued unceremoniously from dumpsters (e.g., R. Spude 2005) and from papers collected from the floors of abandoned structures, but these exceptional cases are also indicative of just how many records have been lost. Even under the best of circumstances, company records go only so far into detailing the lives of working families who spent years—sometimes their entire lives—toiling in and about the mines. Comparatively few chose to write down details of their activities and experiences for posterity.

Similar issues of selectivity hold true for the archaeological record. Cases exist where miners literally walked away from workings never to return, leaving tools, foodstuffs, and work clothing. For the majority of abandoned mines, however, the archaeologist finds collections of pits, waste piles, sections of reworked gravels, and campsites in various states of deterioration. Many sites have seen decades of reworking, salvage, and curio collecting, with an increasing number scheduled also for environmental remediation. Any of these activities can seriously compromise the integrity of what traces remain.

The written and material records each have traditional strengths. The documentary side covers an enormous breadth of subject matter but is arguably treasured most for the direct insights it can allow into people's thoughts and motivations. Artifacts provide a wealth of information into the routines of daily life and sometimes constitute the only information available about those who left no written records. The vicissitudes of preservation add dynamism to an already variable historical situation in which no two sites of human activity are ever exactly alike. Put simply, there is no one way of "doing" historical archaeology. Flexibility in scope and method has proven beneficial and essential. Thus, archaeological contributions have met success sometimes by filling gaps in historical documentation and at other times by comparing written documents against the material record. A third approach examines sources in more codependent ways to develop combined narratives. In nearly all cases, the use of documentary and archaeological data sources enables the development of material-based histories.

There is clear utility in combining the documentary and archaeological records to gain insight into the American experience, as other volumes in this series attest. Most miners left only a limited trace of their toil in company records, but we can improve our understandings about their daily lives by mapping the worlds they built and analyzing what they lost, abandoned, and discarded. Connections between mining enterprises and the more abstract processes of capitalism, colonialism, and industrialization draw upon multiple lines of evidence for similar reasons—for it is typically a combination of different sources that allows us historical insight into lived experiences.

Scope of the Book and a Note on Sources

Archaeological interest in historic mining sites extends back several decades, but syntheses are rare, recent, and pitched at the regional and site level (Hardesty 2010; James 2012; Obermayr and McQueen 2016; Saleeby 2011). This volume reflects a conscious effort to improve the national picture, highlighting key findings and the variety of evidence subjected to archaeological scrutiny. The seven chapters that follow can be divided into three conceptual parts. The first two set the scene with historical treatments. Chapter 1 summarizes the changing expression of American mining over the past four centuries. Particular attention is given here to transformations in the organization of work, to changes in the dominant minerals worked, and to mapping the industry's broader connections with American history and culture. The second chapter chronicles the changing nature of archaeological investigations at historic mining sites since the 1920s. Here again we see revealing transformations in the organization of endeavors, including spatial and temporal proclivities in archaeological research.

Leading archaeological avenues occupy the next three chapters. We look first at the structure of mining communities, examining archaeological findings about the supply networks responsible for sustaining communities and discussing insights into the organization of mining settlements. Chapter 4 tightens the focus further to review archaeological perspectives on miners' livelihoods, paying particular attention to the intersections of class-based and racialized identities. Chapter 5 turns to the workplace, where archaeologists have highlighted a wide variation in American practice reflective of cultural preferences, trial and error, and intentional deception. All three chapters underscore how archaeological contributions reveal the American experience of mining to be far more diversified than usually characterized.

The last section moves the analytical lens closer to the present. Chapter 6 explores how mining sites are remembered and emphasizes important feedbacks between memorialization and our understanding of American mining. Included here are examinations into the selective forces at work in memorialization, the complex ways that films influence perceptions of authenticity at mining sites, and changing perceptions of mining's environmental legacy. The book concludes on prospective ground, identifying new directions for archaeological contributions and noting challenges to archaeological recording and interpretation.

The archaeological findings discussed herein have been gathered from books, articles, theses, and dissertations, as well as from sources less easily accessed, including conference papers and contract reports, that have long formed the bulk of archaeological work on historic mining sites. Findings highlight the efforts of historical archaeologists and industrial archaeologists—another subfield of archaeology that focuses attention on the technological and societal transformations wrought by industrialization. The volume has also benefited from contributions by mining historians, historians of technology, and maritime archaeologists, among others. This is a varied group of practitioners who rarely enter into a collective conversation about their data.

The aim is for synthesis, but selectivity proves inevitable and desirable. The reader will notice, for instance, that examples tend to favor studies of gold, copper, silver, iron, and coal. Some mining endeavors—such as uranium mining, stone quarries, oil drilling, and sand and gravel mining—receive either little mention or no mention at all. Moreover, although examples are drawn from across the United States, there is a weighting in coverage toward western mines. In some cases the examples reflect my own fieldwork, but additionally, the areas emphasized generally mirror the areas where archaeological research has concentrated thus far. Such favoritism is not intended to suggest that underrepresented areas are of little consequence or potential. To the contrary, the approaches outlined here are broadly transferable as examples of how archaeological contributions have enriched an understanding of America's mining past and how they can continue to do so.

1

American Mining in Three Acts

Outside the town of Coloma, on the west side of California's Sierra Nevada, stands a monument to a chance discovery that triggered one of the most dramatic population movements of the nineteenth century. The James Marshall monument is a memorial in the truest sense of the term. Erected in 1890 over the grave of the famed gold discoverer, the likeness of Marshall in statuary bronze clutches a nugget in the right hand and points with the left downhill to the banks of the American River's southern fork (figure 1.1). Plaques distributed around Coloma identify distinct aspects of the famous event. California Registered Historic Landmark No. 530 commemorates the discovery site at Sutter's sawmill in 1848, the statue at Historic Landmark No. 143 celebrates Marshall, and Historic Landmark No. 748 memorializes the road he hurried along carrying news of the find.

The story celebrated at Coloma should be familiar to most readers. The nineteenth-century gold stampedes signaled a watershed event in American history with worldwide ramifications. The stampedes drew hundreds of thousands of prospectors to the western half of the continent and laid the foundations for large-scale, capital-intensive mining in the decades following. The rushes also spurred the rapid development of supply networks and "instant cities," intensified encounters with Native American groups, and generated far-reaching legislation concerning the disposition of the nation's mineral and nonmineral resources (Bakken 2008; Barth 1988; Limerick 1987, 1998; Pisani 1999; Smith 1987).

Marshall's discovery nevertheless represents a latecomer in the historical exploitation of North America's mineral resources. The search for mineral wealth underwrote much European exploration and conquest, and Native American groups had long worked and traded minerals. It follows that tracking the trajectories of mining over several centuries is no

Figure 1.1. James Marshall monument in Coloma, California. Photograph by author.

small task, and the historical overview presented here makes no pretense of being comprehensive. This chapter instead focuses on the industry at three points in time: the 1600s, the 1870s, and the 1950s. These decades correspond roughly with mining during the early colonial period, mining at the height of rush-era expansiveness, and mining as a professionalized and increasingly mechanized industry. For each period, the narrative touches on who performed the mining, how they performed it, and the use made of mineral products, with each section also tracking developments occurring before and afterward. This is an account of mining at a coarse scale of resolution that is nevertheless sufficient to establish a baseline from which to launch archaeological inquiry.

Colonial and Noncolonial Enterprise

In 1600, the opinion that most visitors to North America entertained about the mining industry was that it did not exist, and not for a lack of trying. The plundering of Central and South America by the Spanish in the sixteenth century fueled a sustained belief that mineral riches abounded also in the northern continent. In 1540, Francisco Vázquez de Coronado campaigned 1,400 men around the desert Southwest in search of the Seven Cities of Gold, less than a year after the Hernando de Soto expedition landed several hundred men on the Florida coast with intentions of finding similar riches in the Southeast. The prospect of New World mineral wealth also piqued interest among Spain's European rivals, with the French and English dispatching companies to find gold, silver, and other valuable metals north of Spanish possessions. Jacques Cartier sought out the land of the Saguenay (a fabled land of gold, silver, and copper) in 1541, but the outcrops of diamonds and gold he discovered on the St. Lawrence River unfortunately turned out to be quartz and iron pyrite (Mulholland 1981: 5–10).

English attempts fared little better. Early explorations fruitlessly sought the land of Norumbega, where houses were rumored to rest on pillars of gold. Martin Frobisher's charter to find the Northwest Passage in the 1570s became sidetracked with the discovery of a "black ore" he believed (incorrectly) to be immensely rich in gold. The Virginia Company that founded Jamestown in 1606 instructed the landing party to divide into three equal groups: one to build a fortified village, another to begin clearing and planting the land, and the third to explore the surrounding country for minerals and westward-flowing rivers. Gold fever in the first years of settlement threatened to divert colonists from performing tasks necessary for ensuring subsistence. Again, gold and silver strikes proved unfounded, but the colonists did find ample supplies of glittering pyrites and mica (ibid.: 13–14, 17–22).

For the rare visitor not fixated on finding silver or gold who ventured farther outside of the colonies, mining in North America might have left a different impression. Hardly nonexistent, mining was a widely dispersed, varied, and small-scale activity largely out of the hands of Europeans. Houses supported by golden columns were nowhere in sight, but minerals nevertheless had undergirded aspects of Native American livelihoods for millennia. Characterizing the industry as a whole, chert, obsidian, and steatite (soapstone) quarries abounded, and several Native American groups mined salt for use in food preparation. Metallic oxides, sulfides, and other metal-bearing compounds also found extensive application. Some ores yielded unusual colorings—the reds and vermillion hues of cinnabar, for instance—that made excellent paints and dyes when ground up and mixed with water and fat. Red ochre (iron oxide) found especially wide application for these purposes, as well as use in the burial of the dead. Native American groups residing in the upper Mississippi Valley mined rich galena (lead sulfide) deposits, and these minerals joined quartz and calcite crystals, mica, and chlorite as trade items invested with spiritual power. In the Southwest, the Hopis mined coal to fire pottery and heat their homes. Iroquoian and Algonquian groups south of the Finger Lakes region used petroleum for medicinal cures and body paint. Archaeological evidence in that region indicates the use of timber cribs to enlarge natural petroleum seeps as early as the 1500s (Selso et al. 2000). By 1600, Native American groups throughout most of the lower half of the continent were also tapping clay sources for pottery making.

Turquoise mines in the American Southwest sometimes included chambered excavations (Weigand and Harbottle 1993: 161–64), but underground excavations were rare. The vast majority of hard-rock mines consisted of pits and cuts dug into surface exposures and excavated with hammerstones and hafted picks, complemented possibly with fire and water quenching. A couple of centuries on, Henry Schoolcraft's visit to galena mines controlled by Fox Indians in 1820 near Dubuque, Iowa, documented that women and elder men excavated and transported the lead ore. Women mined the rock using picks and hammers, then loaded the ore into baskets and carried it to the banks of the Mississippi River for sale to traders. This work arrangement—foreign to Europeans, who considered mining a male occupation—followed a division of labor commonly reported among Native American groups. Although Native American men in this case took limited roles in mining and transporting ore, they may have been involved in later-stage processes (Murphy 2000).

Having completed this perambulation of the continent, a European visitor might still have concluded that Native North Americans worked few mines. This perception hinged doubly on the predominance of surface workings and the general absence of refined metals. Metal oxides, as discussed above, were in common use in the 1600s, but indigenous mining technology did not at the time include smelting at the high temperatures necessary to separate out metal from metallic ores. Even so, characterizations of Native American cultures as "premetallic" are inaccurate given numerous accounts documenting the presence of metals. Sebastian Cabot described seeing the native people of Newfoundland wearing copper earrings in 1497. Giovanni da Verrazzano, visiting the island of Nantucket in 1524, met Wampanoag women adorned with copper ornaments. Jacques Cartier learned of the fabled land of the Saguenay in 1535 when people on the St. Lawrence presented him with a "great knife of red copper" (Rickard 1932: 3). During the 1700s, and likely before, the Haidas were the principal traders of this metal along the Northwest Coast. European explorers to the Arctic in the early nineteenth century noted the presence of copper knives among the Eskimos (ibid.: 1–5). Admiral Robert Peary's reconnoiter of northern Greenland in the late 1800s astonished the local Inuits, who had never before seen white men, but Peary was surprised in return to see them carrying iron knives and iron harpoon heads.

The explanation for these curious reports is that *native metal* (metal existing in its pure or nearly pure state) existed in various, albeit relatively few, places in the continent. Native copper is the oldest metal known to have been worked and traded (figure 1.2). A copper projectile point recovered from a site west of Lake Superior dates to a secure context of 4700 BC—old enough to indicate that Native American metalworking developed independent of non-native influence and also that North American copper mining ranks among the earliest evidence of metalworking anywhere in the world (Martin 2004: 8). Archaeological evidence also indicates that native groups across most of the eastern half of the continent were using and trading copper by at least 1000 BC. Native iron, far scarcer, derives almost exclusively from meteorites. The Greenland Inuits had named their iron sources Tent, Woman, and Dog in order of decreasing size. When led to this 30-ton celestial family in 1894, Admiral Peary

Figure 1.2. Native Americans worked and exchanged copper widely, as evident in this early twentieth-century collection of "copper relics." Photograph by J. T. Reeder. Michigan Technological University Archives and Copper Country Historical Collections, MS042-017-261-006.

recalled seeing thousands of basalt hammerstones scattered in the vicinity (Rickard 1941: 58–59).

European observers from the mid-seventeenth century on noted some Native American groups actively refining metals. Smelting techniques may have been learned from Spanish miners, who mined gold and silver ores in the Southwest in secret to avoid heavy taxes (Young 1970: 101). The French reportedly taught Native Americans residing along the upper Mississippi to smelt galena and make molds for casting lead shot (Murphy 2000: 80–81). Still, it is important to bear in mind that mining was an occasional activity and that the quantity of metals in circulation remained fairly small. A detailed knowledge of local and regional environments, including the location of mineral outcrops, nevertheless was long a part of adaptive strategies and social systems on the continent. The European perception that Native American societies were devoid of metals came packaged with connotations that Native American people lacked the cultural achievements of the West and that indigenous use of metal-bearing ores squandered the true economic potential. This paradox between Native American industry and the perceived lack of it helps explain why Euro-Americans engaged in mining activities over the next few centuries relied heavily on native guides to find mineral outcrops yet often dismissed indigenous mineral rights on the grounds that no Indian was, or had ever been, a miner.

The disappointing returns of early European prospecting in North America was partly an accident of geography, but the first colonists also tended to lack the skills essential to identifying the precious metal deposits that sometimes existed under their feet (Mulholland 1981: 17–36). Prospecting efforts in the New World, however, did find greater success with identifying minerals worked contemporaneously in Europe. Iron ore transported as ballast on returning ships yielded some of the first mineral profits realized in the English colonies. The noted abundance of wood for charcoal also opened real possibilities for establishing a colonial iron industry. In 1619, the London Company sent more than 150 emigrants skilled in the manufacture of iron to Virginia to establish ironworks. A Powhatan raid at Falling Creek in 1622 destroyed this first attempt and dampened enthusiasm to develop an iron industry for several years. In 1647, the Saugus Iron Works in Massachusetts began producing iron from bog ores, but a combination of litigation and financial difficulties forced its closure by 1652. Other early efforts to produce iron at an industrial scale likewise proved fitful, the consequence of poor site selection and an overestimation of the iron deposits on hand. Nevertheless, by the 1650s, several English colonies employed smiths and founders to work local iron ores, many of which were recovered from marshes (Gordon 1996: 55–89; Rickard 1932: 8–12).

A wider array of minerals than iron also fell within the purview of colonial enterprise. Clays and sands, for instance, found application for the pottery and glass industries. The Granby copper mine (discovered in 1705) in Connecticut turned a modest profit for several decades before its conversion into a prison. Prospectors mined coal deposits in Nova Scotia as early as 1700 and on the James River in Maryland by 1748. The stone industry centered early in New England (Bowles 1947), where operators supplied building materials for the construction industry as well as memorial stone for masons to carve elaborate Death's Head, Cherub, and Urn and Willow designs.

Outside of the different gender arrangements, the extraction techniques that European miners utilized during the 1600s differed little from their Native American counterparts. In place of hammerstones, European miners employed a single-tined pick and sledgehammer to break rock in an action similar to that of a hammer and chisel. A second method, termed *plug and feather*, drove a wedge into crevices in the rock to split the rock through the grain. A third method used fire and water to break rock through expansion and contraction. A few mines in Europe had adapted the explosive power of black powder to aid excavations by the 1630s. The first black powder mill in the United States opened in 1675, and its application in North American mine workings occurred sometime thereafter (Wyman 1979: 104–7; Young 1970: 187–91, 212–14). Its popular use continued well into the mid-nineteenth century, by which time the scale and scope of American mining practice had transformed so significantly as to be nearly unrecognizable from its colonial origins.

After the Gold Rush

The census of U.S. manufactures for 1870 reported an industry radically different from what returns indicated just a few decades prior. In that year, some eight thousand American mining companies employed 150,000 workers and produced $150 million in raw mineral products. Gold, silver, copper, iron, lead, and other metals contributed to approximately one-third of this production. Coal, which found essential applications for heating, lighting, and steel production, accounted for $73 million, and an astounding 70 percent of this production derived from Pennsylvania mines. Petroleum contributed another $20 million, reflecting its growing importance as a cheaper source of lubricating oils and fuel than camphene or whale oil (U.S. Bureau of the Census 1872). Nonmetallic minerals were not a large supplier of revenue at the national scale, but stone, slate, and clay nevertheless remained important construction materials. Clay (not included under mining totals) found use in the manufacture of common bricks, firebricks, paving bricks, sewer pipes, and roofing, flooring, and wall tiles, with nearly four thousand operators listed for that year (Bowles 1947).

A sea change in the industry is reflected less by these numbers, however, than in the caveat introducing the mining report. Census compilers noted exasperatedly that "the machinery of enumeration is so inapt and so insufficient that the results [from mining] cannot honestly be published without ample admission of errors and defects" (U.S. Bureau of the Census 1872: 748). Coal and iron mines, the report continued, could be documented with reasonable accuracy because they were located near existing settlements and because they concerned essentially low-value products. Gold and silver mines, by contrast, presented intractable difficulties. The remote location of many western mining districts, the thousands of small-scale operators present, and the "thousand opportunities for concealment or exaggeration" of financial returns ranked high among the problems (ibid.: 750). Census takers estimated that gold and silver operations provided $26 million in revenue for the year. Later reassessments by industry practitioners suggest that this figure fell as much as four or five times short of the actual mark. Beyond dispute, however, is a sense of a dramatic turn of events that government officials and industry practitioners struggled to comprehend.

James Marshall's discovery of gold nuggets in the tailrace of Sutter's Mill on January 24, 1848, is the closest one can come to isolating an event that spearheaded this transformation. Marshall's find did not represent the first major discovery of metals—a gold rush to Georgia had occurred two decades prior and a copper rush to Upper Michigan was just winding down—but news of the California strike generated an unprecedented level of interest. In the span of a few months, thousands of novice prospectors set out to try their hand in the western gold diggings. Colonel

Figure 1.3. The "forest of masts" created by ships abandoned in San Francisco Bay, 1851. Photograph by Sterling C. McIntyre. Library of Congress, Prints and Photographs Division, LC-USZC4-7421.

Richard Mason, who ventured to the gold strikes in mid-1848, found the hillsides in mineral areas "thickly strewn with canvass tents and bush arbours" (Mason 1848). Over the next two years, the numbers of rushers to California well exceeded one hundred thousand, most of them men (figure 1.3).

Mining methods in the rush period began with tools not substantially different from what miners had utilized two centuries prior—but the situation soon changed. Prospectors first brought pans, picks, hammers, and shovels to work the goldfields, but the efficiency of placer mining increased with the adoption of sluices, which used the power of water to churn through deposits and sort nuggets from the waste material. Beginning in the 1860s, some large-scale mining operations washed entire banks into sluices using jets of pressurized water, a technique that increased both the profits and adverse environmental consequences of mining substantially. Termed *hydraulicking*, this technique generated debris sufficient in central California to raise the bed of the Sacramento River

20 feet (in places, higher than the surrounding land) and destroy oyster beds in San Francisco Bay (McEvoy 1986: 84–85). This shift to capital-intensive mining became reflected also through the increasing interest in lode deposits, which demanded higher up-front costs but for which developments in mine explosives promised speedier excavations and quicker returns on investments than prior methods (Twitty 2001).

Even if census takers could count every nugget panned, pried, and blasted loose from the western diggings, the consequences of rush-era mining are impossible to assess in dollar value alone. Consider that within two decades of Marshall's discovery at Coloma, prospectors had scoured California for similar finds and stampeded to mineral discoveries in present-day Arizona, Colorado, Idaho, Montana, Nevada, Oregon, Washington, and British Columbia. Other states and territories followed. Consider also the exponential growth of supply centers including San Francisco, Sacramento, and Denver, the infrastructure networks linking these places with mining camps, and the boon that mining gave to suppliers of canned goods and outfitters such as Levi Strauss, whose durable working clothes for prospectors became a cultural icon. The mid-nineteenth-century rushes formed multiethnic, multiracial, and highly mobile communities throughout much of the West. While most people heading to the gold-fields did not find fortune, they left enduring legacies in the places they refashioned and in the place-names they assigned to a slew of landscape features.

For many Euro-Americans, the mineral rushes constituted the first experience with the western territories and the first encounter with native peoples. The converse was not true for Native American groups, although the numbers of prospectors and the broad reach of their activities nevertheless brought interaction at an altogether new level of intensity.

Accounts of native people leading prospectors to bonanza outcrops are legion—one American mining engineer reflected that most mineral discoveries in North America had "rested on the information freely proffered or forcefully wrung from indigenous peoples whose forefathers had found and first worked these occurrences" (Graton 1947: 3). Such assistance could also be indirect. Several copper mines worked in the 1840s in Upper Michigan owed their origins to the discovery of ancient copper pits—one of the deeper pits at the Minesota Mine included a 6-ton mass of copper at the bottom that indigenous miners had left partially raised on a timber crib (Krause 1992: 214–15).

Rush-era accounts also document widespread Native American involvement in mining during the early years. Colonel Mason's 1848 report on the goldfields, for example, estimated that California Indians constituted more than half of the gold diggers. Indeed, historian James Rawls forwards the likelihood that it was James Marshall's Indian laborers rather than Marshall who first found gold in Sutter's tailrace (Rawls 1976: 28–30). The presence of Native American miners more often spurred conflict. In 1851, the blasting of a quartz vein by British entrepreneurs working for the Hudson's Bay Company in the Queen Charlotte Islands met with considerable resistance from Haida people who had to that point controlled the gold trade. The Haidas reportedly stole tools and rushed into the workings after each blast to seize as much gold as possible. W. H. McNeill, a trader accompanying the expedition, described mining efforts as "a regular scramble," in which the Haidas "would take our men by the legs and hold them away from the gold. Some blows," he added dryly, "were struck on these occasions" (McNeill to Douglas, quoted in Rickard 1938: 8). The Hudson's Bay Company ceased mining activities as a consequence, fearing that the fracas would disrupt more-coveted relations in the fur trade. Events unfolding elsewhere in the goldfields mark this as an atypical action. Indeed, the Hudson's Bay Company still looked elsewhere for mining opportunities in British Columbia, and American prospectors took up where the company had left off in the Queen Charlottes (Marshall 1996; Rickard 1938).

Government efforts to protect Native American territories from mineral prospecting proved grossly ineffective. Soldiers were also subject to gold fever, and in several cases, state and federal governments were complicit in violent campaigns to render areas "safe" for prospecting (e.g., Conrotto 1973; Hurtado 1988: 106). Policies of Indian removal tended to follow mineral discoveries on Indian lands, be it justified in terms of serving the "best interests of the Indian" or guaranteeing the safety of American citizens (which did not universally include Native Americans until the Citizenship Act of 1924). Thus, gold discoveries in Georgia in the late 1820s precipitated the removal of sixteen thousand Cherokees to Indian Territory along the Trail of Tears (1838–39), and rumors of wealth in northern Arizona prompted the forced relocation of several thousand Navajo people to Bosque Redondo in New Mexico (1864). These well-known cases are a mere reflection of the smaller, localized, and more widespread disruptions that mineral prospecting fostered. Prospectors reported a sense of adventure in their diaries, but indigenous perspectives draw attention to the violence and dispossession that attended the exercise of such freedoms (Hurtado 1988; Owens 2002; Rawls 1984; Williams 1993).

For those invested in mineral development, the ends justified the means. The mining industry in 1870 represented an industry at the brink of major technological and organizational change. Metal mines to that point had worked high-grade ore deposits with limited chemical complexity, but these easily worked deposits were becoming exhausted. Lower-value resources such as iron, copper, and coal were mined primarily in the eastern half of the continent, where operators took advantage of the lower transportation costs provided by lakes, navigable rivers, and established networks of canals and railroads. The completion of transcontinental railroads in the 1870s altered the economics and geography of exploration by enabling lower-value minerals to be mined profitably at greater distances from industrial centers. The Southern Pacific Railroad is credited in this way with opening up Arizona copper mines. Rail access to Butte, Montana, and Bingham Canyon, Utah, transformed these largely worked-out gold and silver camps into gigantic copper producers. By the 1880s, the largest copper mines had shifted to the western half of the continent (Rickard 1932: 350–52; Robbins 1994: 88–89).

The profitable mining of low-grade ore bodies required working at greater economies of scale backed by significant financial investment. Deeper pockets permitted deeper mines, and deeper mines presented new technical challenges. Technological developments were applied to practically all steps of the mining process. In Nevada's Comstock Lode, investors funneled millions of dollars into completing a four-mile-long tunnel driven just to drain the mines (Young 1970: 254–60). The development of square-set timbering—essentially a system of stackable framing—enabled excavations there to open up vast underground chambers, provided adequate timber could be secured. Duane Smith (1987: 12–13) estimates that the development of Nevada's famed Comstock Lode used an estimated 600 million feet of timber and more than 2 million cords of wood in their construction.

Industry practitioners also warmed to a range of technologies promising to improve the speed and efficiency of the mining process. Compressed air drills increasingly took the place of hand steels in underground workings. The development of dynamite (patented in 1867) provided a more powerful and comparatively safer alternative to the use of powder or straight nitroglycerine for blasting. Underground mapping and regular sampling regimens enhanced the efficient exploration of ore bodies. Mines in rugged terrain adopted aerial tramways to transfer ore, supplies, and workers to and from the diggings. In mineral processing, too, experiments with cyanide, among other reagents, explored the potential for recovering metals from ores that initial techniques had no chance of extracting profitably (Nystrom 2014; Rickard 1932; Trennert 2001; Young 1970: 204–14, 283–85).

Not all these efficiencies translated to across-the-board improvements. Compressed air drills increased the incidence of silicosis and black lung, a chronic respiratory disease caused by the inhalation of fine silica and coal dust. The working of more-complex ores, which often included sulfides, increased environmental impacts because the decomposition of these ores could generate sulfuric acid that in turn entrained heavy metals into watersheds. Deeper and larger mines also increased the incidence of mining disasters. By the late nineteenth century, mining ranked among the nation's most dangerous occupations. Major disasters at underground mines involved fires, flooding, and roof collapses, but more-frequent injuries resulted from explosions, open shafts, and machinery. Coal mining achieved the highest fatalities in the industry, claiming at least six miners per thousand in 1870. Nonfatal injury rates were alarmingly high. In the 1910s, 3 percent of miners suffered major injuries from workplace accidents, and 15 percent received "minor" injuries, which could still necessitate workers taking three weeks off from work to recuperate. Notably, these statistics derived from voluntary reporting. Companies that supplied meticulous records indicated that the actual rate of injury underground was nearly twice as high (Fay 1916: 96).

Mine management seldom compensated workers for injuries sustained on the job, justifying this stance on the grounds of the high wages paid. In western mines, rates of $3.50 to $4 a day were not uncommon, which exceeded what many other laborers made in a week. Yet wages on paper and money in pocket could be different things, and historians note that disruptions in pay were a frequent occurrence in western mining districts. Additionally, many mines maintained wages at $3.50 per day in the early twentieth century, despite substantial increases in the cost of living (Wyman 1979: 61–75).

Miners' unions appeared about the time that rising corporate fortunes increased the social and geographic distance between miners and mine owners. The earliest unions in the western United States appeared in the mid-1860s along Nevada's Comstock Lode. By the 1890s, the United Mine Workers (founded in 1890) and the Western Federation of Miners (founded in 1893) represented mining interests at the national level (Lingenfelter 1974). Well-capitalized mining companies endeavored to stave off union footholds through a carrot and stick approach that varied from supplying housing and entertainment, on one hand, to espionage, intimidation, and blacklisting on the other (Hyde 1986; Lankton 1991). Company housing aimed to retain a loyal workforce. Since married men tended to be less inclined to unionize, they became especially sought after. Families conferred additional advantages to mining companies because women contributed significant unpaid labor in running households and because children supplied the next generation of workers. Depending on the mine, work could begin at an early age. The National Child Labor Committee documented thousands of children under the age of fourteen working in Pennsylvania's coal mines during the early twentieth century, laboring underground as runners, mule drivers, and coal loaders or aboveground as breaker boys (Lovejoy 1906, 1907: 26) (figure 1.4).

Despite company efforts to limit worker resistance, the history of American mining beginning in the 1870s is marked by walkouts, strike-breaking, violent clashes, and high rates of labor turnover (Wyman 1979; Young 1970). Pay reductions served as the common catalyst for worker grievances, but miners also protested against unreasonable working hours and lax safety standards. Several disputes escalated to the involvement of National Guard troops and agents from private security firms to protect company interests. Labor conflicts across the country became increasingly prolonged, more prone to violence, and also far less certain in outcome. Skirmishes between Tennessee miners and the state militia in 1891 lasted for more than a year (Green 1972: 157–68). In 1892, striking miners in the Coeur d'Alene region of northern Idaho resorted to dynamiting company buildings in retaliation for wage cuts and corporate efforts to bust unions. Federal troops responded by imprisoning all men of working age in bull-pens for several months. Resentment against this action was later cited as a factor in the assassination of the Idaho governor in 1905 (Lukas 1997: 98–154). The 1897 massacre at Lattimer, Pennsylvania—in which a posse led by county sheriffs fired on a miners' protest march—and the National

Figure 1.4. Child laborers sort coal at the Ewen Breaker, Pennsylvania, 1911. This Lewis Hine photograph carried the caption "The dust penetrated the utmost recesses of the boy's lungs. A kind of slave-driver sometimes stands over the boys, prodding or kicking them into obedience." Library of Congress, Prints and Photographs Division, LC-DIG-nclc-01127.

Guard assault on a strikers' tent colony at Ludlow, Colorado, in 1914 were shocking as individual events but arguably even more alarming in that violent confrontations had almost come to be expected.

American mining became organized also in terms of resource laws. Sporadic attempts to establish a federal leasing system for mines began as early as the late eighteenth century and continued into the 1840s, but all had failed resoundingly (e.g., Lindley 1903: 49–79). For this reason, miners during the early years of the western mineral rushes were permitted "to work freely." The first federal mining law, passed in 1866 under the title "Right of Way for Canal and Ditch Owners," proposed no major departure from what rush-era miners had implemented among themselves. The act did place limits on the maximum size and number of mineral claims permissible, but local regulations regarding claim size, marking boundaries, and the like otherwise retained precedence (Shinn 1885). An 1872 amendment (which also formally retitled the law as the General Mining

Act) extended miners' property rights to both surface and subsurface resources on mining claims (Bakken 2008). This seemingly small detail had enormous ramifications for federal resource policy because it pertained to the control of water, timber, and soil. The Mining Act established a legal principle of "first in time, first in right"—also known as prior appropriation—that gave the first claimant legal precedence over resources. Court rulings extended prior appropriation to resources such as water, oil reserves, and rangelands, transforming it into the preeminent resource law of the West. Lawsuits between miners and downstream farmers over the siltation of watercourses initiated stricter environmental legislation, among the first statements being the 1884 Sawyer Decision, which effectively ended hydraulic mining in central California (Limerick 1987: 71–73; Pisani 1999; Rohe 1985: 25).

American mining in 1870 also constituted an international enterprise in three senses. First, a large percentage of the workforce was foreign born. Cornish and Irish immigrants had initially dominated underground work, but a wider range of European immigrants—Italians, Finns, Swedes, and Germans among them—worked underground by the 1880s. Second, the development of deep mines placed American metal mining increasingly at the forefront of mining expertise, reflected in part by the establishment of American mining schools, journals, and professional societies, as well as the export of engineers. Third, American mining enterprises increasingly ventured beyond the natural edges of the continent. In 1856, the U.S. Congress allowed U.S. citizens to claim more than one hundred islands in the Pacific Ocean and Caribbean Sea in the hope of breaking a Peruvian monopoly on the mining of guano—a significant source of nitrates (Skaggs 1994). American companies also invested in the development of overseas mines where mining engineers had identified large, untapped ore bodies and cheap supplies of labor. One engineer reported cheerily that in an American-owned mine in Mexico, "The Mexican *barretero* [miner] meets the conditions of mine work admirably, and, if properly treated is a good workman. He stands bad conditions as to ventilation, bad ladders, etc., well and above all, does not strike or allow walking delegates to interfere between himself and the management. . . . There is no necessity to pay high wages to a foreign air-drill man after the Mexicans have learned to run the machines" (Elwes 1910: 662). Through international properties, then, American mining companies made substantial savings to a leading expenditure while undercutting union gains at home. Such forays laid important groundwork for multinational mining corporations in the coming decades.

Cold War and Cool Chrome

During the 1950s, Detroit automakers launched a line of cars costing not much more to build than subcompacts but selling with substantial markups in the showroom. None epitomized the "dinosaur in the driveway" more than the 1959 Cadillac Eldorado, decked in chrome, topped with enormous tailfins, and weighing more than 2.5 tons (Flink 1993: 284–87). This and other gas-guzzlers of the 1950s appeared alongside an expanding system of state and interstate highways. Such developments more than symbolized America's love affair with the automobile. Rather, the automobile industry and its attendant support infrastructure of gas stations and highways had become a key consumer of mining's end products.

All told, American mining between 1870 and 1950 ballooned from a multimillion-dollar to a multibillion-dollar industry. The list of minerals exploited tripled from three dozen to approximately ninety—aluminum, magnesium, and potash were among the newcomers (Pehrson 1947), but iron and other base metals, mineral fuels such as petroleum, and nonmetallics including the aggregate used for concrete assumed primary importance.

The largest growth area occurred indisputably in the exploration of petroleum reserves. Oil revenues jumped from 8 percent of national mineral output in 1870 to 40 percent by 1950. The shift to a petroleum economy began at the turn of the twentieth century, when after years of oil prospecting without success in southeastern Texas, Anthony Lucas tapped a gusher that blew oil 150 feet into the air at a rate of 80,000 barrels per day. The "law of capture," which ruled that oil below an unworked lease could be tapped by one's neighbors, contributed to a climate of frenzied production (Olien and Olien 2002: 19, 34). Nearly three hundred oil wells soon operated on Lucas's discovery site, affording it the name Spindletop (figure 1.5). On the Hogg-Swayne tract alone, lessees worked lots so small that the bases of derrick towers touched one another. Oilfield discoveries elsewhere in Texas and in neighboring states followed the Spindletop strike. As occurred during the gold rushes, oil towns endured cycles of boom and bust. The oversupply of petroleum during the "gusher age"

Figure 1.5. Oil derricks at Spindletop, Texas, in 1915. Detail from a stereoscopic view produced by the Keystone View Company. New York Public Library, b11708972.

encouraged the pursuit of new markets. Oil substituted for coal in heating buildings and in powering locomotives and ships, but promoters found the most profitable market in the budding automobile industry, in which low fuel prices helped tip the balance in favor of the gasoline engine (De-Golyer 1947; Yergin 1991: 209–10).

Changes in the consumption of other mineral products occurred alongside the rapid growth of the petroleum industry. Whereas, for instance, U.S. ironworks produced 84,000 tons of ingots in 1870, annual production in 1945 had increased more than a thousandfold. Steel found use in rails, bridges, and ships, in pipelines for transporting oil and gas, in the canning industry, and also in architecture. The completion of the ten-story Home Insurance Building in Chicago in 1885—an early example of the modern skyscraper—initiated an urban architectural revolution away from the use of load-bearing masonry walls and toward the adoption of a load-bearing steel frame (Fenske 2013). In addition to rising demands for iron and steel, the development and expansion of electricity networks during the late nineteenth and early twentieth centuries generated enormous demand for copper (Curtis 2013: 137–43; Malone 1981: 34–35). In agriculture, farms increasingly adopted mineral fertilizers such as potash and phosphate rock over organic fertilizers—an early ingredient in the radical reformulation of the American food production system (Warshall 2002).

The domestic consumption of mineral products also increased to unprecedented levels during the postwar era. American families purchased home appliances such as washing machines and vacuum cleaners, each of which promised savings in household chores while ultimately creating more work for American housewives (Cowan 1983). Carmakers fostered continuing demand for automobiles through car styling, whereby surficial adjustments to side panels cultivated a sense of newness and, with it, the obsolescence of earlier designs (Gartman 1994).

Mining in the postwar period also became an important supplier to America's postwar military-industrial complex. That political-economic conditions exerted important influences on mineral production should come as no surprise. During the 1870–1950 period, base metals, fuels, and nonmetallics (such as cement, talc, and sand and gravel) rose in demand during the two world wars because they had strategic uses. Gold and silver mining showed the reverse trend, booming during the economic depressions of the 1890s and 1930s and ebbing during wartime (Miller 1998).

After the power of the atomic bomb was devastatingly proven at Hiroshima and Nagasaki in 1945, the U.S. government embarked on projects to utilize atomic energy for both domestic and "peacekeeping" purposes—among them developing an arsenal of atomic and thermonuclear weapons (Blustain 2013; Hanson 2016). The U.S. government authorized the stockpiling of strategic materials as a precaution in case of another global conflict. Congress passed laws encouraging citizens to explore uranium sources. In addition to spurring the development of towns such as Moab, Utah, and Grants, New Mexico, the excitement became evident through the staging of Miss Atomic Energy and Miss Atomic Bomb beauty pageants and the marketing of the Uranium Rush board game in which "Your 'Geiger Counter' Lights and Buzzes Your Way to Fun and Fortune" (Amundson 2004: 11, 17–35, 53–103). Still, in 1952, a report by the President's Materials Policy Commission found that domestic mineral reserves had become insufficient to meet the high national standards of living, encouraging American investment in foreign mines and raising the specter that resource-rich countries in the developing world could otherwise fall prey to communism (Lynch 2002: 304).

Historical associations between American mining and Native American land dispossession advanced in step with the widening range of exploitable minerals. From the late nineteenth century to the mid-twentieth century, legislators approved the redrawing of several reservation boundaries to exclude known deposits of precious metals, base metals, and key fuel resources (McDonnell 1991: 10–12; Miner 1976; White 2008: 40–86). Indian reservations became targeted for minerals once again beginning in the 1950s—this time for reserves of strategic metals and deposits of low-sulfur coal (Snipp 1986a, 1986b).

All told, American mining at midcentury could be characterized as professional, mechanized, capital intensive, and scientific—in a word, rationalized. The attraction of rationalization lay principally in maintaining profitability in the face of the widespread exhaustion of rich ore reserves. Early accounts of inexhaustible and easily recovered wealth notwithstanding, the richest high-grade deposits in the United States had largely been discovered and worked out by the turn of the twentieth century. In its place, however, mining geologists had identified immense bodies of low-grade ore deposits that, for some metals, measured in concentrations less than a single ounce per ton. Outside of relocating operations to high-grade ore bodies outside the United States, profitability hinged upon lowering production costs.

Technological solutions ranked among the most visually evident changes. In 1870, one typically entered a coal or metal mine via portals and shaft houses. By the 1950s, an increasing number of mines were open entirely to the air, the excavation consisting of an immense pit or strip mine worked by mechanized diggers and dump trucks. Companies working the profitable Mesabi Iron Range west of Lake Superior were among the first in North America to adopt open-pit methods at the scale now prevalent in mining regions. The Hull-Rust-Mahoning Mine began production during the late nineteenth century and, when production peaked between the two world wars, accounted for one-quarter of national iron production. Open-pit techniques became widely employed in western states to unlock vast reserves of copper. The enormous Berkeley Pit in Butte, Montana—measuring 1.5 miles long and nearly 1,800 feet deep—was excavated in just

Figure 1.6. Mining writ large. A view of Bingham Canyon Mine, Utah, in 2003. The haul trucks, barely visible as small dots on the truck ramps, average 24 feet high and are capable of moving approximately 300 tons of rock in one load. A landslide in 2013 cascaded 70 million tons of material into the pit. Photograph by Spencer Musick.

twenty-seven years. Even-larger excavations in Bingham Canyon, Utah, began in the early 1900s and continue to this day (Goin and Raymond 2004: 3–13, 97–103) (figure 1.6).

The transformations wrought by mechanization and scientific management notably impacted employment structures. At the managerial level, the university-trained mining engineer increasingly replaced the self-taught entrepreneur. Down in the mine, workers specialized in running one piece of equipment took the place of the jack-of-all-trades miner who had hammered, blasted, and hauled out rock, in addition to other tasks (Hovis and Mouat 1996). This reconfiguration of labor ultimately eroded job security. Mechanization increased capital expenses but also brought substantial cost savings to mine owners. The attendant deskilling of labor ended the reliance on coveted and high-paid skills that mining crews had closely guarded to protect their position and wages in the mines.

While the industry was subject to dramatic changes, three consistencies with earlier periods are also apparent. First, western mining remained a predominantly male profession, although this is not to say that women were absent from mining communities. The miner was often a married man, and by the twentieth century, his wife and children typically accompanied him to the camps. Mining families took in boarders to supplement income. Women found informal work in coal-mining regions picking coal from waste piles for domestic use, and they also became involved in mining strikes and labor activism. Some took up mining during World War II, but women did not gain the right to find employment as underground miners until the passage of affirmative action legislation in the 1970s. Historical research has also identified women who rejected social conventions and carved out an independent life of prospecting in the west (Zanjani 1997).

Second, disputes between capital and labor continued. The establishment of a conciliation board under the Roosevelt administration had reportedly eased grievances between workers and mine management, but as a general manager of a coal company reflecting on the situation in 1947 put it, "This improved method of handling grievances did not end petty strikes . . . which have plagued the industry ever since its beginning" (Evans 1947: 268). By the 1950s, the United Mine Workers, Progressive Miners of America, and Industrial Workers of the World, among other labor organizations, had scored hard-won victories in establishing an eight-hour day and collective bargaining rights. Indeed, few mines in the coal industry remained nonunion in 1950, but this situation was not to last. The continuing decline of mineral resources of any sort, combined with the increasing internationalization of the industry, has led to a present-day resurgence in the number of nonunion mines.

The third continuity is that mining remained a dangerous profession. In 1907, an explosion of firedamp at the Monongah Mine in West Virginia killed 362 miners—the worst mining disaster in American history. The Monongah Mine catastrophe led directly to the formation of the U.S. Bureau of Mines to improve mine inspections (Curran 1993). Mining engineers in 1950 could identify signs of a diminishing fatality rate, yet the industry's track record still gives one pause. Between 1900 and 1950, more than five hundred mining disasters each claimed 5 or more lives. The Mine Safety and Health Administration indicates that more than 110,000 fatalities occurred in coal, metal, and nonmetal mines during this period. Total fatalities are likely to have been greater, because not all deaths were reported through the same channels and deaths from work-related diseases (such as silicosis and pneumonia) were typically excluded from tabulations. Arguably the most unsettling truth is that not all deaths in mining are directly knowable.

Staging the Questions

Such a brief accounting of American mining practice simplifies complicated trajectories of change. Suffice it to say that American mining practice in 1600 differed profoundly from mining in 1950. Over the course of three centuries, mining witnessed fundamental transformations in organization and operative scale. Mechanization introduced new mining techniques that reorganized labor tasks. The professionalization of mining, including the establishment of technical journals and mining schools beginning in the late nineteenth century, marked the rise of the mining engineer and the incorporation of scientific management principles into mine work. Shifts in extraction from high-grade ores to vast low-grade ore bodies expanded the physical imprint of mining and escalated the profits possible to secure from a traditionally risky enterprise.

The transformations wrought by mining were also profoundly social in character, for America had become a mining society. The mineral rushes had urbanized the western states in rapid order and fueled the development of a robust consumer economy. By the 1950s, the mining industry undergirded everything from electricity networks to the materials used in appliances, consumer goods, and the fashioning of urban streetscapes. Metals and plastics found ubiquitous, everyday use, and agricultural yields became increasingly tethered to the application of mineral fertilizers.

We now have a sense of the general contours that mining historically took, but finer resolution is desirable and necessary. Mineral extraction dovetailed with a rising American standard of living, yet the benefits were unevenly distributed. For instance, mining had advanced colonial agendas that dispossessed Native Americans from their land base, and the environmental impacts of mining disproportionately impacted the lifestyles of those living about the mines as well as the types of land use possible for downstream users. A closer look at the technical transformations in the industry also reveals that the shifts to mechanization did not happen all at once, in the same ways, or across all minerals. There remained plenty of places in 1950 where mining practices continued largely unchanged since the late nineteenth century. For small-scale metal mines especially, tried-and-true technologies served most purposes adequately, and several technologies used in 1870 continued to be effective because small-scale operators worked pockets of high-grade ores. Underground work in larger mines continued to present difficulties to scientific management. Hand sorting persisted in many mines, and machines still required tenders to assist the separation of waste from wanted materials. Thus, it is also the case that an immense amount of variability occurred in local practice.

It is precisely at this local scale that archaeology is well positioned to make contributions. Archaeological fieldwork, after all, inherently works with the material remains left at sites and locales. Contributions traditionally have a strong foundation in revealing the fundamental aspects of daily life that people seldom recorded, but it is also the case that research emphases have changed over time. Indeed, just as miners approached ore bodies with different tools, so, too, have archaeologists varied the tools for analyzing the sites that miners left behind.

2

Historical Archaeologists
and American Mining

The exploration of a mineral deposit and the exploration of a new field of research can trace similar evolutionary paths. Both actions tend to begin with a flurry of interest in which the rush to claim new ground provokes turf wars. Both also involve an element of risk, since the true value of a set of claims is ultimately proven only through further testing. Let us take the analogy a step further. During the life of a working mine, a mineral property undergoes successive stages of prospecting, development, and extraction. *Prospecting* involves the examination of the property to search for minerals and to assess whether further effort is warranted. On the basis of encouraging finds, miners *develop* the property by driving openings into the deposit to block out an ore body and prepare it for removal. *Extraction*, the final phase, entails removing the ore from the mine so that returns on investment can finally be realized, be what they may.

In this chapter, I apply this three-stage mining model to loosely characterize how archaeologists have investigated mining sites. Prospecting here typifies the period of early interest, 1920–60, marked by occasional excavations at historic mines and exploratory writings on potential archaeological contributions. Development usefully portrays the drawing together of "mining archaeology" after the 1960s, when archaeological attention to western mines pursued a more cohesive agenda. The extraction phase, 1990 to the present, is evidenced primarily by the appearance of synthetic studies drawing data from multiple sites and framing interpretations in broader historical and anthropological contexts. As with experience in the mines, the organization of scholarship is always messier in reality than in the model. Prospecting and development work continue as essential parts of archaeological investigations just as they do with mineral exploration. It is also the case that initial prospects have not always predicted the main veins and that changing circumstances continue to identify new areas for profitable exploration.

Early Prospects in the Archaeology of Mining, 1920s–1960s

Archaeological interest in North American mining sites began in circumstances similar to those typifying interest in other historic places, which is to say that research concentrated first on sites associated with famous people and key events. The historic-sites archaeology of the 1930s focused on Euro-American settlements such as Jamestown, Virginia, the location of the first English settlement in America (1607), and military outposts including Fort Necessity, Pennsylvania, the site of the first engagement in the French and Indian War and the site of George Washington's only military surrender (1754) (Orser 2004). If finding the proverbial spot where George Washington slept proved elusive, early excavations nevertheless added texture to historical understandings and a material authenticity to commemorative activities. Details about building phases and historic lifeways all supported a burgeoning heritage and museum industry.

James Marshall's statue at Coloma (described in the previous chapter) is noteworthy in this respect because Marshall's finger points to the location of one of the earliest excavations of a mining-related site in the United States. In 1924, a period of extreme low water on the South Fork of the American River exposed the log foundations of a dam presumed to be associated with Sutter's Mill. Phil Bekeart, the director of the Society of California Pioneers and the son of a forty-niner, directed the society's excavations of a portion of the site farther downstream for the purposes of erecting a monument. Through pick and shovel work, the investigators located one end of the sawmill and recovered a slew of artifacts including a straight saw, the wheel of an ore car, and a half bag of sawdust (figure 2.1). Excavations even recovered gold (Neasham 1947: 23), albeit not in quantities sufficient to impel archaeologists en masse to investigate historic mines.

Archaeological work at Sutter's Mill resumed two decades later when nearby gold-dredging operations rerouted the river and reexposed a portion of the sawmill's foundation. Archaeologists from the Department of Anthropology at the University of California, Berkeley, undertook investigations at the request of the California State Park Commission,

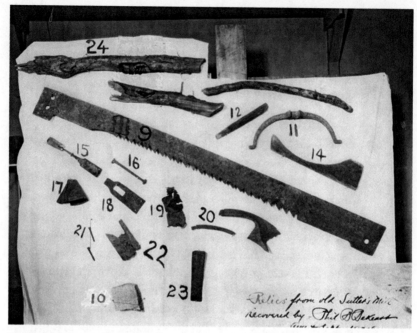

Figure 2.1. Selection of artifacts recovered during excavations at Sutter's Mill, California. Depicted here are a jigsaw blade (9), a bedrock fragment (10), an end iron for keeping logs in place (11), a wooden peg (12), a wheel brake (14), a chisel (15), a bolt and nut (16), a leather funnel (17), an unidentified iron piece (18), a fragment of a canvas belt (19), wheel parts (20), wooden screws (21), a timber fragment (22), a wedge (23), and the roots of twin pine trees located near the mill (24). Photograph courtesy of California State Library, record 001507332, view 3. Inventory from Philip B. Bekeart donor file, Alice Phelan Sullivan Library, Society of California Pioneers.

which had recently acquired the property. Led by Robert Heizer, the 1947 excavation uncovered enough foundation timbers to permit a detailed architectural reconstruction of the mill's lowest floor. Further digging located the wood-lined tailrace and recovered nineteenth-century artifacts including decorated pipe stems, Chinese porcelain, glass bottle fragments, square-toed boots, and tools associated with the construction and operation of the mill (Fenenga 1947; Heizer 1947). These materials, along with artifacts from the 1924 excavation, found their way to the California Pioneers Museum in San Francisco and eventually went on display at a museum erected on-site.

Heizer worked again with one of his graduate students, Franklin Fenenga, in the following year to record gold rush-era structures along the Sierra Nevada's western slope. Funded by the California Division of Mines as part of the centennial celebrations of California statehood, the study documented more than sixty gold rush towns by photographing storefronts and house ruins, drawing attention also to quarry sites, stables, and miners' dams (Heizer and Fenenga 1948). Although Fenenga is remembered more for work on Great Plains cultures, among others, he continued to investigate early mining sites. Fenenga recorded mining sites for the Georgia Historical Commission where gold discoveries in the northwestern part of that state in 1828 initiated North America's first mineral rush. Possibly as a high school student, Fenenga had also assisted in an archaeological survey of Mine La Motte, Missouri's earliest European lead mine (Fenenga 1967: 81; Riddell 1997; Wallace 1999).

Reconstruction-guided efforts dominated, but did not totally capture, archaeological work at historical mining sites during the 1940s and 1950s. Charles Hunt (1959), for instance, looked to tin cans and bottles—among the most ubiquitous components of mining sites—as having a high diagnostic potential for dating occupational periods. Though less interested in examining aspects of miners' diets (Hunt was primarily a geologist by trade and his tin can article appeared in a geology journal), Hunt still drew broader connections. Knowing the dates of mining camps, he contended, might permit comparisons between local conditions and economic boom-and-bust cycles. He also postulated that a dated site would enable geologists to correlate the grade of ore mined historically with broader temporal and technological trends in the mining industry. This is to say that Hunt recognized the potential for archaeological analyses to add a new level of detail, which could potentially diverge from accepted narratives of the industry.

By the 1960s, then, the study of historical mining sites had made inroads as a small but nonetheless legitimate field of historical inquiry alongside the archaeology of missions, fur-trading sites, military posts, ranches, postcontact Native American sites, and urban settlements. The first professional assessment of this subfield, authored by Fenenga, appeared in the inaugural issue of *Historical Archaeology* (1967), the first publication of the newly minted Society for Historical Archaeology (SHA). The assignment of Fenenga's article to the journal's back pages may reflect a lesser interest among practitioners in mining sites. Indeed, Fenenga's opening sentence takes an almost apologetic tone in declaring, "Mining camps [a term he extended to workplaces] are certainly a minor one of the kinds of historic sites with which we are occasionally concerned" (Fenenga 1967: 80). His prospectus for the historical archaeology of mining was also somewhat bleak. Fenenga noted that mining's destructive character combined with the continued reworking of old claims tended to obliterate the types of sites that archaeologists and historians were most interested in finding. His personal experiences in Georgia as well as pre–Sutter's Mill work in the Midwest had both failed (his term) to relocate discovery sites, because subsequent mining had churned up the ground. Fenenga also considered that archaeologists would be best to skip the subject of technology. Mining technologies recovered in archaeological contexts, he reasoned, could contribute only minimally to understanding human behavior, because much of this information was better documented in the technical literature, in which mining tools and equipment had enjoyed centuries of careful documentation by engineers (ibid.: 81).

Fenenga projected greater returns for archaeological studies into the social aspects of mining. First, social conditions in early mining camps were often poorly documented in written records. Second, and anticipating a core direction in historical archaeological scholarship on pattern recognition and settlement frontiers (e.g., Lewis 1984; South 1977), Fenenga suggested that the male-dominated material culture of mining camps would leave an assemblage quite distinct from one expected at ranch houses, military outposts, and other historical sites. Along similar lines, he argued that the ethnic divisions in mining towns could also leave material residues and permit the study of acculturation processes. Fenenga thought that adaptive reuse would also be a productive area, since expediency in mining districts often ruled the day. Lastly, he encouraged archaeologists to seek broader connections to the American historical experience. The mineral rushes had spurred the rapid and total depopulation of settlements far removed from mining districts, and such instances of abandonment should be evident materially.

At the time that Fenenga authored these remarks, the number of published archaeological reports on mining sites could be counted on two hands. Judging only by academic journals, we can see that the situation did not change much—other foci of archaeological research, together with the strident debates over whether historical archaeology belonged properly to the discipline of history or anthropology, left little oxygen for an extensive examination of Fenenga's outline for a mining archaeology.

Indeed, the next reference in print to Fenenga's prospectus did not come until a decade later (Baker 1978).

The seeming dearth of discussion belies a substantive increase in archaeologists' actual engagement with historical mining sites after the 1960s. Changes to heritage legislation were partly responsible, but a burgeoning interest in industrialization and its consequences also afforded mining sites more attention. These new conditions also lent the historical archaeology of mining a different character than Fenenga's projections. Indeed, it helped advance the study of mines as a specialization.

Development: Mining Archaeology in an Age of Acronyms, 1960s–1980s

Frank Fenenga's assessment of the archaeology of post-1800 mining sites had drawn upon the state of the field prior to the passage of the National Historic Preservation Act (NHPA) of 1966 (Public Law 89-665). This legislation, still in effect today, became enormously influential in directing subsequent archaeological practice because it mandated that federal agencies evaluate adverse effects on historic properties for any federally funded or permitted projects. In addition to calling for assessments of site significance, the NHPA expanded the temporal range of potential archaeological sites to include a moving wall of fifty years. Given the extensive federal holdings in the United States, the act vastly expanded opportunities for archaeological encounters with all cultural sites, and old mining locations were among them.

The ramifications of the NHPA on archaeology are difficult to overstate. Archaeological sites became included within the broader category of "cultural resources," encompassing the tangible and intangible aspects of cultural systems such as sites, structures, districts, objects, and historic documents (Kerber 1994: 2). The subsequent rise of cultural resource management (CRM) dramatically increased the number of archaeological practitioners. Changes were evident also through the expanding scale of investigations. Through CRM-based initiatives, the scope of archaeological work on mining sites moved beyond the investigation of single sites to incorporate mining landscapes and districts.

Archaeological work initiated by the construction of the New Melones Dam and Reservoir (1966–83) on the Stanislaus River in central California provides a representative example. Here, preparatory work by the U.S.

Army Corps of Engineers included funding thirty separate archaeological surveys in areas projected to be flooded after the dam's construction. Beginning in 1968 and conducted over the course of twelve years, these surveys ultimately inventoried upward of seven hundred archaeological sites, of which two-thirds related to the historical period, and a sizable number of these were formed during the California Gold Rush era (Greenwood 1992; see also Teague 1987: 146–47, 157–58 regarding similar projects).

Rising gold prices in the 1970s intensified survey work. The reopening of mines throughout the western United States generated the need for cultural resource assessments because many proposals concerned public lands. With mine operators increasingly favoring open-pit excavations over underground exploration, the areas of potential effect could be sizable. An open-pit operation could impact several square miles, obliterating not only underground workings but also the surface remnants of communities and infrastructure.

One consequence of the rise in mining-land surveys is evident in the nomination of mining sites for listing on the National Register of Historic Places, a list of historic properties considered significant to national heritage. Eligibility to this list requires that nominated sites meet at least one of four significance criteria: (A) association with significant events; (B) association with significant persons; (C) embodying distinct characteristics of a type, period, or mode of construction; and—the roomiest of them all—(D) information potential. Placement on the list does not legally protect sites, but the modification or destruction of listed properties could result in archaeological testing, excavation, or public interpretation.

For the most part, historical mining resources were inventoried but seldom mitigated, and rarely were they considered of greater value than the minerals lying beneath them. Archaeologists and historians experienced difficulties in nominating some mining sites to the National Register (e.g., Spude 1990b: 31), but eligible sites increased as register criteria expanded to recognize vernacular landscapes (Feierabend 1990; Hardesty and Little 2000; Noble 1990; Noble and Spude 1997). By 1990, the National Register included approximately 250 mining-related sites. Listings focused nevertheless on standing structures and domestic sites rather than industrial features, and there was a clear dominance also in the selection of gold mines over sites that exploited other minerals. The majority of sites had become eligible under criterion A, because of their association with the western mineral rushes (see Barker and Huston 1990: app. B).

The concerns for archaeological site protection that gave rise to this revision in heritage legislation had also spurred the development of organizations geared specifically to documenting and preserving industrial sites. In 1969, the federal government established the Historic American Engineering Record (HAER) to document America's disappearing engineering and industrial heritage. HAER modeled its organization and recording methods closely after the Historic American Building Survey (HABS), a division of the National Park Service established in 1933 as a federal make-work project during the Great Depression. Both HABS and HAER emphasized the preservation of sites through documentation. Both organizations adopted a tripartite recording structure, with sites documented through architectural drawings, large-format photography, and historical research, and with final reports housed in the Library of Congress. But whereas HABS focused on recording American architectural treasures, broadly construed—Montpelier, the U.S. Capitol, and Arizona cliff dwellings among them—HAER focused on structures such as bridges, factories, canals, and coal breakers and also emphasized the recording of industrial processes. HABS tended to work on properties in near-original condition, while HAER documented sites that, even if well preserved, had by their very nature undergone complex changes over time. These differences encouraged HAER recording teams to draw from a broader range of practitioners, including archaeologists and historians of technology (DeLony 1999: 10). In execution, and especially in terms of its products, the HABS/HAER methodology came to set the standard for industrial site documentation in the United States and internationally (Martin 2009: 287).

HAER projects began as statewide surveys to catalog historical industrial sites potentially eligible for the National Register. In hindsight, mining sites were underrepresented in these early efforts (DeLony 1999: 19), but documentation projects during the 1970s and 1980s at places such as the Quincy Mine, Michigan, Butte, Montana, and Kennecott, Alaska, began correcting the balance. The mines HAER targeted for documentation tended to be large scale. The Quincy copper mine, for instance, which operated from the mid-1840s to the mid-twentieth century, had employed more than two thousand people at its peak and extracted 1.5 billion pounds of copper over its operative life. Although technically considered a "medium-sized" operation, at its closure, miners had excavated the copper deposit down more than ninety levels. The mine bottomed out

Figure 2.2. Quincy Mine Hoist, Michigan. This immense device was responsible for lowering skips of men and mining equipment down the ninety-two levels of the mine and for returning skips of men and ore to the surface. Photograph by Jet Lowe, HAER MICH, 31-HANC, 1, photo 59.

at 1.7 miles below the ground surface, making Quincy the world's deepest mine at the time (Lankton and Hyde 1982). (The deepest today, the Tau-Tona Mine in South Africa, descends another two-thirds of a mile into the earth's crust.)

HAER documentation of the Quincy Mine included the recording of the mine complex, mill, and smelter locations in addition to company housing (figures 2.2 and 2.3). All told, project historians authored seven reports that emphasized business, economic, labor, and technological histories (Hyde 1990: 91). Architects drafted nearly three dozen measured drawings that included profiles and floor plans of mine structures, graphic representations of technical processes, details of select equipment, and base maps illustrating landscape change over time. Completing the set were more than ninety large-format photographs of extant structures and equipment and nearly two hundred copies of original plans and photographs of operations above- and belowground.

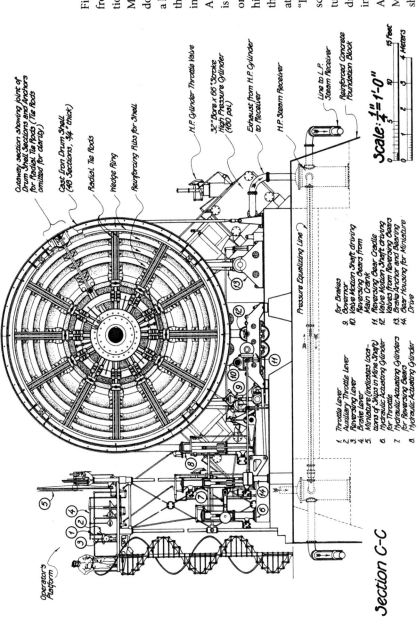

Figure 2.3. Detail from HAER illustration of the Quincy Mine Hoist. HAER documentation set a high standard for the recording of industrial places. A humorous touch is the depiction of one of the project historians beside the hoist controls at upper left. The "Larry Lankton scale" became a fixture on other HAER drawings. Drawing by Richard K. Anderson Jr., HAER MI, 31-HANC, 1, sheet 15.

A second organization promoting the documentation of industrial heritage was the Society for Industrial Archeology (SIA). Formed in 1971, the SIA was influenced heavily by developments across the Atlantic, where industrial archaeology had emerged as a vibrant field. Concern for industrial heritage arose in Britain out of a growing public awareness that the industries that had been central to the Industrial Revolution (textiles, mining, ironworking) no longer occupied a prominent position in British life. Moreover, the physical sites were prone to destruction during the postwar building boom, and there had been little attention paid to the information that the physical remains of industrial sites could provide. Industrial archaeology developed partly as a popular movement, engaged just as much in the survey and preservation of industrial monuments as with research into the social and technological transformations that industrialization promulgated (Buchanan 2000; Hudson 1963).

Industrial archaeology in the United States adopted a similar conceptual charge and likewise brought together a broad base of practitioners, including historians, archaeologists, curators, architects, and engineers. However, site recording in the United States tended to be conducted more by paid professionals than by the wider corpus of volunteers who dominated early field research in the United Kingdom (Hyde 1991; Martin 2009).

The first issue of *IA: The Journal of the Society for Industrial Archeology* (1975) included mining-related articles examining a black powder factory and a copper and lead smelter. As with HAER, journal submissions emphasized technological histories. Both mining-related articles, for instance, recorded the technical processes involved, although neither was exactly "asocial" in delivery. Robert Howard (1975) noted how the danger of black powder manufacturing was reflected in the architecture, including an outhouse on factory grounds constructed with boilerplate. T. Allen Comp (1975) framed his analysis of the Tooele Smelter, Utah, in terms of company responses to the threat of lawsuits from neighboring farmers. Assessing the field a decade later, George Teague (1987: 37) noted that the editorship of *IA* had "passed from specialists in technology and engineering to those in history and anthropology, with an attendant softening of topics from machinery and monuments to more humanistically inclined subjects."

Industrial archaeology's mixture of avocational experts and employed professionals came to mark a difference in approach to historical archaeology. Whereas industrial archaeologists favored maintaining a wide spectrum of practitioners, historical archaeologists by the 1970s had become aligned with a more explicitly anthropological and social-scientific agenda. Divisions between anthropological and historical perspectives in historical archaeology came to the fore in answer to Clyde Dollar's provocative stance that archaeology served history (Dollar 1968). Friction between historical archaeology and industrial archaeology occurred contemporaneously in a debate published in the journal *Historical Archaeology* (Foley 1968, 1969; Vogel 1969). Here, Vincent Foley objected to the term *industrial archaeology* on the basis that its practitioners emphasized preservation more than the recovery of scientific information and that they paid little attention to subsurface investigation. Robert Vogel's impassioned rebuttal took issue with the elitism behind these more restrictive definitions. Later reflections indicate how much of the Foley-Vogel debate rested more on perception than actual scholarship. Comparisons between the works of self-titled "historical" and "industrial" archaeologists, for instance, reveal little difference in the engagement with material culture (Martin 2009; Teague 1987).

Even so, a division of labor developed in the sorts of material culture investigated. Industrial archaeologists tended to focus attention on mining workplaces, with analyses emphasizing mining systems, plant layouts, technological change, and assessments of process efficiency. In contrast, historical archaeological research focused on the settlements associated with mining enterprises; typifying early research were examinations of ethnic communities and studies of the frontier processes revealed through domestic artifact assemblages. The separation of interests between historical archaeology and industrial archaeology arose from no formal pronouncement but derived instead as a consequence of myriad research avenues, different preservation priorities, and the pragmatic parsing of skill sets. As such, reports incorporating the research emphases of both fields were comparatively rare (Teague and Shenk 1977 being one example).

Reviewing the state of mining archaeology in the mid-1980s, Donald Hardesty lamented the lack of an organizing research agenda. Archaeological investigations had increased dramatically, but the majority of site research could be classified as surveys and inventories, with some attention to settlement patterns and select ethnic communities following traditional lines of anthropological inquiry (Hardesty 1986: 47). The mounting pile of reports showed few indications of a coherent "archaeology of mining," despite the enormous potential.

Hardesty marked out three broad-scaled themes to better unify archaeological research at western mining sites. The first and broadest of these concerned the connections between mining and the expansion of global capitalism. Mining districts existed as extractive colonies in service of a world system. The archaeological investigation of labor movements, technological systems, and supply systems could all detail the localized characteristics of this broader relationship. A second theme centered on the ability of mining communities to inform about Victorianism and the rise of conspicuous consumption. The westward expansion of mining during the Victorian era (1837–1901) and the short life-spans typical of mining camps offered snapshots into changing value systems, as well as baselines for interpreting later, post–gold rush era sites (e.g., Baker 1978). A third, related theme, framed mining sites in terms of understanding frontier processes (e.g., Hardesty 1986; Ostrogorsky 1982).

Hardesty's *The Archaeology of Mining and Miners* (1988), probably the most referenced archaeological work on American mining, explored these themes in the context of nineteenth-century mines and mining camps of Nevada. In addition to providing a needed review of the range of historical documents available for mining, the work demonstrated the intimate connection between mining locales and world systems. Hardesty pointed to how ethnic groups employed at the mine, the domestic goods consumed, and the technological processes selected were part of global flows of people and materials. Hardesty's research referenced the twin foci of mining archaeology by drawing attention first to how technological processes could be interpreted from partial remains, and second to the interpretations possible from the domestic material culture of mining camps. Important to both was the necessity of developing comparative frameworks informed by anthropological theory and mining history.

Developments outside of archaeology also contributed to a converging interest in mining sites. Beginning in the 1960s, a small set of practitioners developed mining history into an immensely productive field of research. This included overviews of the mineral rushes (Greever 1963; Paul 1963), as well as more-selective forays into mining camp life (Smith 1967; West 1979), the politics and lifestyles of the mining elite (Malone 1981; Peterson 1977), the rise of labor movements (Brown 1979; Lingenfelter 1974; Wyman 1979), and the transformations in mining techniques, investment, professionalism, and environmental impact (Smith 1987; Spence 1958, 1970; Young 1970). Such developments suggested profitable directions, too, for an archaeology of mining.

Despite concerns over a lack of unity, the majority of archaeological research from the 1960s still bore the stamp of NHPA stipulations. Eligibility for the National Register rested on making determinations of significance—be it unique or representative—and this implied that historic properties could be ranked and compared using some objective criteria. Archaeological attention to mining typologies sought to standardize recording procedures, improve overall assessments, and enable comparative research (Cunningham 1990; Hardesty 1988). Even research undertaken on the more explicitly anthropological approaches, such as evaluating Victorian material culture or frontier processes, developed contexts for gauging historical significance and broadened the range of potentially applicable National Register criteria.

The influence of the NHPA became plainly evident in a workshop on managing historic mining sites organized by National Park Service historian Robert Spude and HAER chief Eric DeLony in 1989. An escalation in mining activity, combined with a growing number of government initiatives targeting abandoned mining lands for environmental remediation, had, as Spude (1990a: 3) remarked, created a "compliance nightmare" for those involved in the management of historic mining sites. The conference brought together a wide spectrum of professionals: historians, archaeologists, historic architects, environmental consultants, mining engineers, reclamation specialists, land managers, and agency representatives. Conference themes included addressing the significance of mining sites in ways that moved beyond the "criterion A" bias that accounted for almost 80 percent of mining sites listed on the National Register (Barker and Huston 1990: app. B). Conference attendees advanced HAER as a documentation standard and also presented case examples of successful heritage preservation. Connections forged by the end of the conference led to HAER's development of a Hard-Rock Mining Initiative to increase the recording of mining sites (particularly in national parks). Site selection also broadened to include the smaller mines that were more representative of the historical mining sites actually encountered (Andrews 1994; DeLony 1999: 21).

It is fair to conclude that archaeological engagement with American mines looked very different in 1990 than it had just two decades prior.

Although mines remained one of numerous areas of archaeological concern, changes in legislation in combination with a growing body of interested specialists developed firm footing for an archaeology of mining. The passage of the NHPA, in particular, set many of the terms for archaeological encounters with mining sites. Mining archaeology developed through a preservation context, but it would be mistaken to imply that interests began and ended with site conservation. Implicit to any discussion about what mining sites should be protected is the consideration of why they should be preserved in the first place. This resulted in a revision of research priorities as well as a push, continuing at present, to synthesize findings and explore new possibilities for interpretation.

Toward Extraction: Mining Archaeology, 1990s–Present

Casting an eye over the past twenty-five years of publications on mining sites shows, above all else, that there is more of it. Exact numbers remain difficult to quantify, in part because archaeological scholarship works its way into diffuse forms of reporting, but some measure of the increase can be gauged through journal articles. Representation in *Historical Archaeology* has been boosted by thematic issues on the American West (1999), the Intermountain West (2001), labor camps (2002), and Chinese-American experiences (2008). *IA* has published well over a dozen articles on mining-related sites since 2000, increasing from a single article published in the decade prior. Articles on historic mining sites have appeared also in the *International Journal of Historical Archaeology*, as well as in regionally based journals including the *Nevada Archaeologist*, *Southwestern Lore*, and *Tennessee Anthropologist*, among others. The *Mining History Journal*, first issued in 1994, adds significantly to this tally since many contributors make reference to material culture and because the journal's back pages include an annual summation of historical, archaeological, and historic preservation reports.

The uptick in publications indicates that historical mines have increased as foci for archaeological research, but it may still be premature to intuit any change in research agendas. *Mining archaeology* continues as neither a formally recognized term nor a formally defined specialization. The nature of submissions to *Historical Archaeology* and *IA* continues to show a general division between the study of mining communities (Adams et al. 2001; Dixon 2006; Schmitt and Zeier 1993; C. Spude 2005) and the study of workplaces and landscapes (Landon and Tumberg 1996; Quivik 2000, 2003; Van Bueren 2004; White 2003, 2010). Areas of crossover nevertheless exist. For instance, treatments of the legacies of the coal and iron industry as seen through monuments and artwork (da Costa Nunes 2002, 2008; Kierstead 2002; Langa 2002; Schruers 2002; Shipley 2008) complement articles appearing in *Historical Archaeology* concerning the memorialization of the Ludlow massacre and the Colorado Coalfield War (Shackel 2004; Walker 2003). However, historical and industrial archaeological findings are rarely reviewed together, and examinations of technology tend to be downplayed in historical archaeological overviews (Paynter 2000: 174; Shackel 2009: 1–3).

Where we begin to see signs of a qualitative shift is in the recognition that maintaining hard distinctions between industrial archaeology and historical archaeology has become detrimental to a holistic understanding of industrialization (e.g., Beaudry 2005; Cranstone 2005)—a line of reasoning similar to calls for bridging methodological and theoretical gaps between historical and prehistoric archaeology (Lightfoot 1995). Indications of a shift become clearer first through a rise in the number of syntheses of historical and material evidence. Richard Francaviglia's *Hard Places* (1991) documents the distinct vernacular material culture of American mining landscapes. Robert Gordon and Patrick Malone's *Texture of Industry* (1994) distills historical trends in American industrialization with case studies drawn from well-preserved archaeological and historic sites, including mining sites throughout North America. Other works (Gordon 1996; Rolando 1992) draw detailed national and statewide portraits of the iron industry from historical and archaeological evidence, with Gordon also incorporating the archaeometallurgical analysis of iron artifacts. Archaeologically based overviews include evaluations of rush-era camps at local and regional scales (Hall et al. 1997; Hardesty 2010; Obermayr and McQueen 2016; Spude et al. 2011), evaluations of Chinese American experiences in the West (Chung and Wegars 2005; Wegars 1993), and a compilation of findings from excavations at Ludlow, Colorado (Larkin and McGuire 2009; Saitta 2007), Virginia City, Nevada (James 2012), and Skagway, Alaska (Saleeby 2011), where investigations ranged from several field seasons to work conducted over three decades. Conference papers published under the title *Social Approaches to an Industrial Past* (Knapp et al. 1998) offer the broadest anthropological synthesis by integrating archaeological and anthropological approaches to the study of mining sites worldwide, with contributors exploring class, gender, and power relations in mining communities as well as the social contexts of technology.

Indications of a qualitative shift stem also from a jump in graduate research. Online databases indicate that at least 180 theses and dissertations on the material culture of American mining sites have been completed since 1970, with 90 percent filed after 1990 (figure 2.4). The University of Nevada, Reno, has steered almost three dozen mining archaeology projects since the 1980s, most of them under the direction of Donald Hardesty (Fowler 2006). Michigan Technological University, another primary contributor, initiated a master's program in industrial history and archaeology in 1991 and a doctoral program in industrial heritage in 2005 (Martin 1998; Seely and Martin 2006). Archaeological work shows expected regionalization to the extent that the location of graduate research tends to occur in the same state as the university. With the notable exception of Michigan, the majority of research locales for mining theses and dissertations are sited in the American West.

Although academic theses derive from comparatively few academic programs, the jump in numbers indicates that mining sites are recognized as legitimate sites for historical archaeological inquiry. Moreover, because a common component of theses involves linking material culture to a specific body of anthropological theory or line of historical inquiry, such works have both tested and broadened interpretive possibilities for mining settlements. A leading line of investigation concerns the formation of identity in mining communities. This includes the closer examination of ethnicity, gender roles, class, and status relations, as evident in several doctoral dissertations that subsequently appeared as standalone publications (Cowie 2011; Dixon 2005; Johnston 2013; Metheny 2006) or in compilations (Larkin and McGuire 2009; Spude et al. 2011).

The general trend toward the study of power matches a broader shift traceable in archaeological practice from processual to postprocessual and interpretive approaches (Johnson 2010), but thesis directions also mirror investigative trends in allied disciplines. Developments in four historical subfields have exerted a significant influence. First, beginning in the 1960s, labor historians increasingly adopted a "bottom-up" perspective that emphasized workers' actions and contested class relations (see Gutman 1976). Second, environmental history emerged about the same time to examine interactions between societies and the environment through more-contextual readings of terms such as *ecology* and *nature* (see Morse

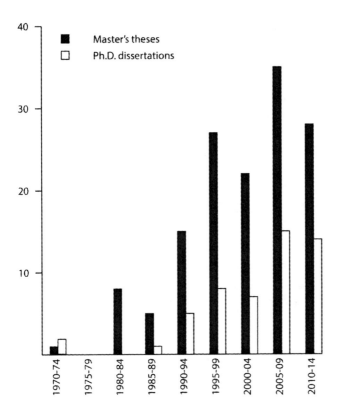

Figure 2.4. Graduate theses on mining archaeology from American universities. Data from author's review of ProQuest Dissertation Abstracts database and library catalogs from universities with graduate degree programs in anthropology and historic preservation. Numbers err on the conservative side in part because determinations are dependent on the titles, abstracts, and keywords used for cataloging theses. Chart by author.

2003 and Smith 1987 for applications to mining history). Third, beginning in the 1980s, New Western historians dislodged a long-reigning historical focus on frontiers to emphasize instead histories of conquest and appropriation, diverse cultural experiences, and the central importance of place in shaping historical events (Limerick 1987; see Hardesty 1991). Fourth, historians of technology increasingly emphasized the external social, political, and economic factors responsible for technological change, differing from an earlier focus on internal technical considerations (Staudenmaier 1985). Additionally, sociological and cultural anthropological studies have long drawn attention to mining communities as a unique organizational form, recording ways that indigenous peoples have incorporated the regimen of industrial work into their lives and the ways that mining sustains relations of economic dependency (Ali 2003; Ballard and Banks 2003; Culver and Greaves 1985; Finn 1998; Gedicks 1993; Godoy 1985; Kirsch 2014; Nash 1993; Snipp 1986a, 1986b; Taussig 1980). The net result has been an expanding pool of ideas with which to frame archaeological investigations at mining sites.

The National Register context, which proved influential in increasing historical archaeologists' encounters with mining sites beginning in the 1960s, continues to undergird the bulk of archaeological investigations (e.g., Hardesty and Little 2000). Section 106 compliance continues as a main "vein," yet new scenarios are also raised by the rapid expansion of environmental remediation programs. The Environmental Protection Agency, National Park Service, U.S. Forest Service, and Bureau of Land Management, for example, all have initiated inventories of abandoned mining sites to identify environmental threats and safety hazards preparatory to cleanup work. The Comprehensive Environmental Response, Compensation, and Liability Act (CERCLA) of 1980, also known as "Superfund," is the most well known of these initiatives because it targets the worst cases of contamination. Since the 1990s, the scope of these initiatives has shifted from attention to worst cases to a wider consideration of entire mining districts. Archaeologists have not always been apprised of these occurrences, yet there are notable differences in the ways that cultural resource and natural resource managers approach historical mining landscapes. As explored in later pages of this volume, such areas of contestation are also areas with enormous promise for informed interdisciplinary collaboration.

The Conceptual Toolkit

It goes without saying that archaeologists have a more extensive set of tools at their disposal today than what was available even a decade ago. However, whereas archaeological attention to historical mining sites has kept pace with general shifts in the discipline over the past five decades—adopting more-rigorous excavation protocols, incorporating spatial analysis, and exploring new technical applications among them—contributors have devoted less space to detailing the theoretical underpinnings guiding exploration and facilitating analysis. A range of theoretical approaches and position statements have informed the archaeology of mining over the years (Costello et al. 2007; Hardesty 1986, 1988, 1991, 1994, 1998, 2003; Simmons 1989; Vermeer 2006), and these generally ally with a dominant framework in historical archaeological scholarship concerned with the study of capitalism (Leone and Potter 1999; Matthews 2010; Orser 1996; Paynter 2000; Shackel 2009; Wurst 2006).

Capitalism is an economic system with a broad reach in the modern world. At its core, capitalism involves an unequal exchange between two parties: those who own facilities, tools, and other items necessary for producing commodities (referred to as the "means of production") and those who sell their labor for a wage. Labor, in this sense, has, like the items being produced, become transformed into a thing for sale. Because capitalism concerns the pursuit of profit, the capitalist endeavors in all interactions to buy cheap and sell dear. It follows that the exchange of commodities is never fully balanced: the worker produces more than what is remunerated, and this difference translates into revenue that the capitalist either reinvests in the enterprise or taps to improve his or her standard of living (Marx 1967).

What has made capitalism of particular interest to social theorists is that the simplicity of its operating principle belies the complex social and political conditions that capitalism arose from and set in motion. Viewed in historical perspective, capitalism did not introduce social inequality as much as reconfigure its expression. Capitalism's inroads in sixteenth-century Europe marked the expansion of global commerce and the establishment of a mercantile class. Beginning in the mid-eighteenth century, the rise of industrial production systems created a working class whose members also became key consumers of the goods being manufactured in prodigious quantities (Wallerstein 1974). The industrial transformation was wrenching because of its rapidity and because the underlying profit motive generated new forms of social friction. Profitability rested on the ability to tap new markets and expand one's market share, with the ultimate goal of eliminating competition. In daily transactions, profitability hinged on continually finding ways to reduce costs, and this often targeted workers. Capitalists were drawn to mechanization because it promised dramatic increases in the quantity of production without a concomitant increase in labor. Indeed, the act of simplifying production processes into sequences of repeatable tasks broke down the very skills that commanded high wages. This constant chipping away at the market value of human labor brought the capitalist and working classes into a dependent but antagonistic relationship.

Capitalism and mining have entwined and lengthy historical roots. The deepening of underground mines beginning in the Middle Ages seems to have laid the groundwork for capitalism's early expansion in Europe. Lewis Mumford (1963) reasoned that because the underground environment offered nothing to sustain life, any consideration of mine work as an occupation necessitated viewing labor abstractly as something that could be bought and sold. Underground mining ventures also involved considerable capital investment and highly uncertain outcomes. In all these aspects of labor and risk taking, mining exemplified and served as an agent for modern capitalism (Mumford 1963: 65–77).

Capitalism categorically underlay American mining endeavors from the inception of European interest in the continent, but there would arguably be little archaeological interest if it looked the same everywhere. Mining functioned successfully at a wide range of profit margins and proved highly adaptive to additional rules of engagement provided that the twin premises of exacting a profit and allowing for continual growth could be met. American mining was shaped through colonial policies that appropriated land and deemed who could be considered a legitimate miner. Federal resource laws, despite being very lenient toward mining interests, still set criteria for what constituted a legal mineral entry and appropriate use. Even if we envision capitalism operating in some truly unfettered form, its contractual conditions still had to be learned. These are critical points to contemplate, for it is only through the exploration of such dynamics that we come to connect an abstract economic principle to its lived realities.

Marxist perspectives emphasize the interrelationships between material conditions, ideology, and the individual, and it is not surprising that a profession as engrossed in the study of material culture as archaeology finds the materialist bent of Marxist theory compelling (Trigger 1993). While room exists between Karl Marx's seminal treatise and later iterations of Marxist theory, there can be no doubt that Marx was first and foremost a contemporary observer of events and that his works detailed the mechanics and systemic abuses of industrial capitalism. There is, then, a conceptual elegance in employing a perspective historically generated in response to industrialization to further the examination of capitalism's historical expressions and consequences. The archaeology of mining has not always made this connection explicit, but research into frontier dynamics, acculturation processes, and the creation of American identity has encouraged the delineation of supply networks, ethnic neighborhoods, consumption patterns, and technological systems. All ultimately furnish data points useful in the historical analysis of capitalism.

Beginning in the mid-1980s, Donald Hardesty (1986, 1988, 1991, 1994, 1998) outlined prospective takes for investigating different facets of capitalism at mining sites, including attention to world systems, gender, and power dynamics. In retrospect, however, excavations at Ludlow, Colorado, in the late 1990s (Larkin and McGuire 2009) marked the clearest turn toward the visible implementation of Marxist frameworks. The site of a short-lived strike camp that ended in a massacre presented a case of the harshest consequences of class conflict. Investigators recognized Ludlow's importance from the outset; the tent colony had come into existence because of class antagonism, and its investigation offered a way for archaeologists to engage with labor history and critical theory, a Marxist-informed approach concerned with exposing the power inequities perpetuating in the present (McGuire 2014; McGuire and Reckner 2009; Saitta 2007).

Theses and dissertations on mining continue this core focus on power relations and identity formation. This includes investigations of race and ethnicity, with several theses exploring Chinese encampments and neighborhoods (Axsom 2009; Dale 2011; Knee 2012; Norman 2012). Studies of gender in mining districts reveal a widening thematic interest from rush-era camps to more-diverse settings where miners were permitted and encouraged to bring their families (Hardesty 1994). Studies of red-light districts continue as a strong thread (Horobik 2011; Vermeer 2006), and archaeologists have also made inroads into exploring the interplay between working-class ideals and notions of domesticity, masculinity, and status (Banks 2011; Burnette 2014; Cowie 2011; Horn 2009; Ogborne 2013; Thurlo 2010; Wood 2002). Fundamental here is an acknowledgment of agency, which emphasizes that social relations are always negotiated. This is not to state that all parties are on an equal footing or that arrangements are arrived at amicably. Rather, agency draws attention to how identities are deployed in strategic ways and how people become habituated to circumstances through daily practice.

Examinations of the workplace reveal signs of a similar interest in social dynamics through the study of "sociotechnical systems" and operational chains (Lemonnier 1986; Pfaffenberger 1988, 1998). The former, and conceptually broader, approach frames technology in terms of the cultural preferences and sociopolitical networks that influence selections, maintain technological systems, and direct the course of technological change. Investigations of operational chains (*chaînes opératoires*), by contrast, tighten the focus to observe how a given technological practice comes to be organized into specific procedures and tasks. These complementary perspectives have promising application to mining sites, for both permit finer insight into capitalist transformations of work and the cultural factors shaping capitalism's expression (DePasqual 2009; Hartnell 2009; Holman 2016).

While the study of capitalism remains a primary theme in the archaeology of mining, it is apparent that research directions are increasingly attuned to investigating capitalism's variable expressions, such as the tangled ways that cultural factors worked outside of, intermeshed with, and butted directly against capitalism's fundamental mechanics. Attention to these dynamics recognizes that although capitalist principles have become deeply incorporated into our livelihoods, capitalism is not the only tenet through which people make their lives and the places they inhabit into something meaningful.

Assaying a Half Century of Results

Fifty years of archaeological research into American mining reveals proclivities toward the documentation of surface features and toward sites located in the western half of the continent, sites formed between the mid-nineteenth and early twentieth centuries, and sites concerned with the extraction of either precious metals, copper, or coal. Commodities such as lead, mercury, and a plethora of nonmetals including oil, uranium, and talc have seen limited examination by comparison. Studies of the iron industry resist this simple categorization, for although few archaeological studies concern mining workplaces and associated communities (Cowie 2011; Sportman 2011), research on iron furnace and forge sites is extensive (e.g., Gordon 1996; Kotlensky 2009; Pollard and Klaus 2004; Rolando 1992; Ryzewski 2008).

What accounts for such a selective sampling of the American experience? The limited number of underground surveys (Blankenship 2007; Poirier and Harper 1998; White 2016; White and James 1991) is

Figure 2.5. Abandoned dynamite at a mine in south-central Alaska: a nightmare scenario. Photograph by Logan Hovis.

understandable because of the formidable safety risks that abandoned workings present. Mines were dangerous places during their operation, and the dangers hardly lessen with age. Support timbers rot, roof bolts weaken, and water and gas accumulate in workings. Excavation methods such as robbing pillars leave workings unstable and prone to collapse (see, for example, James 2012: 14). Miners also left explosives secreted in niches, loaded in drill holes, or scattered among rock debris and dust (figure 2.5). Dynamite sticks and blasting caps (small explosives inserted into dynamite to trigger the charge) are dangerous items in any circumstance, but they behave unpredictably with age—sometimes detonating at the slightest disturbance. The dangers presented by abandoned explosives were tragically realized at a mine near Kremmling, Colorado, in the 1950s, when a work crew encountered cases of dynamite left beside a mine portal just a few years earlier. After a cursory inspection of the cases, an experienced blaster opted to move the first box. All the crew found of him after the explosion was an arm and a part of his lower leg (Hovis and Shields 1999).

Bear in mind that surface features at mining sites are not necessarily "safe" by comparison. Mining sites can include open shafts, deteriorating structures, toxic waste dumps, and mine explosives that might be stashed anywhere. Surprisingly, hazard awareness training has yet to be made mandatory for surveying mining sites. Archaeological approaches consequently have been ad hoc, if not cavalier (Reno et al. 2001). In the interest of full disclosure, the author admits to having fallen partway through the floor of more than one collapsed mill building, having stepped unknowingly onto a rotten platform cantilevered over the lip of a shaft, and once having handled heavily deteriorated objects that turned out to be seventy-year-old sticks of dynamite (the hazard removal team later offered thanks because they learned thereby that the explosives were safe to move). These are not especially proud moments. Obliviousness and complacency in these situations need not have afforded this occasion for self-reflection.

One explanation for a bias in mine documentation toward the western states is that the actual record of mining on the continent is itself skewed. The vast majority of American mining sites were formed during the rushes of the nineteenth century and early twentieth century, when hundreds of thousands of prospectors scoured the American West for minerals. Archaeological studies thus reflect what is there. As indicated by Fenenga's efforts, the comparative paucity of attention to mining during earlier periods (including historic French, Native American, and Spanish efforts) has not been for lack of trying. The tendency for miners to rework sites limits the preservation of early examples. The scarcity argument nevertheless does not explain why archaeological coverage of twentieth-century mining remains spotty. Attention to gold mining during the Great Depression is increasing (Barna 2008; McMurry 2007; Smith 2006), but archaeological interest in post–World War II–era sites and, with it, the documentation of industry shifts toward mass mining practices remains rare (e.g., Blustain 2013).

A second factor contributing to the selectivity of archaeological coverage concerns the uneven geographic distribution of public lands. Federal agencies including the Bureau of Land Management, National Park Service, and U.S. Forest Service administer large parcels of public land in the western region. Federal land parcels have aided the preservation of a wide range of archaeological sites partly because of land-use restrictions and partly because the comparative aridity of western lands lessens some of the forces responsible for structural deterioration. Forest reserves arose from the desires of farmers to protect western watersheds, and legislators established many western national parks in areas considered worthless but for their scenic value (White 1991: 406–12). Public lands are nevertheless also where present-day mining tends to concentrate. Archaeologists have thus found considerable work on western lands either compiling cultural resource inventories or conducting surveys and excavations as part of the Section 106 process in advance of mining operations.

The current foci of archaeological research on the western mineral rushes and the coal wars of the nineteenth and twentieth centuries dovetail with some of the classic images of American mining—of the independent prospector washing gravels beside a creek bed and of coal miners and Pinkerton detectives. Archaeological investigations on these types of sites have provided a needed means for subjecting our national narratives to closer scrutiny. Such actions generate a few ironies of their own, given that paying attention to select minerals and time periods does little to broaden public awareness about the enormous depth and breadth of American mining.

While there is clearly much work to do, the temporal and geographic selectivity of archaeological research provides us with firmly situated data by which to assess the quality of archaeological contributions to date. The remainder of this volume takes up this charge by shifting the focus from *how* archaeologists have examined mining sites to *what* archaeologists have found. Suffice it to say, the returns from mining sites have proven far less bleak than they appeared to Franklin Fenenga at the inception of the field. Archaeological investigations of mining communities remain an immensely productive area for archaeological investigation, as Fenenga predicted, but investigations of mining workplaces have proven richer than his generally unenthusiastic outlook. As will be seen in the chapters that follow, archaeologists have also widened the scope of a post-1800 mining archaeology by examining relationships between mines and the environment and by investigating processes of memorialization, among other lines of inquiry. We begin our survey of findings, however, with the type of site most responsible for fixing a romantic image of American mining: the ghost town.

3

Roaring Camp and Company Town

Boom and bust: this pithy characterization of economic cycles finds dramatic expression in the life of mining communities, where makeshift towns could appear virtually overnight and changing fortunes at the mine could empty out even substantial urban centers. Today little meets the eye at Rhyolite, Nevada, beyond the ruins of a bank building, a school, a railroad depot, and a house constructed of bottle glass. In 1907 the town had four thousand residents; today it has none. Situated in a shallow basin of the Bullfrog Hills beside the Montgomery-Shoshone gold mine, Rhyolite in 1907 showed all the signs of becoming a metropolis. Concrete sidewalks, electric lights, water mains, and telephone and telegraph lines accessorized the streets (Lingenfelter 1986: 219). The town included an opera house as well as a stock exchange, churches, bars, and brothels. In the heart of it all, on the corner of Golden and Broadway, stood the three-story Cook Bank (figure 3.1). Completed in 1908 at a cost of $90,000, the building included a staircase fashioned from Italian marble, stained glass windows, and interior walls trimmed with Honduran mahogany (ibid.). The building's concrete exterior at street level mimicked the appearance of dressed stonework, and what remains of the roof line today reveals a decorative cornice. Despite the investment, this bank failed within a year, and the town followed not long afterward, spurred by the decline of the Montgomery-Shoshone Mine. The Cook Bank ruin evokes an urban scene now out of place in the quiet of the surrounding desert. Like the broken statue of Ozymandias, "Round the decay / Of that colossal wreck, boundless and bare, / The lone and level sands stretch far away" (Shelley 1819: 72).

Rhyolite joins literally hundreds of towns that have succumbed to a similar fate. Like the logging industry, American mining often fostered the development of single-industry communities that struggle for viability

Figure 3.1. Ruins of the Cook Bank building, Rhyolite, Nevada. Photograph by author.

when operations close. In the western half of the continent especially, the string of ghost towns left by mining ventures seems equaled only by the number of guidebooks describing them.

A survey of American mining communities quickly reveals immense variation in scale, from the remnants of expedient camps and way stations to fully fledged metropolises. Archaeological investigations of these settlements have provided foundations for understanding how miners and their families organized their lives. This chapter focuses on the structure of mining settlements, drawing out patterns in architecture, common institutions, and the ways that social power operated even amid the surface uniformity of company towns. We begin, however, with a closer examination of the supply systems responsible for enabling so many mining settlements to spring into and out of existence.

Reconstructing Mining Supply Networks

Mining is an industry well adapted to working in remote places, but few mining camps exist in total isolation. Historian Jerome Steffen (1980) usefully characterized mining districts as "cosmopolitan frontiers"—a term chosen to emphasize the critical linkages that mines and other extractive industries maintain to outside sources of labor, material, and capital. In short, it takes more than minerals to make a mine, and mining operations satisfy most of these additional needs through imported goods and services. Because the mineral stampedes in the western United States occurred in areas that had seen limited Euro-American exploration, the development of mining districts required the establishment of entire supply chains connecting entrepôts to mining locales.

Alighting at different points along this supply network provides a better sense of the archaeological picture. An exceptional glimpse from the supplier end of the equation is provided by the remnants of several gold rush–era mercantile stores beneath the streets of San Francisco (Delgado 2009; Pastron and Hattori 1990). In the 1980s, excavations for a new building exposed old wharf piers and, with it, an extensive assemblage from the Hoff Store, which had burned during one of six major city fires occurring between 1849 and 1851 (Pastron 1990: 2). Preserved by the anaerobic conditions of harbor mud were baked goods, dried vegetables, and rice, some of which had likely come from China. The recovery of more than five hundred pig bones also identified packed pork as one of the staples of the western frontier (Hattori and Kosta 1990: 86–89). Equally spectacular finds derive from the remnants of buried gold rush–era ships. During the early years of the California stampede, enterprising merchants repurposed the vessels that crews had abandoned upon arrival in San Francisco Bay. Whether left at anchor or hauled onto the mud flats and connected by piers, these forlorn hulks gained renewed life as storehouses, offices, and

Figure 3.2. Excavation of the *General Harrison*, one of many ships converted into warehouses during the California Gold Rush. Photograph by James Delgado.

even lodgings. Dozens of store ships later became incorporated into the city's fabric as land reclamation projects gradually filled in Yerba Buena Cove. Salvage excavations of the *Niantic* and *General Harrison* (figure 3.2) recovered evidence of their later use as warehouses. The assemblages included construction supplies and more barrels of salt pork but also crates of wine and champagne. San Francisco's early warehouses thus furnished both the essentials and frivolities for miners and the burgeoning port city (ibid.: 113–61).

Historical and archaeological evidence indicates that miners' dependence on imported goods and domestic meats increased as they traveled inland. Robin Mills's (1998) investigation of advertisements and street directories during the Alaska rush, for instance, indicates that wholesalers of manufactured goods established businesses in only the largest settlements. Prospectors disembarking from Fairbanks soon encountered few businesses related to food production other than the occasional bakery (Mills 1998: 304–15). Beyond those establishments, the diet atrophied to coffee, bacon, beans, and flapjacks.

A detailed picture of rush-era supply chains midroute comes from materials left along the Chilkoot Trail, a rugged 33-mile-long path linking southeastern Alaska with the Yukon Territory. Approximately twenty thousand stampeders used the trail in 1897, the first year of the Klondike gold rush (Spude 2011: 9). Canadian regulations required prospectors to each bring supplies sufficient for lasting a year in the remote Yukon. Disembarking from Dyea at the head of Chilkoot Inlet, prospectors hauled one ton of gear up 3,500 feet of elevation to reach the Chilkoot Pass and then on to Lake Bennett and eventually the goldfields. Time on the trail averaged three months. Prospectors left in their wake a 33-mile-long midden deposit, punctuated by at least five townsites and more than a dozen transportation nodes (Griffin and Gurcke 2011: 148). A summary of artifacts inventoried along a small section of the trail near Chilkoot Pass indicates the sheer variety of imported goods, including the following:

> restaurant ceramics, food and fuel cans, boots, suspenders, an umbrella, hats, parts of an acid battery cell, portable boats, a pencil, prune pits, dog and horse harness parts, sleds, dog and horse skeletons, a candle, vests, shoelaces, a pigskin valise, a box of wooden matches, a drawstring tobacco pouch, barrel parts, an ax, a pair of blue jeans, a comb, a mattress, a perfume bottle, a wooden milk crate addressed to Dyea, a long-distance telephone service sign, and fragments of newspapers dated February 1898. (Ibid.: 157)

Closer inspection of the foodstuffs indicates how industrialized the American food system had become. Condiments heralded from New York and Pennsylvania, and canned milk from California, Illinois, New York, and Washington, as well as Nova Scotia. Meat paste bottled in Chicago and discarded on a trail 2,000 miles distant indicates the wide distribution of this city's meatpacking industry (Murray and Hamilton 1986: 211–20).

Materials recovered from a riverboat that wrecked in 1865 en route to the Montana gold strikes have provided archaeologists with an unparalleled opportunity to observe a shipment of goods sent to the frontier. Punctured by a submerged log on the Missouri River 25 miles upriver from Omaha, Nebraska, the *Bertrand* sank in a matter of minutes. Remarkably, no lives were lost, but the sediment-laden Missouri buried the steamboat in riverine mud and foiled attempts at the time to salvage cargo below the deck.

When the ship was relocated a century later, 30 feet below an Iowa cornfield, excavators were astonished to find most of the ship's hull intact, and with it approximately 10,000 cubic feet of goods and supplies in a remarkable state of preservation (Petsche 1974; Switzer 2013). The archaeological assemblage—the largest single collection of Civil War–era artifacts in the United States—reveals a wide variety of items channeled to the mining frontier. Among the commodities were five thousand barrels of whiskey; building supplies such as nails, tar paper, and doorknobs; foodstuffs; tablewares; agricultural implements; and mining supplies including black powder, pickaxes, shovels, and cylinders of mercury. Also preserved were approximately twenty-seven thousand textile items ranging from bolts of cloth to ready-to-wear apparel (Petsche 1974; Switzer 2013).

Most clothing items were hard-wearing (Guilmartin 2002). Shoes and boots tended to be of sturdy design, and the plain woolen vests on board the *Bertrand* differed from the light, brocaded garments marketed in Sears catalogs (Guilmartin 2002: 59–61, 93–99). Even so, several types of clothing displayed modern cuts, revealing that mining districts also kept apace with Victorian fads. Examples included men's trouser legs cut with less dramatic tapers and work shirts sporting rounded shirttails and bright plaid designs (ibid.: 54–58, 127, 167). Reflecting the gender imbalance of rush camps, men's clothes constituted 80 percent of recovered garments.

Artifact assemblages recovered from mining camps support the trend observed at earlier points in the network, namely, that urban fashions reached the frontier with little delay. Roberta Greenwood's analysis of several gold camps in California's Mother Lode region notes how shifts in ceramic types from British-made to American-made wares occurred in lockstep with shifts in major supply centers (Greenwood 1992: 73). Artifacts recovered from saloons in Virginia City, Nevada, similarly affirm that new commodities spread rapidly into the arid interior. There, bottle fragments and residue analysis suggest that Tabasco sauce made an appearance in Virginia City within a few years of its invention. Pieces of coral, seashells, and a crab claw also recovered from one of the saloon assemblages imply the presence of a fish tank, indicating that even some desert saloons joined in the nineteenth-century aquarium craze (Dixon 2005: 66, 95–97, 140–42). Such tastes seem out of place given the rough and burly image of the frontier, but they nevertheless reveal a desire among camp residents to enjoy the trappings of urban life (Baker 1978; Greenwood 1992; Ostrogorsky 1982; Toulouse 1970).

The cosmopolitan frontier model does not, however, account for many sources of variation seen archaeologically in mining camps.

Archaeological investigations indicate, for instance, that even though camps focused heavily on external supplies, miners still tapped local resources extensively. Marcia Rockman's (1995) analysis of faunal assemblages from the gold camp of South Pass City, Wyoming, identified a drop-off in the number of rabbit, elk, deer, and bison within a few years of the mining rush that likely was the consequence of overhunting. Because the demand for supplies continually adjusted to the fortunes of the camp and news of other strikes, the analysis of supply networks must also consider the dynamics occurring after the initial rushes. Archaeological investigations have been helpful here in identifying the signatures of abandonment. Leaving an area with the expectation of return generates a different material record than the gradual abandonment of a region—the former leaves behind portable, reusable items and the latter leaves mostly structural, nonportable artifacts (Spencer 1994; Stevenson 1982). Allyson Brooks's (1995) investigation of mining camps in White Pine, Nevada, and Deadwood, South Dakota, concluded that miners' anticipation of mobility affects what the archaeologist finds. Rush-era districts, where miners expected to move on to other areas, encouraged a minimalist material culture—such as dugout housing and tin tableware. By contrast, the material culture left at more-established camps is more diversified, suggestive of the presence of families and also of class stratification (Brooks 1995).

But abandonment could also be a very slow process. The material culture of mining settlements after the rush era reveals that miners continued to depend on imported equipment and supplies and also found novel ways to extend the use life of artifacts. Benjamin Barna's (2008) examination of the Rabbithole Mining District in northern Nevada provides an in-depth examination of one such small-scale community eking out an existence during the Great Depression. There, evidence abounds of materials reprioritized to fit the needs of making do. Old railroad ties found use as retaining walls, tent pads, machine platforms, cabin walls, and even an anvil base. Barrels became makeshift stoves, automobile hoods became repurposed for siding, newspapers found use for chinking in log cabins, cardboard served as lining for dugout interiors, and beer bottle caps found use as fasteners (Barna 2008: 58–136).

The close connection between mining camps and urban settlements during rush periods presents a marked contrast with rural assemblages, for which stylistic change tends to "lag behind" or occur independently of urban fashions (e.g., Deetz [1977] 1996: 103–24; Turnbaugh 1983). When longer settlement histories can be traced, however, the material culture from mining sites and agricultural assemblages come into closer alignment. Parallels exist, for instance, in the material culture of Rabbithole District miners with those of ranchers in Paradise Valley, situated just 100 miles distant. Among the ranchers, Margaret Purser (1999) charts a general shift in material culture from locally produced and modified goods to a greater reliance on catalog goods produced at distant locations—a consumption pattern that miners developed early. During the lean years, Paradise Valley residents, like those burrowing for riches in the Rabbithole District, maintained livelihoods by recycling materials. Among the archaeological contributions here is the identification of unique and localized adaptations amid the wash of mass-produced artifacts.

The Structure of Mining Camps

The rush-era camp often elicited a sense of "having gotten there before it was sent for" (*La Plata Miner*, November 8, 1879, quoted in West 1979: 28). Without horticultural plots, agricultural fields, or ranches to buffer the edges, mining camps presented a jarring juxtaposition between the urban bustle of commerce on Main Street and the howling wilderness just beyond the privies. Mining camps materialized at alarming speeds and grew at a pace that had few precedents. The shock is readily apparent in the journal of a prospector returning to a Californian mining camp in 1851 after a two-month hiatus only to find the settlement beyond recognition. In place of the dozen canvas tents he expected to see come into view at Rough and Ready was "a street nearly three-fourths of a mile in length, compactly built up on both sides with frame houses, many of them two stories high, with handsome exteriors" (Street 1851: 32). For large mining supply centers such as Helena, Montana, the transition from log cabins on Main Street to a downtown complemented with streetcar lines and multistory stone and brick buildings occurred in twenty-five years, an extraordinarily rapid transition when compared to the growth of East Coast cities (Barth 1988; Rohe 1984: 104–7; Rothschild and Wall 2014).

The singular purpose of the mining camp, the high mobility of prospectors, and the spirit of laissez-faire individualism all contributed to the atmosphere of expediency. The result is no more dramatically evidenced than in what came to pass for initial accommodations. Upon venturing into one encampment in 1851, Daniel Woods noted the presence of stone cabins, log cabins with canvas roofs, wood-framed canvas tents, dugouts, brush shelters, hide shelters, and even more-haphazard arrangements of branches and blankets and "tree nests" (Woods 1851: 121). Rush-era mining sites preserve other novel forms, such as Rhyolite's extant bottle house—a three-room gable-roofed structure completed in 1906 and constructed from fifty thousand liquor bottles scavenged from the back lots of saloons (Lingenfelter 1986: 219). Archaeological inventories have documented how miners fashioned expedient accommodations from water tanks, repurposed packing crates, and scrap metal (Barna 2008; Greene 1981). In the camps of Darwin and Shoshone, California (80 miles, respectively, west and south of Rhyolite), miners overcame the shortage of construction materials by digging accommodations into the sides of arroyos, improving the appearances of their caves with framed doors and windowpanes. Elsewhere, cots and tables placed into old mine workings effected much the same result with considerably less effort (figures 3.3 and 3.4).

Among the more surprising findings is that a sense of order could still undergird this chaotic variety. Based on his survey of mining towns throughout the United States, Richard Francaviglia (1991: 84–85) estimates that 70 percent of mining settlements reveal some form of urban planning, even if most communities never achieved greater permanence than the tent frame. Rush camps tended to be chaotic, but even in such settlements, the later a mineral outcropping was discovered, the more likely the associated camp was to adopt a pattern of gridded streets and saleable lots. Within ten years of James Marshall's discovery at Coloma, the straight lines of Main Street, Back Street, and High Street had organized California's first rush camp (Reps 1975: 275–76). On Nevada's Comstock Lode, miners had formed a local government and implemented a town plan for "Virginia City" within a year of the mineral discovery. Lettered streets ran perpendicular to the steep hillside, with the first of them, A Street, tracing the line of the Comstock Ledge (ibid.: 276; Francaviglia 1991: 151).

Urban planning also expressed the social order of camp life. In Virginia City, as elsewhere, position on the hill correlated with social attainment (Reps 1975: 277). Mine owners and merchants sited their residences primarily in the highest sections of town, upslope of C Street, the town's primary commercial strip. Boardinghouses were located along B, C, and D Streets. Low- to middle-income neighborhoods, including the town's

Figure 3.3. Water tank repurposed by a borax miner into an accommodation. The structure now resides at the Tonopah Historical Society Museum, Tonopah, Nevada. Photograph by author.

Figure 3.4. Mine workings repurposed into sleeping quarters in Death Valley, California. Miners adapted a nearby adit into a kitchen and pantry. Photograph by author.

red-light district, began on D Street. By the mid-1860s, the Chinese quarter had become situated between G and I Streets (Schablitsky 2002; Thompson 1992). Farther down the hill and below everyone else, Northern Paiute families set up their camps beside the mine dumps (Hattori 1975). Archaeological examinations indicate that ethnic neighborhoods could arise even in small camps. Miners' dwellings at the camp of Shoshone Wells in north-central Nevada (1860s–1900s) echoed nineteenth-century observations on the variability of rush-era camp architecture, with accommodations including stone, adobe, and wood-frame buildings, tent platforms, and dugouts (Hardesty 1988: 84–87). Artifacts collected from the site's surface nevertheless revealed a divided community; the western half marked by the usual assortment of cans, tobacco tins, and alcohol bottles and the eastern section peppered with a suite of materials of Chinese manufacture, suggesting the presence of at least two distinct neighborhoods.

Business districts tended to be extensive in mining towns because of the heavy reliance on external provisions (Francaviglia 1991: 34–35). The fortunes of any business in a mining camp were ultimately linked to the success of the mine, and this relationship came to be expressed doubly in architecture. As mining camps increased in size, the tents gave way to log cabins, and log cabins, in turn, to multistory structures fashioned from more permanent materials.

A common development in this transition was the appearance of the false-fronted building. Despite being neither unique to mining districts nor particular to the West, a line of false fronts became a frequent sight in the western mining town. In common with other facades, the false front created an illusion that the building was constructed with the same care on all sides. What made the front architecturally "false" is how the street-side face of the building implied a larger structure than actually existed.

Business owners utilized the extra height of the false front for advertising, but the appeal extended beyond merely the pragmatic idea of a bigger sign. Kingston Heath (1989) argues that the blocky appearance performed symbolic work by evoking the look of buildings constructed from stone and brick. Additions such as pilasters, crenulations, and arched windows drew their inspiration from the Greek revival, Gothic revival, and Italianate styles present in cityscapes. In this way, streets lined with false-fronted buildings presented an appealingly urban scene. If the urbanity seemed incongruous with the surroundings, false fronts partly advanced hopes that the oddness would dissipate as the community and its mines became a long-term fixture on the landscape.

This end did not befall Bannack, Montana, a gold rush settlement that vanished into obscurity, leaving a line of false fronts standing "like a banner of defeat" (Heath 1989: 201). Bannack started life in 1862 as little more than a collection of tent frames near a mineral strike. Before the first winter set in, residents had erected several log structures. False-fronted buildings appeared the following year, corresponding with a drop in the price of sawn lumber. Heath's (1989) closer examination of the remaining false fronts reveals additional details on the evolution of this architectural style. Bannack's earliest false fronts appended a sawn-board facade onto the log wall fronting the street (figure 3.5). This contrasted with a later technique in which the false front replaced the front wall entirely. Such modifications to log buildings compromised structural integrity, but they carried the advantage of allowing the use of large sheets of plate glass to create an attractively modern storefront (Heath 1989).

Commercial listings in mining towns typically reveal a wide assortment of trades as well as a disproportionate number of drinking establishments. Within a year of Garnet, Montana, being founded, regional newspapers advertised the presence of at least seven saloons (Hall 1997: 17–19). In Virginia City and neighboring Gold Hill, Nevada, a hundred saloons are estimated to have been in operation during the 1870s, servicing a population that never exceeded twenty-five thousand (Dixon 2005: 25). Elliott West's examination of 1870 and 1880 census returns for fifteen western mining towns (including settlements in Arizona, Colorado, Idaho, and Montana) identified 466 saloonkeepers (West 1979: 52).

The popular image of entertainment in the western mining town is one of drunken brawls, outlaws, and prostitution, but historical and archaeological investigations have highlighted that the character of saloons was far more diversified. Kelly Dixon's (2005) comparison of four saloons in Virginia City, Nevada, reveals that this fixture of the mining camp catered to a wide spectrum of residents and budgets. Piper's Corner Bar, situated below the town's opera house, served the higher society of Virginia City. Archaeological excavations there revealed a well-appointed establishment furnished with brass wall sconces. Similar sorts of materials were found at the site of the Boston Saloon, which had been owned and operated by an African American proprietor and became a local haunt for nonwhites. Trendy fixtures such as gas lighting and decorative tin ceilings indicate

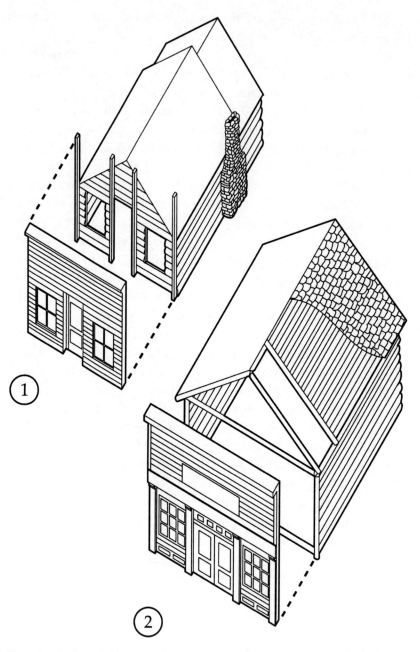

Figure 3.5. Evolution of false-front architecture in Bannack, Montana. The first false fronts (1) appended a sawn-board facade directly onto a log front, but in later styles (2), the facade served as a structural wall. Adapted with minor modification from illustrations by Michael Ludovico in Heath 1989.

that patrons at this bar enjoyed a fairly sophisticated atmosphere (Dixon 2005: 30, 59–62). The same could not be said for patrons at the Hibernia Brewery and O'Brien and Costello's Saloon and Shooting Gallery, located in a rough section of town nicknamed the "Barbary Coast." Whereas Piper's Corner Bar and the Boston Saloon were fitted with gas lighting, the Barbary Coast bars were lit dimly by kerosene lamps (ibid.: 62–64).

While architectural elements suggest that each bar occupied a defined place in the city's social scene, archaeological findings also reveal additional complexities. Excavators recovered decorated tea services from all saloons, suggesting that a measure of gentility reached even the seedier establishments. Faunal analysis indicates that the Boston Saloon, rather than the more opulently appointed Piper's Corner Bar, served the most expensive cuts. Most saloons were male only, but DNA recovered from a tobacco pipe stem at the Boston Saloon indicates the presence of women among the clientele (Dixon 2005, 2006).

A fine line existed between saloons and that other veritable institution of the mining camp—the brothel. All brothels sold liquor in addition to sex, and historical accounts indicate that some saloon owners employed prostitutes to supplement income (C. Spude 2005; West 1979: 49, 78–79). Oral traditions in Skagway, Alaska, for instance, note that prostitutes lined up dolls with their names along the edge of the bar's piano—the seated or prone posture providing patrons with a graphic indicator of availability (Dixon 2005: 132). Thus, the recovery of doll parts from some of the saloon assemblages may hint at the presence of children or, alternatively, at seedier activity occurring on the premises. Complicating matters further, saloons could also double as bakeries, restaurants, barbershops, general merchandise suppliers, and boardinghouses, and in new camps, the list of functions could extend to holding town hall meetings and church services (West 1979: 27–33). All this can make it problematic to identify saloons only from the presence of alcohol bottles (C. Spude 2005: 103).

Victorian literature depicted prostitutes as "fallen women," but historical and archaeological research notes that the respectability of prostitution differed according to established social hierarchies (Foster et al. 2005: 352–56; Hardesty 1994; Simmons 1989). Houses of prostitution could occur anywhere in a mining town. Parlor houses, for instance, provided comfortable and discreet settings of an upper-class home, with some enterprises also employing servants and bringing in clients on an appointment-only basis. Brothels provided a cheaper alternative and tended to be located in designated red-light districts. Location alone, however, does not always make it possible to discern a brothel from historic documents. Fire insurance maps can lack the coverage and resolution necessary to identify "bawdy houses," although spatial proximity provides some hints. In Silver City, Idaho, nineteenth-century insurance maps identify an area of downtown populated with "female boarding houses," a few of which tellingly shared common walls with saloons (Simmons 1989). The preservation of "cribs" in mining towns such as Bisbee, Arizona, and Butte, Montana, provides an unambiguous marker of red-light districts. Cribs were typically constructed as a narrow row of one-room dwellings, each room including a door to the street. Decorations tended to be scant, comprising a bed, a stove, and a washbasin. Expedience reigned in such instances, with building form following function (Francaviglia 1991: 35).

Paternalism and Order in the Company Town

Because mines needed amenities to attract and retain a workforce, many companies with operations in remote regions came to function doubly as landlords. At a bare minimum, company-built facilities consisted of bunkhouses and a commissary where employees purchased food, clothing, equipment, and tobacco. More-substantial settlements could include a thriving business district in addition to rows of cottages and duplexes (Allen 1966). Finances, existing infrastructure, and stage of mine development were influential factors in directing the amenities offered and the physical form that company towns took. Wood-frame houses were common in American company towns because they were cheap to construct, easy to modify, and purchasable direct from catalogs. Many companies additionally took advantage of materials at hand by repurposing waste rock for house foundations. The epitome of these economizing efforts was reached in places such as Mineville, New York, where house walls were fashioned from a mixture of cement and tailings (Peele 1918: 1544). Mineville's miners thus slept amid the very rock in which they toiled.

Company towns accentuated an already intimate connection between work and home life in American society. Managerial policies could transform this association into outright exploitation or, at the other extreme, into experiments in progressive social engineering. Policies differed, for instance, on which workers could arrive with families, what outside businesses were allowable in the town, whether wages were to be paid in money or company-issued scrip, and whether rental from the company was a condition of employment (Allen 1966; Crawford 1995; Dinius and Vergara 2011; Green 2010; Hoagland 2010).

Company towns in the eastern coalfields leaned toward more exploitative conditions. Inspectors of West Virginia's coalfields during the 1920s documented frequent price gouging in company stores, effectively reducing the standard of living for miners, which was already lower than urban industrial workers (U.S. Coal Commission 1925: 1525). Restrictions on liberties also abounded. Many of the surveyed companies had made rental a condition of employment, banned outside businesses from operating inside camps, and even required that workers obtain passes for entering and exiting the community (Green 2010: 57–58). Analogies to a prison were not entirely out of line. Indeed, in coal mining states such as Alabama and Tennessee, coal miners and prisoners had become somewhat interchangeable entities by way of convict-lease systems that continued into the 1920s (ibid.: 58–59; U.S. Coal Commission 1925: 1430).

The copper town of Tyrone, New Mexico, stood in contrast to the stark conditions documented in West Virginia by the United States Coal Commission. Tyrone embodied the principle of corporate paternalism, a relationship between management and worker in which the company adopted the role of a benevolent father figure concerned with the welfare of his children. The Phelps-Dodge Copper Company planned the town in the mission style, complete with a plaza, arcades, and a large Catholic church modeled after the Panama-California Exposition's (1915–17) California Building. Town facilities included a hospital, a school, a theater, and one of the largest department stores in the state (Crawford 1995: 138–40). Tyrone received accolades from architects as well as social reformers. Phelps-Dodge kept the streets swept and collected garbage regularly. The company also banned dance halls and the sale of alcohol to reduce vice (ibid.: 143–44). In Tyrone, as in other company towns, landscaping and green space softened the edges of what remained a town constructed for a single purpose (e.g., Alanen and Bjorkman 1998; Malone 1998).

Cradle-to-grave policies of corporate paternalism shaped life in intimate ways, from funding sports teams and music bands to providing fire and police services, and from training the next generation of mine workers in schools to paying pensions. But corporate benevolence extended only so far. Eviction from the job—whether from incompetence, injury, or involvement in union organizing—spelled eviction from the home and often from the community (Crawford 1995; Lankton 1991).

Company towns carried an economic undertone even when operating under the aegis of enlightened social reform. Historical architects note how the streetscapes of company towns emphasize economic consider-ations by the choice of identical house forms, limited color palettes, and a general lack of architectural ornamentation (Hoagland 2010). Manag-ers justified expenditures on amenities such as recreation facilities, public baths, schools, libraries, and indoor plumbing by reasoning that better living conditions attracted "a better class of worker," namely, a worker who stayed with the job and was disinterested in unionizing. Town libraries provided enlightenment through a carefully selected range of texts that conveyed American values. The American Library Association proposed to aid this end by translating books that extolled the "greatness of this country and the advantages of living in it" into different languages (e.g., Da Ponte 1920: 211–12).

The landscapes of company towns provide avenues for understanding the structures of social control. Inequalities took on literal dimensions in the company town because pay grade translated directly to square foot-age. In Calumet, Michigan, the Calumet and Hecla Mining Company pro-vided the families of miners with a comparatively generous five-room, two-story house, affording approximately 460 square feet of living space on the ground floor. The general manager's family, by contrast, lived in a two-and-a-half-story, twenty-room mansion. Although plain in outward appearance, the general manager's living room alone accommodated the footprint of a miner's house with room to spare. Marks of distinction ex-tended to the finer details of higher ceilings, a better-quality wood used for flooring and wainscoting, and the presence of indoor plumbing (Hoa-gland 2010: 22–23, 41–54; Lankton 1991: 153). Signs of status were hardly novel in American society, but company towns made the connection stark, accustoming an often foreign-born workforce to American values that linked hard work with social attainment.

The appeal to a "melting pot"—whether conceived as the blending of ethnic traditions to form a new composite society or as an acculturative process toward white values—seldom translated to the company town. In mining communities, racial prejudices drew tight linkages between ethnicity, skill set, and pay grade. In the copper town of Ajo, Arizona, for

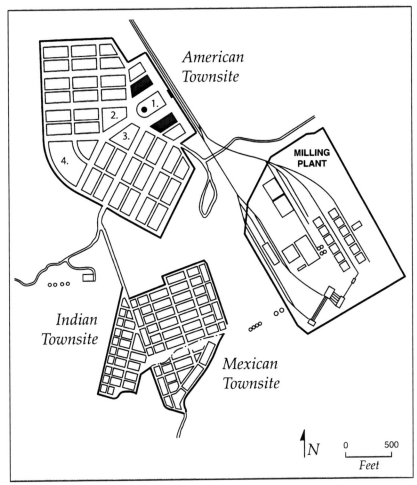

Figure 3.6. Racial inequities expressed in the town plan for Ajo, Arizona. (1) Town square with railroad station, theater, stores, and band rotunda; (2) Catholic church; (3) club and swimming pool; (4) school. Drawing adapted from the architectural plan (Kenyon 1919: plate XI).

instance, census records for 1920 indicate that among the men, whites took positions as managers, administrators, and foremen. Mexican workers found employment as miners, and Native Americans (primarily Tohono O'odham) worked as general laborers (Meeks 2003: 485). Racial segregation in the workplace extended to the creation of distinct "American," Mexican, and Indian sections of town (Roth 1992: 183–84) (figure 3.6).

Ajo's town center included a company store and post office, a theater, a picture house, and additional retail stores arranged around a colonnaded town square. Community amenities also included a pool, schools, and a band rotunda. Ajo's architecture blended Puebloan and Spanish elements, with the use of stucco and flat roofs. The southwestern motif was evident in both the American section and the Mexican section, but allusions to equality ended there.

Company policies actively maintained social distance between Ajo's American residents and other community members. American residents, for instance, could purchase houses and building lots, but Mexican workers had to rent. Mexican and Tohono O'odham families enjoyed fewer company-sponsored social events, sent their children to separate schools, sat in a designated section of the theater, and were permitted use of the town pool at limited times—only after use by American families and before the pool was cleaned (Meeks 2003: 485).

The unequal reach of paternalism was manifested just as bluntly in the provision of space. The size of the domestic areas allocated for American, Mexican, and Native American workers had little relation to population numbers. Mexican workers constituted up to 80 percent of Ajo's workforce, but the American settlement—Ajo proper—occupied double the space of Mexican Town (Meeks 2003: 486). The American section also included a varied streetscape of single- and multibedroom house designs, with houses including exterior porches and interior bathrooms (Kenyon 1919: 9). Mexican Town, separated from Ajo by a low ridgeline, included simpler, unpainted houses and outdoor privies. This nevertheless represented a step up from "Ajo Indian Village," where the Tohono O'odham were required to construct their own housing on undeveloped lots leased from the company (Meeks 2003: 486). Lot size, house size, distance to market, and even the presence of sidewalks all externalized social and economic inequalities. The banality of it all contributed to naturalizing these differences.

Such policies were expressed just as blatantly in American ventures overseas. The development of the Chuquicamata copper mine in Chile by the Anaconda Copper Corporation, for example, advertised the mine as a model of free enterprise for all Chileans to emulate (Finn 1998: 73–75). The Guggenheim family funneled millions of dollars into the mine in the 1920s, and this included developing a settlement for tens of thousands of workers in the remote Atacama Desert. Housing policies at Chuquicamata varied by pay grade, but the town also maintained a caste-like division between "American" and "Indian" workers. This included separate stores and schools, as well as a club for Americans that included a reading room, a ballroom, a billiard room, a bowling alley, and a swimming pool (Guggenheim 1920: 207). The company allotted heads of department 1,500 square feet of furnished living space, complete with bathrooms and a kitchen. Chilean laborers received dwellings approximately one-fifth the size and devoid of furniture and amenities. For those workers showing "more than the usual interest" in raising the standard of their homes, the company granted permission to add a bath to their dwellings. The result, to owner Harry Guggenheim (1920: 209), was that "instead of the ragged, barefooted, irresponsible laborer of five years ago, there is a well-dressed, well-shod workman with the spark of ambition burning within him." Such statements echoed the language of American Indian reformers like Merrill Gates, who two decades earlier had proposed that acculturation could occur only by awakening want. Only by lighting the fires of discontent, Gates contended, would the American Indian change "out of the blanket and into trousers, and trousers with a pocket in them, and with a pocket that aches to be filled with dollars!" (Gates in Prucha 1973: 334).

It is tempting to suggest from these examples that company towns approached the status of "total institutions," which like boarding schools or prisons provided an enclosed social system that controlled most aspects of people's lives. But mining companies rarely achieved this in any strict sense of the definition. First, companies entered into the landlord business reluctantly because company towns were seldom, if ever, profit-making entities (Allen 1966). Company towns tended to experience decreasing levels of corporate investment as infrastructure aged. Ben Ford's (2011) analysis of worker housing at the Ely copper mine in Vermont may offer one archaeological indicator of this general apathy. While historical photographs indicate a row of identical worker tenements, archaeological surveys revealed that the tenements were built atop a variety of cellar arrangements, ranging from full cellars to partial cellars established at each end of the building (Ford 2011). If mine owners seemed focused on appearances, the concern evidently stayed at the surface. The real money, if it was to be made, always came from the mine.

Second, company towns rarely accommodated all employees. During the early twentieth century, the workforce for Upper Michigan's copper mines is estimated to have outstripped company housing three to one

(Lankton 1991: 148–55). Access to company houses correlated positively to pay grade and negatively to need. Managers and upper-level staff typically enjoyed first priority, with accommodations provided free of charge. Administrators and other surface workers took preference over underground workers, and so on down the pay scale. At Michigan's Champion Mine in 1912, for example, miners occupied 140 of the 162 company houses, while timbermen took 16 and wallers and pickers resided in another 6, but management assigned houses to none of the 207 trammers on the payroll (ibid.). These workers lived in tents, paid rent as boarders, or resided in satellite settlements outside of company property. Satellite towns became havens for businesses and vice that companies had banned under the auspices of social reform. Such communities could, in this way, share much in common with early mining camps. Richard Goddard's (2002) investigations of Steptoe City, Nevada, suggests, however, that even satellite settlements complied with social norms the longer they were occupied.

Third, planned communities were subject to reinterpretation if not outright resistance by their residents (Herod 2011: 37). Karen Metheny's (2006) examination of a Pennsylvania coal town provides one glimpse into how individualized actions modified the structural uniformity of the company town. In Helvetia, the Rochester and Pittsburgh Coal Company had followed a typical plan of accommodating managers and administrators in freestanding houses and lodging workers in rows of plain doublehouses. Over time, Helvetia's residents made additions and alterations to these basic templates to fit their needs. Inside the doublehouses, residents increased available living space by expanding cellars and crawl spaces and enclosing front porches and rear stoops. Employees also constructed stone ovens in their backyards, connected their units to water and sewer lines, planted vegetable gardens, and converted barns into car garages. Archaeological excavations of front and backyards revealed small beautification projects such as the laying of brick walkways and the establishment of flowerbeds, actions suggestive of budding community pride as well as a claim to ownership (Metheny 2006).

On the Archaeology of Best Laid Plans

Mining camps, company towns, and the networks of infrastructure supporting them provide a record of ambitions made manifest, reflecting the hopes of making fast fortunes from minerals and miners, as well as corporate efforts to engineer model communities. Among the most significant archaeological contributions has been an appreciation of the diverse forms that mining communities ultimately took. The stereotypical image sees the mining camp as chaotic and lawless. The archaeological record indicates that even frontier camps could submit to planning and order, sometimes right from the start. Conversely, where the image of company towns is of ordered streets and identical houses, historical and archaeological research draws attention to a wider scope of corporate models, the exporting of these principles abroad, and the fact that diverse arrangements still occurred at its edges. Now that we have canvassed the perimeter of camps and observed the differences in the forms of miners' housing, it seems high time to begin knocking on a few doors.

4

Meeting the Miners

Blasting caps, two tins
Box of playing cards, empty
Box of Jell-O
Klim powdered milk, 5-pound can
Small crowbar
Hills Brothers coffee, three 2-pound cans
Christmas card, blank
National Geographic, April 1936
Prince Albert–type tobacco, two tins
Nutmeg

When it comes to meeting miners in person, archaeologists have made a profession out of arriving late. Most often, the passage of time rules out the possibility of face-to-face interaction, but a surprising amount of information can still be communicated across time through the materials that survive. The above list draws from an array of items found stashed in a historic bunkhouse in Alaska's rugged Chugach Range. Miners had finished the 1941 season with the expectation of returning, but it was not to be. When the bunkhouse was visited more than a half century later, archaeologists found the shelves still stocked with foodstuffs, work clothes hanging from hooks, and magazines and books lying where miners had left them. Miners in this isolated spot had spent their days toiling underground in the cold and dark, and their evenings playing cards, catching up on *Reader's Digest*, and flipping through images of Japanese gardens and English lakes in *National Geographic*. Objects as humble as these—be they cans of coffee and tobacco or a well-thumbed magazine—draw us immediately to the lived experience and suggest something about what it meant to be a miner on and off the job. Here, intermixed with the tools of the trade also lay miners' aspirations to know something else of the world.

Figure 4.1. Alabama coal miners, 1937. Photograph by Arthur Rothstein. Library of Congress, Prints and Photographs Division, FSA/OWI Collection, LC-DIG-fsa-8a08362.

Just who was the American miner? Historical and archaeological research reveals this to be a deceptively simple question. One starting point is to recognize from the outset that mining brought into its orbit a much broader range of people and activities than the images that first spring to mind. Even a classic depiction, such as Arthur Rothstein's evocative close-up of a group of coal miners waiting to start their shift (figure 4.1), hints at differences in age and prompts one to think about whether variation might also have existed in background and outlook. The archaeological record provides a means to investigate these sorts of questions and to explore such fluid concepts as social identity. This chapter provides a sampling of findings by selecting three key areas of contribution: ethnicity, class, and health.

Mining Ethnicity

Though rarely thought of as such, mining towns in their heyday ranked high among America's most cosmopolitan communities. In 1870, one encountered more ethnic groups per square mile in an out-of-the-way mining camp in Idaho than in the cities of Boston, Brooklyn, and Philadelphia (West 1982: 118). Census returns for that year indicate that two-thirds of miners in southern Idaho were foreign born, and half of the remainder had at least one immigrant parent. Most foreign-born miners had originated from Ireland, Germany, Britain, Canada, and China, but the census also documented Danish, French, Norwegian, Polish, Scottish, Swedish, Swiss, and Welsh émigrés (West 1982: 110–11). Such variety was endemic. A survey of anthracite districts in the eastern states in the 1920s reported more than half of the miners being foreign born, half of whom came from Poland and Russia (Obenauer 1925: 535). Much of the initial variety in mining districts occurred as a consequence of the international attention that news of the mid-nineteenth-century mineral strikes had generated. But the industry sustained a measure of diversity over the longer term because the hard labor and dangerous conditions of mining work matched the type of work generally left to new immigrants.

Census recorders categorized all the above-listed ethnicities as "white" except the Chinese, whose othering in the census hints at more-formalized forms of social exclusion. Sharing a "W" in a census column, however, neither effaced discrimination nor ruled out ancestry from having social utility. As occurred in other industries, mining companies often divided tasks by ethnicity, with the lowest-paid tasks typically falling to the newest group. Language barriers contributed to workers being categorized according to stereotypes of ethnic character and general disposition. Disparaging labels such as *irresponsible* and *clannish* tended to be applied to the most recent immigrant groups. For example, Italians, some mining engineers argued, could not "be depended upon to hold positions requiring a cool head," and consequently they found employment in minimally skilled positions (Brinsmade 1907; Murray 1907: 1059). Mexican laborers were characterized in similar ways as "irresponsible, happy, fatalists" (Tays 1907: 623) who looked only to satisfy daily needs. Such judgments seemed to have eased the conscience of mine operators on the issues of low pay and poor working conditions. The common tendency to cluster a given ethnicity into a neighborhood also encouraged ethnic groups to develop tight-knit networks of support.

Sarah Sportman's examination of Scandinavian, Irish, and French Canadian workers employed at the Crown Point Iron Mine in Hammondville, New York (circa 1870–90) highlights key ways that ethnic identity undergirded community life. Nearly one-third of Hammondville's families supplemented wages by taking in boarders, and census records indicate that boarders and the host family shared the same nationality in 80 percent of cases (Sportman 2011: 117). Marriage records repeated the pattern. Intragroup marriage among Scandinavians accounted for more than 90 percent of unions over a seventeen-year period. Cross-checking of time sheets and census records reveals that the composition of work gangs tended to reflect family ties, boarding arrangements, and even one's neighbors (ibid.: 151–59). Swedes at Hammondville, in other words, rented rooms to Swedes, married Swedes, and worked alongside Swedes, and these tendencies occurred also among the town's Irish and French Canadian residents.

Ethnic identities are often expressed through clothing, food, and living arrangements, but a couple of factors tend to complicate their visibility in mining camps. First, consumer purchases were necessarily influenced by what was provided and what was available. Mining camp assemblages show considerable overlap in materials such as tin cans, cookware, and furnishings in part because company stores and supply towns stocked only a limited range of goods. Mail-order catalogs made greater choice available to consumers beginning in the late nineteenth century, but this also required money on hand.

Historical archaeologists have looked particularly to tobacco pipes, clothing, and other portable items for positing ethnic identities because these materials relate to personal expression and were more likely to be brought into the camps. Bottles and knickknacks of Italian manufacture, for instance, tend to be found in communities with known Italian residents (Costello 1981; Hardesty 1988; see also Reckner 2009: 395–98), and tobacco pipes embossed with the words "Home Rule" or the sign of the Red Hand often dovetail with a historical Irish presence (Brighton 2004; Reckner 2004). Such assignments are used cautiously, for few items were ever used exclusively, and the same item could have multiple social meanings. Moreover, not all ethnicities have equal archaeological representation. Test excavations at Hammondville did not conclusively identify a Swedish presence, although surface finds at the "Swedetown" location for Michigan's Quincy Mine (Martin 1992) identified artifacts likely attributable to Scandinavian households. The assemblage of smoking pipes from the Quincy Mine's "Swedetown" included several curved pipe stems decorated with a scale design and pipe bowl fragments held in the grasp of sculpted claws (figure 4.2). Sherds of white- and green-slipped

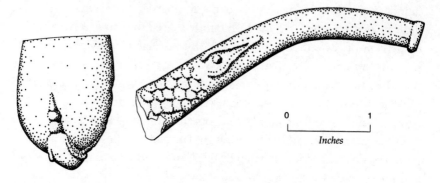

Figure 4.2. Fragments of curved tobacco pipes recovered from the site of Swedetown, Michigan. Drawings by author.

earthenware, not seen elsewhere in the region, matched a folk pottery style popular in western Finland and eastern Sweden during the nineteenth century. The recovery of Swedish and Finnish coins additionally affirms the presence of Scandinavian groups in the area (Martin 1992: 209–10).

This broadening of resolution from Swedish to a Scandinavian identity is partly a consequence of labor turnover and the cycling in of new ethnic groups. The Quincy Mining Company had begun operations with English, Irish, and German miners and with French Canadians and Swedes working as surface laborers. By the 1890s, however, the Finnish predominated in the underground work in Michigan mines. Twenty years later, Slavic groups increasingly occupied these positions (Hyde 1986: 4–5; LeDuc 2005). In this way, the communities of "Limerick," "Frenchtown," and "Swedetown" that the company established in the mid-nineteenth century as a nod to, respectively, the Irish, French Canadian, and Swedish workers on the payroll gradually lost their specific ethnic associations. By 1910, Swedetown remained Swedish in name only. Recorders that year listed six Swedish families in a community that was also home to three English and three German households, ten Slavic families, and more than two dozen Finnish households (Hoagland 2010: 52; Lankton 1991: 156). Frenchtown, Limerick, and Swedetown may never have been single ethnic communities to begin with, but shifts in employment patterns over time created situations whereby the same company house saw occupation by multiple ethnicities.

Herein lies the rub, for archaeologists strive in their interpretations to go beyond verifying the presence of ethnic groups to understanding what these material remains say about how people fashioned lives on the mining frontier. Questions of interest here include considerations of how ethnic groups adjusted to novel circumstances, be it through cultural continuities or innovations or the formation of new identities, and the extent to which such responses were common or highly localized (Costello et al. 2007: 81–82). Inquiries of this nature become more feasible where mining camps existed only briefly, where ethnic and racial marginalization maintained ethnic neighborhoods over long periods of time, or where corporate policies sought expressly to downplay ethnic difference.

An example of the latter occurred in Buxton, Iowa (1900–1925), where the Consolidation Coal Company racially integrated schools and businesses well before those of other mines and surrounding communities. In Buxton, African American residents could dine in any restaurant, swim in the town pool, and try on clothes at the company store without experiencing prejudice (Gradwohl and Osborn 1984: 193). Neighborhood designations of "West Swede Town" and "East Swede Town" indicate that integration did not necessarily extend to all facets of camp life. Although archaeological testing did not extend to all areas of town, test results did not indicate marked differences in artifacts across sites, affirming the lack of distinction seen in historic photographs (ibid.: 190–91).

Overseas Chinese settlements, by contrast, provide one of the clearest opportunities for examining racial marginalization in mining towns. Prior to James Marshall's gold discovery in California, fewer than fifty Chinese were residing in the United States (Voss and Allen 2008: 9). Within a few years of the strike, however, the number of Chinese arriving annually in San Francisco exceeded twenty thousand. Upwards of 90 percent of the Chinese venturing to America during the mid-nineteenth-century rushes emigrated from Guangdong province in southeastern China, and most of these were from the counties neighboring the city of Guangzhou (Canton)—an area about the size of Texas (ibid.: 6).

Chinese immigrants were initially tolerated because after Mexicans, Chileños, Peruvians, and the French had left the goldfields, the Chinese were among the only groups from whom county officials could collect a foreign miners tax (Chan 2000: 74). However, Euro-American attitudes changed once the Chinese were perceived as being willing to work for lower wages than whites (ibid.; Orser 2007: 130). Six years after the gold discoveries at Sutter's Mill, the California Supreme Court bolstered the anti-Chinese faction by declaring Chinese and Chinese American testimony inadmissible in court, adding one more group to a ruling that already disallowed testimony from Native Americans, African Americans, and "mulattos." Congress tightened restrictions against the Chinese further with the Page Act (1875), which limited the immigration of Chinese women and prohibited the immigration of forced labor on the national level. The Chinese Exclusion Act of 1882 added a provision explicitly barring those seeking employment in mining. Anti-Chinese sentiments became expressed also through local ordinances prohibiting the Chinese from mining new mineral strikes or forcing Chinese households and businesses to relocate into Chinatowns.

Hostile conditions encouraged the maintenance of strong ethnic ties, and it is no coincidence that sites occupied by the Overseas Chinese tend to be distinctive across a broad set of artifact classes. Ceramic assemblages include imported brown-glazed earthenware ranging in size from storage vessels to small, spouted jugs formerly holding liquids such as soy sauce, vinegar, and honey. Tableware features jade-colored celadon bowls and cups as well as imported porcelains decorated with Four Seasons, Bamboo, and Double Happiness designs. Common finds also include pipe bowls, lamp fragments, cleaning utensils, and storage tins associated with the recreational smoking of opium. Variation in the designs of opium pipe bowls may reflect regional differences, but it draws attention to multiple suppliers and a degree of choice (Thompson 1992; Wegars 1991; Wylie and Fike 1993).

The Overseas Chinese carried more than material goods to the mining frontier, for they also brought cultural preferences. Faunal remains from Chinese sites, for instance, indicate the processing of the animal largely by cleavers rather than saws and also suggest strong preferences for pork (as high as 80 percent) (Bowden 1999; Langenwalter 1980; Longnecker and Stapp 1993; and see Gust 1993 for variation). Belief systems such as fêng shui likely influenced the domestic arrangements of mining camps. Idealized conditions promoting good energy flow (including shelter from the north wind, a protective surround of hills, a view out to water or open ground, and location near a moderately flowing watercourse) were not possible to achieve in all situations, especially because anti-Chinese edicts meant that Chinese people did not have much choice in where "Chinatowns" were sited. Still, miners generally built their own accommodations

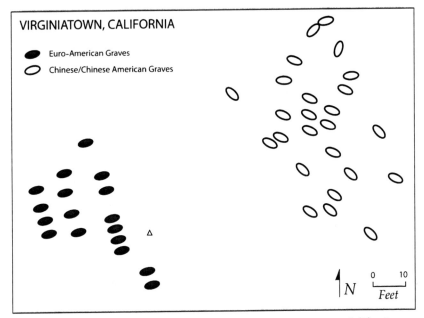

Figure 4.3. Segregation in life and in death: a cemetery in Virginiatown, California, with Euro-American burials to the left and Chinese burials to the right. Burial orientations also suggest different religious practices. Drawing by author, adapted from Rouse 2005.

in the camps, and criteria for promoting good ch'i (energy flow) could be selectively applied. Archaeologists note that the internal arrangements of some Chinese accommodations show an inclination for chimneys to be constructed beside doorways, differing from European patterns of positioning the chimney opposite the entrance (Ritchie 1993; Sisson 1993; Stapp 1990). Other potential characteristics include the setting of buildings at different angles and a propensity for few doors to face one another. These latter two arrangements minimized straight lines, which fêng shui principles associated with the passage of evil spirits (Ritchie 1993: 366).

Similar principles informed the layout of cemeteries (figure 4.3). Archaeologists have noted the orientation of Chinese cemeteries toward favorable winds and a view of water and with the graves arranged perpendicular to the hillside, in contrast to Christian cemeteries, which tended to orient burials along an east-west axis, with the head to the west (Couch 1996: 192–94; Rouse 2005: 84–86). Chinese burials, moreover, were often exhumed historically to fulfill the wishes of the deceased that their remains return to Mainland China. Excavations among the exhumed grave pits at a cemetery in Virginiatown, California (Rouse 2005), indicated shallow burials—on the order of 2–3 feet deep, and in which the coffin lid sometimes lay less than a foot below the ground surface. Archaeologists found evidence of grave offerings including buttons tied on a leather string and coins placed at grave corners. Rice bowls, stoneware jars, wine cups, and metal food tins found in and around the grave pits indicate that the graves remained sites of continuing veneration. Clothing fragments also indicate that not all members were buried in Chinese clothing—the recovery of jean rivets from one of the graves indicates that at least one individual went to ground decked in a pair of Levis (Rouse 2005: 93–95).

As this suggests, archaeological examinations reveal points of variation in Overseas Chinese experiences and, with it, a more complex rendering of ethnic relations. Although archaeological attention gravitated first to an inventory of exotic materials, store account books readily document that the Chinese acquired Western goods ranging from food and clothing to tools of the trade (Gust 1993: 190–91; Russell 1991: 25–26; Stapp 1990: 192–94). Excavations of Chinese businesses likewise recover goods of both Euro-American and Chinese manufacture, a reflection of adaptations to the mining frontier and a diverse clientele. Excavations also reveal how Chinese goods filtered into a wide range of non-Chinese sites. Thomas Layton's (2002) investigation of the *Frolic* shipwreck charts the wide appetite for Chinese commodities in nineteenth-century America, from fake pearls and camphor chests to prefabricated houses, game tokens, and opium (see also James 2012: 49–51). The Hoff Store assemblage in San Francisco included at least five toiletry sets of Chinese export porcelain, with designs for soap dishes, water bottles, and brush boxes identical to those exported to East Coast consumers (Terry and Pastron 1990).

There remains considerable room, also, for understanding interactions between miners and ethnic groups often assumed to be minimally associated with the industry. Eugene Hattori's (1975) pioneering study of a historic Northern Paiute encampment in Virginia City, Nevada, identified a range of ways that Northern Paiute families adjusted to the arrival of miners onto their lands. Nineteenth-century newspapers documented Northern Paiute women working as housekeepers, laundresses, seamstresses, and hawkers of small game, pine nuts, and floral bouquets, while their men worked as woodcutters for area mines (Hattori 1975: 74, 1998: 234; Queen 1987: 112–18). Non-native miners also took local wives, but many such marriages were never formalized and were terminated when

Figure 4.4. Paiute encampment below a mine dump at Virginia City, Nevada, 1891. Photograph by William Cann. Nevada Historical Society, photo no. 704.

the miners left. Epithets such as "squaw man" and "half breed" highlight both the commonality of mixed unions and the general derision with which they were received.

In Virginia City, Northern Paiute families resided in at least three distinct encampments on the outskirts of town, including one positioned at the foot of a mine dump (figure 4.4). Investigations at one of these encampments indicated that Northern Paiute residents built accommodations from a wide variety of available materials. In constructing wickiups, for instance, residents substituted iron pipes for a framework of willow branches, and canvas, carpet, burlap, and sheet metal in place of brush siding (Hattori 1975). Surface surveys found metates and flaked bottle glass intermixed with an array of mass-produced items that included buttons, nails, cartridge cases, and doll parts. Animal bones suggest a comparatively high reliance on waterfowl, rabbit, and other wild game, which were in keeping with cultural tastes but may also have reflected continued economic marginalization (ibid.). Census records indicate that one or two extended families lived in the encampment, a social structure in line with general Northern Paiute residence patterns (Hattori 1998: 237–38). Thus, one finds amid the detritus of the settlement evidence for cultural preferences working through other forms of prejudice.

Laboring Identities

I have been a miner for seventeen years. I am now twenty-eight years of age. My father was a miner, and his father before him. I did my first mining under my grandfather.

THOMAS LEE (OHIO MINING COMMISSION 1872: 136)

Bury me beside Jim Dayton in the valley we loved. Above me write: "Here lies Shorty Harris, a single blanket jackass prospector."

GRAVESTONE EPITAPH, DEATH VALLEY, CALIFORNIA

As an occupation doubling as a way of life, mining fostered different takes about what it meant to be a miner. Like many other desert rats, Frank "Shorty" Harris had been hooked as much by the independence that the prospecting life afforded him as by the chance of discovering a rich prospect, of which he found and squandered quite a few (Lingenfelter 1986: 203–4, 284–85, 313–14). One gets a different impression about mining from Thomas Lee, a third-generation coal miner whose early start in the industry was unexceptional and probably obligatory. A survey of coal mines three decades later in a neighboring state estimated at least nine thousand boys (some just eight or nine years of age) working as pickers, mule drivers, and gate tenders (Lovejoy 1906: 36–37). Lee's deposition before a state commission went on to identify areas for improving underground safety, explain his involvement in union activities, and express support for an initiative to improve the frequency of mine inspections (Ohio Mining Commission 1872: 136–37)—a very different take on an industry that also included solitary prospectors and their trusty burros.

Lee's recitation of his mining family history reveals another source of variation. Employee records underscore that mining was a male profession, but the listing of fathers, sons, and grandsons on payrolls is a telling indicator of the presence of women. Work in the mines developed a shared experience among men, but mining identities were also nested within broader working-class identities, in which women were neither isolated nor insignificant. Women commonly contributed unpaid labor as wives and mothers in maintaining households. Girls also found occasional employment in and around the mines, and women volunteered as community organizers, owned businesses, and worked as prospectors and miners, too (Gier and Mercier 2006; Moore 1996; Portelli 2011: 157–61; Wood 2002; Zanjani 1997).

Because archaeological investigations so often center on domestic sites, interpretations of the laboring life also draw attention to the composition of the mining household. Domestic arrangements in mining camps could be diverse, ranging from single- and multiple-occupancy bachelor cabins to boardinghouses and family homes. Such variety opens multiple research avenues for exploring the intersection of class and gender ideologies, including an emergent interest in conceptions of masculinity and domesticity (Costello et al. 2007: 82–86; Hardesty 1994; Lawrence 1998; Wood 2002). The following section illustrates some of these directions by taking a closer look at differing conceptions of fraternity and brotherhood.

Rush-era accounts indicate that a shared sense of identity formed quickly among prospectors on the goldfields. Letters home highlight the dual sense of competition and solidarity among those venturing to the newly discovered mines. Historian Charles Shinn (1885: 110) noted that once at the camps, "Clothes, money, manners, family connections, letters of introduction, never before counted for so little," and yet distinctions invariably formed between in-groups and out-groups. Despite perceptions of "all men for once [being] upon a level" (Shinn 1885: 110), local laws set conditions for who was and was not a legitimate miner. The miner defended by the first mining laws was not necessarily a U.S. citizen, but he was male and white. Edicts against Chinese, Mexican, and Native American miners were both early and commonplace on the California goldfields (Paul 1947: 69; Shinn 1885: 212–18).

Class structures also found their way into mining camps, where they became evident in miners' leisure behaviors. The dulling routines of work and diet made miners receptive to splurging on fine dining and entertainment as opportunities arose. Meeting this demand for the glamorous, restaurants in as decidedly noncoastal settings as Tombstone, Arizona, and Virginia City, Nevada, offered appetizers of oysters on the half shell, which patrons could chase down with champagne (Conlin 1986: 119). Miners also developed a taste for the heavily sauced dishes of *la cuisine française*, popular otherwise on the dining tables of the upper classes.

Although it is impossible to know how such dishes truly compared in quality, even a feigned opulence mimicked social norms for demonstrating success (ibid.: 120–23).

But mining communities constituted more than a collection of preestablished social identities, for the act of mining itself created new forms of camaraderie that were also expressed through material culture. Early visitors to the California diggings remarked on how the "red or gray flannel shirt, old trousers, high boots that were pulled up over the pant-legs, and a dilapidated slouch hat" marked someone as a miner (Paul 1947: 69). Gaudy shirts recovered from the *Bertrand* wreck (chapter 3), among them a loud plaid of black, white, and bright blue with magenta piping, suggest that the fashion for being seen at a distance continued to the Montana fields. Indeed, given the lopsided male to female ratio of rush-era camps—some settlements as staggeringly unbalanced as 123 to 1 (Schlatter 1997: 336)—men might have pursued these embellishments to stand out from the pack. Women's clothes from the *Bertrand* followed a muted color palette by contrast, making an analogy to hens and peacocks not out of line (Guilmartin 2002: 55).

Social distinctions also formed according to experience and outlook. In arid regions, the terms *jackass prospector* and *desert rat* came to designate hard-living loners who enjoyed the independence that the prospecting life afforded them. During the Klondike rush to the Yukon and Alaska Territory, the terms *sourdough* and *cheechako*—the latter borrowed from the Chinook language—distinguished veteran prospectors from inexperienced and unwanted newcomers. Marc Stevenson's (1989) examination of mining camps in Yukon Territory concludes that sourdough and cheechako identities created separate archaeological patterns. Veteran prospectors minimized investments in infrastructure, with a typical sourdough cabin featuring an earthen floor and light, unpeeled local spruce for bunks, tables, and benches. These features contrasted with the imported sawn boards, dressed furniture, and costlier ceramics seen in the remains of contemporary boomtown dwellings (Stevenson 1989). Group distinctions extended to diet as well, with sourdough camps indicating the purchase of larger sizes of canned goods and a greater reliance on local game than seen among boomtown residents. Such differences, Stevenson argues, related to more than merely the amount of cash on hand for each group, communicating differences in lifestyle choice and a local knowledge borne from experience. Andrew Higgs and Robert Sattler's (2011) comparison of miners' cabins along Fish Creek north of Fairbanks never-theless indicates that investment in structures increased with the length of occupation. There, even sourdough cabins introduced wood flooring among a modicum of other comforts to ease the "roughing it" lifestyle.

The maturation of mining districts introduced more-formalized identities in the form of churches as well as through the establishment of specifically labor-based identities such as unions and fraternities. The presence of several such institutions in mining communities points to multiple meanings of brotherhood, and the central location and often-or-nate facades of society halls reflect the respectability and investment that these organizations achieved in town life (Francaviglia 1991: 43). Unions and fraternities offered services that ranged from hosting social events to the provision of financial support for injured miners and assistance with funeral arrangements. The latter task was of particular importance in mining towns because companies rarely provided compensation for workplace deaths and many mining communities consisted of single men with no relatives present to bury them. Silver Terrace, the largest of several cemeteries servicing Virginia City, Nevada, included sections maintained by the Free and Accepted Masons, Pacific Coast Pioneers, Independent Order of Odd Fellows, Virginia Exempt Fire Association, Knights of Py-thias, and the New and Improved Order of Red Men, to whom no Native American need apply (Wheeler 2008). As this suggests, fraternal brother-hood reached across some social divisions while entrenching others—and quite literally when miners took these identities to the grave.

Labor unions and fraternities overlapped in some services but they also embodied fundamentally different philosophical outlooks. Fraterni-ties looked to precapitalist trade guilds as an organizational model, in which a member could ascend to higher positions in the organization irrespective of his actual employment. Labor unions, by contrast, were class-based organizations, in which mine administrators were typically barred from membership (Jameson 1998: 88). The first miners' unions had not necessarily formed in opposition to capitalism, but the corporatiza-tion of mining endeavors during the late nineteenth century ultimately sharpened distinctions between those shoveling rock in the mines and those shuffling papers at the company office. It was obvious from the start that many burdens of the mining life—be they unsafe working conditions, inadequate housing, poor sanitation, or threats of layoffs—were carried unequally between managers and laborers. But were certain risks and inequities acceptable provided there was room for personal advancement, or did the nature of the inequalities demand systemic change? Fraternities and unions took different stances. Unions supported labor strikes and provided strike relief; fraternities did not.

It follows that fraternities and unions wove different social networks through mining communities. Fraternal organizations spun warp threads by strengthening connections within specific ethnic or religious groups. Unions formed the weft, linking an often-diverse set of nationalities within a social class to a common cause. Despite the different ideological foundations of these organizations, miners frequently belonged to both. The interrelation of their memberships opened possibilities for resolving some tensions between capital and labor before they came to a head (Jameson 1998: 87–89). Even so, disputes between corporate and worker interests became increasingly intractable during the nineteenth century. In Colorado alone, an estimated 92 percent of the more than seven thousand miners employed in the state had walked off the job at least once between 1881 and 1888 (Wyman 1979: 158). Miners in Colorado's Cripple Creek District staged nearly three dozen labor strikes between 1899 and 1903 (Jameson 1998: 70).

Circumstances such as differential pay scales nevertheless complicated the expression of class identity. Variable pay rates fragmented class consciousness first by creating a degree of mobility based on achievement. Wages for underground work in the Cripple Creek region, for example, varied from three dollars to five dollars per day, depending on the task performed, but workers could potentially move up the ranks. Different pay rates were also effective wherever ethnic groups worked particular tasks because they provided a justification for those higher up on the pay scale to consider themselves better than those below them. The United Mine Workers became the first national union to remove racial barriers from membership, but this was itself a complex struggle. Western miners' unions had objected vociferously to the presence of Chinese labor in mines and mills during the 1870s, and eastern unions protested against the use of African American strikebreakers (Finn 1998: 126–27; Gutman 1976: 121–23; Jameson 1998: 140–60; Lingenfelter 1974: 107–27). The Cripple Creek District had a reputation during its heyday as being a "white camp," open to white Americans and western and northern Europeans but few others. Companies capitalized on this friction between ethnic groups to secure victories in wage reduction and labor deskilling.

From an archaeological perspective, variation in take-home wages translates to differences in household assemblages. Archaeological interpretations of class and status work from the idea that commodity purchases usually involve a measure of consumer choice. Ceramics, for example, vary widely in quality and price range, with porcelains exceeding the cost of plain, undecorated earthenware. Middle-class social mores dictate that a matching dinner service sets a "classier" table than a miscellany of patterned wares. For food items as well, meat cuts are finely differentiated, with short loin and other slices "high off the hog" being more valued and expensive than necks, shanks, and trotters. Tastes changed over time, but historical documents allow a detailed assessment of the range of values for a given time period. This makes it possible to compare contemporary archaeological assemblages in terms of relative value, even in circumstances where choice may have been limited.

We have already seen how companies manifested and reified class structures in the physical layout of mining towns (chapter 3). Assemblages from domestic sites follow suit, with artifacts from the residences of managers and administrators differing in variety and quality from those recovered from worker tenements. As Sam Sweitz (2012: 233) observes, there is value also in analyzing differences within a given social class. After all, a 50 percent difference in the take-home pay among underground workers impacted the purchasing power of their respective households.

Archaeological testing at five former townsites in the Cripple Creek District furnished a substantial body of data for analyzing consumer purchases. Sweitz's (2012) comparison of several working-class households affirmed the tendency for assemblages with higher-quality ceramics to also have higher-priced meat cuts. However, the exceptions—in which four households dined well off cheap plates while another household ate rougher cuts off finer china—suggest different strategies by which householders negotiated status. The broader point is that consumer purchases reveal complex interplays of identity. Consumption patterns point to the ways that miners' households sought to improve their standing within the class system. Class consciousness was certainly present in Cripple Creek, and class was one of many identities being negotiated.

The archaeological picture appears to differ at sites more directly associated with class resistance. Donald Hardesty's (1998) analysis of Reipetown, Nevada, a satellite community that developed between the company towns of Ruth and Kimberly, suggests that class consciousness leveled out differences in consumption patterns. Nothing remains of Reipetown today, but its establishment in the early 1900s offered an alternative to the regulated environment of neighboring mining towns. Businesses in Reipetown included the requisite range of saloons, brothels, and gambling houses, but the town also developed a reputation for labor organizing. C. E. Mahoney, vice president of the Western Federation of Miners, served as the town's mayor for the one year that Reipetown was incorporated (Hardesty 1998: 90).

Archaeological testing at Reipetown identified little in the way of wealth disparities or other forms of social distinction. Even with a diverse historical population that included eastern and southern Europeans, Mexicans, and Japanese, the archaeological picture showed few markers of ethnic difference that excavations at other sites would lead us to expect. Hardesty posits that the town's history of union activity formed the social glue that ultimately downplayed other points of difference among community members (ibid.: 92).

To date, the most thorough archaeological inquiry into class conflict in mining communities has centered on the strike camp of Ludlow, Colorado—a site connected with the bloodiest labor struggle in United States history. The coalfield strike of 1913 originated from a set of commonly expressed grievances. In August of that year, the United Mine Workers threatened a general strike against the Colorado Fuel and Iron Company if demands for union representation, improvements in pay, reductions in work hours, and the right for workers to choose their boarding place and doctors were not met. One month later, approximately ten thousand men (constituting 90 percent of the workforce) walked from their jobs in protest. The United Mine Workers of America established the Ludlow colony shortly afterward as the largest of several camps to shelter the striking miners and their families following their eviction from company houses (Saitta 2007: 49–54).

The strike lasted more than a year, and tensions escalated as it wore on into the winter months. Hostilities reached a tipping point on April 20, 1914, when shots exchanged between militiamen and striking workers initiated a bloody melee at the strike camp. At day's end, the death toll stood at twenty-five, with the tent colony left a smoldering ruin (figure 4.5). The casualties included two women and eleven children who had sought refuge in a cellar hole during the fighting and suffocated when the tent above them caught fire (ibid.: 54–60). News of the Ludlow tragedy

Figure 4.5. Ludlow tent colony after the massacre on April 20, 1914. Photograph by Bain News Service. Library of Congress, Prints and Photographs Division, LC-DIG-ggbain-15859.

sparked a guerilla war between union miners and the militia that lasted several months. All told, the Colorado Coalfield War is estimated to have claimed from sixty to two hundred lives.

Archaeological investigations at Ludlow (Larkin and McGuire 2009; Reckner 2009; Saitta 2007) found surface evidence for approximately one-quarter of the strike camp's historical extent (Saitta 2007: 68–69). Residents had dug shallow ditches and berms around the perimeter wall of their tents, which revealed not only the gridded arrangement of the camp but also the location of specific tent sites. In addition to mapping the site, archaeologists sought to investigate how the strike situation influenced the expression of identity. Ludlow's strikers had resettled from company camps where ethnic neighborhoods existed. Although oral histories collected decades after the massacre noted that people "all got along," interviewers did not record the voices of Hispanic, Asian, and African American families also present during the strike. Paul Reckner's (2009: 313–23) analysis of interview transcripts suggests that some social distance may have existed, given that whites tended to be identified by personal names and nonwhites by ethnic terms.

Recovered artifacts suggest the presence of several ethnic groups. Excavations at a tent site in the northwestern part of the colony, for instance, identified suspender buckles inscribed with "Society of Tyrolean Alpinists" and a medicine bottle with embossed Italian writing that implies that the tent residents were Italian (Saitta 2007: 73). The recovery of a Knights of Pythias pin, among other fraternal pins recovered from excavations (Reckner 2009: 423–25), draws attention to the operation of multiple identities in the camp and, ultimately, suggests that even contradictory identities could reside within an individual. Had the pin belonged to Louis Tikas, a member of the fraternity killed during the massacre, he might have introduced himself to us variously as an American citizen and a Greek citizen, as a citizen who had been shot once before in the defense of citizens' rights, as a miner who worked as a strikebreaker before becoming a labor organizer, and as a member of a union that espoused racial equality and a member of a fraternity that did not.

Connecting Mine and Body

> Ellen, darling, Good Bye for us both. Elbert Said the lord had Saved him. Do the best you can with the children. We are all Praying for air to Suport us but it is getting so bad without any air. Horace, Elbert Said for you to wear his shoes and clothing. It is now half past one.
>
> JACOB L. VOWELL TO HIS WIFE, MAY 19, 1902

Hardship shadowed the mining life wherever it occurred, and nowhere was it more fundamentally realized than on miners' bodies. Jacob Vowell and his fourteen-year-old son, Elbert, had survived the explosion of methane and coal dust at the Fraterville Mine in Tennessee on May 19, 1902, only to suffocate in the toxic gases while awaiting rescue. More than 200 miners died that day, leaving hundreds widowed and approximately 1,000 children fatherless. The explosion catapulted an average mine into lasting notoriety as one of the nation's worst mining disasters, but Fraterville ultimately ranked as just one more incident in a disaster-prone industry. Seven weeks earlier, an explosion in Dayton, Tennessee (75 miles to the southwest), took 16 miners. Seven weeks after Fraterville, a Pennsylvania coal mine claimed 112 lives, and five days later, 34 miners died in a lead mine in northern Utah (Humphrey 1960: 22). Industry statistics indicate that still more miners died from events claiming just one or two at a time and that for every death, workplace accidents maimed or incapacitated greater numbers (Fay 1916: 96–98) (figure 4.6).

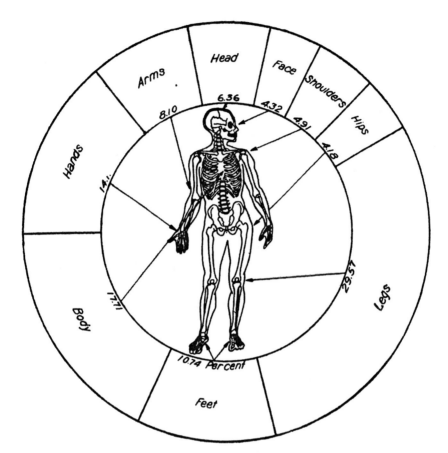

Figure 4.6. An evocative depiction of locations of nonfatal mining injuries on the body, based on 6,719 cases (Fay 1916: 98).

Tragedy and working-class identity were closely linked, for the hazards of the job forged bonds between generations of mining families and between those working in different mines. Folklorists point to the rich traditions of songcraft that developed in mining regions as both a coping mechanism and a vector for channeling outrage (Green 1972). Archaeologists observe the interconnections through different sorts of evidence, ranging from patterns in health-care practices to those directly imprinted on miners' bodies.

Bioarchaeological studies indicate that the human skeleton chronicles traumas, illnesses, and even toxins accumulating over the life of an individual. Archaeological assessments of historic mining populations remain scant, and rarer still in the United States, but the results confirm that mining has a signature. Chemical testing, for instance, has identified contaminants likely introduced into the bone through association with mineral processing. Skeletons recovered from two late eighteenth-century cemeteries in northeastern Nebraska contained lead concentrations ten to one hundred times higher than background levels. Of the thirty-six individuals analyzed, significantly higher lead concentrations among adult males (185 micrograms per gram, as opposed to 23.8 micrograms per gram for females) implied that Omaha men had handled lead artifacts regularly and were probably involved in lead smelting and casting (Reinhard and Ghazi 1992).

Fractures, depressions, and other traumas visible on the bone underscore the dangers common to mine work. A study of one hundred burials (Van der Merwe et al. 2010a, 2010b, 2011) associated with the Kimberley diamond mines in South Africa, for instance, identified healed fractures and blunt force trauma in over one-quarter of the burial population. Six individuals had endured amputations, and nearly all suffered from poor dental hygiene, suggestive of the impoverished diet that the mining company provided to African workers. Chinese miners laboring some 300 miles distant at the Witwatersrand gold mines fared little better. Between 1904 and 1910, the Witwatersrand mines had employed more than sixty thousand Chinese indentured laborers to resolve a short-term labor crisis. Nearly one in twenty died during their tenure, with one-third of deaths directly attributable to injuries on the job (Meyer and Steyn 2015). The analysis of three dozen skeletons unearthed at Witwatersrand during salvage excavations in the 1950s corroborates the high incidence of trauma reported among the Chinese workers. Thirty percent of the skeletons showed fractures occurring either at or close to the time of death. Most damage occurred to the leg bones, and the presence of multiple and spiral fractures is suggestive of falls and severe impacts (Meyer and Steyn 2015).

Such results do more than affirm industry statistics, for archaeological analyses are able to catalog the traumas accumulating over an individual's life. Miners' skeletons often show signs of multiple traumas. Because the skeleton responds to injury in only so many ways, not all injuries can be attributable simply to mine work. This said, an expanded definition of mining-related injury recognizes the concurrence of other forms of violence in mining communities. Records for Kimberley and Witwatersrand indicate heightened tensions between miners and area residents. Among the causes of death for 189 Chinese miners who died at Witwatersrand in 1905 were 14 lost to opium poisoning, 4 murders, 4 executions, and 5 who committed suicide (Meyer and Steyn 2015). It would not be farfetched to suggest commonalities between miners and other populations subjected to hard labor and racial oppression (e.g., Burnston and Thomas 1981; Harrod et al. 2012).

Falls, cave-ins, and machinery accidents accounted for the greatest numbers of workplace fatalities, but they were not the only risks. The archaeological exhumation of five prospectors who had perished during an ill-fated attempt to cross Colorado's San Juan Mountains in the winter of 1874 revealed the perils that went with being unprepared for conditions. The party became stranded ten days into the trek, and only Alferd Packer made it out alive. Packer later confessed to cannibalism but admitted to killing only one of his companions. The reassessment of the victims more than a century later enabled a closer reading of the tragic event. Cut marks on the skeleton—from 80 to 106 cuts per individual—were located in places consistent with the removal of the largest muscle groups. Inconsistencies in the orientation of cut marks suggested processing at different time periods, and the preponderance of cuts on the back of the bodies suggests an intentional avoidance of the victims' faces (Rautman and Fenton 2005: 336). Whether all men had been killed by Packer's hand remains undetermined, but all five had assuredly met violent deaths. The skulls of each showed the telltale marks from a hatchet, and defensive wounds on the arm bones indicate that at least three victims had been aware of the attack (Rautman and Fenton 2005). But mining tragedies could also occur quietly. Recent surveying in central Nevada recovered the remains of a 1930s-era prospector who had died from a self-inflicted gunshot wound (Obermayr and McQueen 2016: 135–39). Such unfortunate fates highlight that the pursuit of elusive minerals could spell much more than financial ruin.

Historical medical records indicate that mining populations suffered rates of pneumonia and infectious disease higher than their urban counterparts did (Ferris 1991; Zanjani 1990). Poor working conditions certainly contributed to the problem, especially for mines without sanitation policies in place. The situation in Pennsylvania's Hazelton Mine had become so dire in the 1890s, for example, that rats gnawed at mules not quick enough to trample them, and miners had resorted to burying their dinner buckets in a desperate attempt to have something to eat during their shift (Long 1989: 34–35). A far more common vector for illness stemmed from such banal causes as miners walking home in their sweat-soaked clothes at the end of the shift. The installation of dry rooms at mine entrances reduced part of the problem, but silicosis proved to be a deeper and more difficult issue to solve. The onset of silicosis compounded matters because the scarring of lung tissue reduced lung capacity, and this in turn increased the lethality of tuberculosis, bronchitis, and pneumonia, among other respiratory diseases (Holman 1947).

Aboveground conditions also provided conditions ripe for the spread of infectious disease. After all, rush-era camps seldom invested in public works, and cramped quarters and poor sanitation were commonplace. Nor did the situation necessarily improve with company towns, for housing shortages resulted in overcrowding, and the short life projected for many ventures discouraged companies from making substantial investments in infrastructure. Indeed, company towns could fare worse than independent settlements in the provision of basic sanitation (Obenauer 1925: 539). A widely circulated study of West Virginia coal patches by the United States Coal Commission in 1925 noted several communities for which a single water pump serviced more than thirty families and in which miners' accommodations were heated by either an open fire or a single coal stove. Few communities connected miners' houses to sanitary sewer systems or had developed regulations for privy construction and cleaning (U.S. Coal Commission 1925: 612–13). The construction of some privies over streams answered why these communities suffered disproportionately from typhoid outbreaks (Green 2010).

Archaeological studies of historic privy soils have revealed that historic populations were additionally burdened by the presence of parasites such as hookworms and tapeworms (Fisher et al. 2007; Reinhard 1994). These pathogens indicate that the fecal contamination of food and water in urban areas was quite common, but it has also opened possibilities for seeing health disparities across different populations. Investigations of privy soils at the nineteenth-century iron-smelting town of Fayette, Michigan, suggests that class differences found expressions beyond architecture and ceramic purchases. Soils sampled from the manager's privy showed no sign of parasites. Soils from a two-story privy associated with a hotel and boardinghouse, however, recovered the eggs of *Trichuris trichiura*, a common parasite causing diarrhea and abdominal cramps for its hosts (Faulker et al. 2000).

Domestic deposits provide us with valuable insights into the ways that miners and their families treated various ailments. Privies again serve as useful sites for investigation because vaults served as convenient trash receptacles. Glass assemblages recovered from the red-light district of Ouray, Colorado, indicated a preference for discarding bottles in the privy but also that the privy discard was selective. Medicinal and alcoholic bottles were found two to three times more frequently in the privies than in the corresponding back lots of a theater and boardinghouse (Horobik 2011: 64, 67). Fully three-quarters of the 219 bottles excavated from a theater privy were classified as medicinals. The boardinghouse followed suit, with medicines accounting for 43 percent of the 46 identified bottles, among them several homeopathic vials and a medicine targeting genital diseases (Horobik 2011). While high volumes of alcohol and medicines are common in red-light districts (C. Spude 2005: 99), intrasite variation at Ouray suggests that concerns for privacy still prevailed amid the revelry.

Among the frequent historical medicines recovered from domestic assemblages are the proprietary, or "patent," formulas promoted during the mid- to late nineteenth century as cure-all tonics, blood purifiers, and cathartics. The immense popularity of cure-alls rested in part on long-held notions about the importance of maintaining the body's humors (Estes 1988; Toulouse 1970: 62–63). By this logic, an imbalance in one's overall health could cause a wide range of otherwise disconnected ills (Estes 1988). Hamlin's Wizard Oil, for example, attacked rheumatism, toothache, headache, sore throat, lame back, sprains, bruises, and burns; Hostetter Bitters alleviated dyspepsia, dysentery, and malaria, among other problems; and Drake's Plantation Bitters, "unequaled for family, hotel, and medicinal use," treated diarrhea, constipation, cholera, liver complaints, and headaches, prevented fevers, purified the breath, and "enlivened" the mind. The last of these claims arguably came closest to the mark. Most patent medicines included liberal doses of alcohol, because many originated as a means for alcohol manufacturers to circumvent payment of a whiskey tax. Drake's Bitters clocked in at 38 percent alcohol.

Although cure-alls were often packaged in distinctive bottles, the broad spectrum of cures proclaimed by a given medicine frustrates attempts to discern specific complaints. Nevertheless, the presence or absence of patent medicines at mining sites affords insight into changing ideas about medical practice. During the nineteenth century, the medical profession gave increasing attention to bacteria and viruses as primary disease vectors. The adoption of germ theory prescribed different forms of preventative care, among them an emphasis on improving municipal sanitation, developing immunization programs, and disseminating information about personal hygiene.

Claire Horn's (2009) research on the Colorado Fuel and Iron Company has tracked how shifts in medical practice became integrated into corporate policies at coal camps. Beginning in the 1900s, the company unveiled a series of health-care initiatives in which employees paid one dollar per month for the provision of doctors and medical services. The company established a Sociological Department that, among other tasks, issued bulletins on cleanliness and hygiene and ran competitions for "best garden." Despite denouncements of patent medicines appearing in company bulletins, archaeological investigations reveal that old habits died hard. Excavations at the company camp of Berwind and the strikers' camp at Ludlow found medicines accounting for at least 20 percent of the bottle assemblage, and patent medicines constituted the majority of these (Horn 2009: 264–71). Here, archaeological findings indicate that changes in practice were neither immediate nor uniform in implementation. Departures from proscribed company policies may imply a lingering mistrust of company physicians. After all, strikers encamped at the Ludlow colony had included among their demands "the right to choose our own boarding place and our own doctor" (Horn 2009: 251).

One point that archaeological findings drive home is that the difficulty of accessing medical professionals impeded but did not close off options for health care. Alcohol bottles, tobacco tins, mineral waters, and opium paraphernalia to a lesser extent are common finds at mining sites, and all provided palliative care in the absence of alternatives (Horobik 2011). Moreover, the occasional survival of bottle contents and handwritten labels has also documented the reuse of bottles for a range of medicinal preparations. Jane Russell's (1991) inventory of the Chew Kee mercantile store (1860s through 1930s) in Fiddletown, California, identified condiment and whiskey bottles refilled with remedies for bruised muscles, a Mason jar packed with headache powder, a bottle of vanilla essence containing cologne, and bottles filled with powders for treating knife wounds. Excavations at other historic sites have identified bottles refilled for applications ranging from cleaning detergents to male virility enhancements (Staski 1993: 134–37; see also McDougall 1990: 69). It is also the case that beginning in the mid-nineteenth century, mail-order businesses supplied

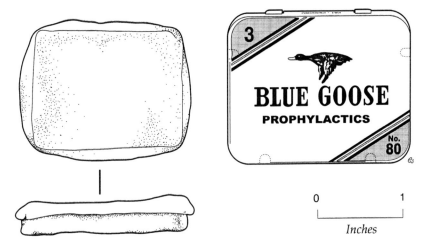

Figure 4.7. Small tin recovered from Goodsprings, Nevada, that approximates the dimensions of aspirin containers and condom tins. The Goodsprings red-light district was colloquially referred to as Blue Goose. Drawings by author; drawing at left adapted from Becker 1981: 154.

patent medicines, herbal preparations, and, following an amendment to the Comstock Act in 1918, prophylactics (Heffner 2012: 257–59; Valentine 2003). Archaeological investigations in Goodsprings, Nevada, suggest that residents made use of this availability in the town's red-light district of Blue Goose, in existence from 1916 to 1921. A surface survey in the 1980s had recovered several small tins initially interpreted as aspirin containers (Becker 1981). David Valentine's (2003) reassessment, however, notes the similarity of form to condom tins (figure 4.7), including the Blue Goose brand that evidently gave the district its name.

Broadening the Narrative

Given that mining camps were cosmopolitan places dependent on external ties, it might be presumed that social identities arrived at mining camps prepackaged like so much of the food. Archaeological sites certainly abound with evidence of imported goods, down to the minutiae of personal effects. Irrespective of whether people ventured to the mineral strikes or sought employment at an established mine, most came from somewhere else, and they did not simply discard these identities and class-based aspirations upon reaching their destination. Mining for most practitioners remained a job. It was a means to an end, and one of the commonly envisioned ends involved materially improving one's lot in life.

This said, attention paid to only external connections falls short of producing an understanding of the dynamics occurring within communities. The industry brought ethnic groups together in new combinations and concentrations, and the dangers common to mining work forged bonds among miners, left common signatures on their bodies, and also laid the groundwork for organizations that contested the arrangements of industrial capitalism. Archaeological studies help draw attention to how the business of mining generated these new identities. Diverse takes existed on what it meant to be a miner, and the expression of identity left different signatures in the material record. I have focused to this point on the patterns seen in domestic arrangements, but mining workplaces were just as prone to variation and transformation over time. As we shall see, cultural value systems also shaped the basic act of removing rock.

5

Into the Mines

I only remained in the milling business one week. I told my employer I could not stay longer without an advance in my wages; that I liked quartz milling, indeed was infatuated with it; that I had never before grown so tenderly attached to an occupation in so short a time; that nothing, it seemed to me, gave such scope to intellectual activity as feeding a battery and screening tailings, and nothing so stimulated the moral attributes as retorting bullion and washing blankets—still, I felt constrained to ask an increase of salary. . . . I said about four hundred thousand dollars a month, and board, was about all I could reasonably ask, considering the hard times.

—MARK TWAIN, *ROUGHING IT*

For all but the most fortunate, the dream of venturing into the hills and finding riches for the taking lost its sheen when faced with the drudging reality. Samuel Clemens did not take to mining. His early prospecting efforts in Nevada proved to be a failure, and he experienced firsthand that mining did not get easier with shift work. He summed up his stint at a stamp mill in Aurora, Nevada, as being "the most detestable work I have ever engaged in," suspecting also that it had given him a mild dose of mercury poisoning (Branch et al. 1987: 225; Paine 1924: 258). Clemens ultimately spun the straw of his mining experiences into literary gold as Mark Twain, but the same cannot be said for whoever filled his vacancy on the stamp floor. We have not even a name.

Industrial workplaces are often impersonal. On the one hand, high rates of labor turnover and the uncertainties of documentary preservation tend to decrease the visibility of individuals at the workplace. On the other, the immense scale of landscapes created by hydraulicking, dredging, mountaintop removal, and open-pit mining, among other techniques, seem at odds with the scale of the individual. Looking over the ruins of a stamp mill, we may find it hard to envision the choreographed labors of Clemens or his replacement feeding a stamp battery, washing corduroy blankets, and screening tailings while half covered in the stuff.

What we do see in abundance is technology, whether manifested in remnant equipment strewn about a site, in the outlines of foundation pads designed for specific machines, or in the general contours of a worked landscape. Even at this removed level, one can gain an inkling that close connections existed between the rhythms of the workplace and the pace of community life. When mills and mines prospered, so did the towns. But archaeological investigations of the workplace also draw attention to themes other than the leitmotif of boom and bust. Here, among the foundations, lie records also of cultural assumptions about appropriate technologies, of changing relationships between capital and labor, of repeated trial and error, and of attempts by speculators to fleece investors. The workplace, it turns out, is not so impersonal after all.

The Culture of Technological Practice

In the summer of 1995, archaeological testing at a mid-nineteenth-century mine in Michigan's Upper Peninsula unearthed milling floors in a remarkable state of preservation. Residual copper in the stamp sands covering the mill's lower levels had acted as a biocide limiting the effects of decomposition. Among the 140-year-old detritus, archaeologists recovered leather boot uppers, wooden launders, and the tongue-and-groove tabletops of two Cornish milling devices in near-immaculate condition (figure 5.1).

The buddles uncovered at the Ohio Trap Rock mill (1848–58) were comparatively simple contraptions, each consisting of a gently sloping surface over which a slurry of ore was introduced. In operation, heavier, metal-rich material settled onto the upper slopes of the buddle, while lighter (and lower-value) sediments flowed off the slanted tabletop and out of the mill. Buddles varied in design and could be as low-tech as an inclined trench cut into the ground. During the 1850s, however, Cornish millers increasingly favored the construction of a circular table fitted with mechanical sweeper arms to agitate the material. The devices unearthed at Ohio Trap Rock followed suit, being circular in form and installed with center bearings for the attachment of sweeping brushes (Landon and Tumberg 1996). Evidently, the transfer of buddle technology from the windswept Cornish coast to the mosquito-swept Michigan woods had

Figure 5.1. A Cornish buddle exposed at the Ohio Trap Rock Mill, Michigan. Copper present in the stamp sands had worked as a biocide to preserve the wooden timbers. Photograph by Patrick Martin.

occurred with little delay. The use of entirely different construction materials for the buddles—stone in Cornwall and locally available timber in Michigan—strongly implies that this transfer was the consequence not of purchasing parts from England but of employing Cornishmen who had carried the idea in their heads across the Atlantic.

The international character of mining injected a great deal of variation into American technological practice. Patterns of ethnic migration on the continent corresponded, at least initially, to patterns in practice. Thus, the appearance of buddles in a Michigan mill dovetailed with the influx of Cornish immigrants into the Lake Superior region (ibid.; Rowe 1974). Mining districts in southern California and the American Southwest, by contrast, exhibited a tendency to favor Spanish mining methods (Young 1970: 55–101). Such associations became muddied during the mid-nineteenth-century mineral rushes when the flood of people and machines, proliferation of mining textbooks, and growth of mining societies all disseminated awareness of available options to broader audiences.

Patterns in technological practice nevertheless continued to occur, and in ways not explainable in terms of only economic efficiencies or available finances. Social, cultural, and political factors influenced where certain ethnic groups could and could not mine, as well as the technologies able to be employed. Many western mining districts as early as the 1860s instituted laws to collect a foreign miners tax from Chinese miners and ban "Celestials" from working virgin placer ground. Anti-Chinese sentiments thus relegated Chinese miners to the poorest placer ground, ensuring that whites retained the first opportunity to win easy fortunes. Heavy taxation limited the funds Chinese miners had available for investing in equipment, and most adopted hand methods. Among the more common tools utilized by the Chinese was the rocker box—a screening and sorting device that miners moved back and forth like a cradle. Its use among the Chinese became so pervasive that it was commonly (and mistakenly) believed to have been a Chinese invention (Limbaugh 1999: 30).

Archaeological surveys of Chinese work sites in Idaho, Oregon, and Montana have identified scatters of heavily worn equipment including picks, axes, shovels, and rocker screens in addition to neat rows of hand-stacked tailings (James 1995; Merritt 2010: 323–24; Steeves 1984; Valentine 1999: 164–65; Valentine 2002: 46–47 [outside the United States, see Mc-Gowan 1996; Ritchie 1986]). While distinct ethnic signatures cannot be attributed to such deposits on this evidence alone, a common denominator at Chinese work sites is the prevalence of labor-intensive methods. The comparative rarity of Chinese hydraulicking operations (but see LaLande 1981, 1985) and the absence of Chinese-run dredging operations further underscore this history of political and economic marginalization. Suffice to say, contemporary descriptions of the Chinese "thriving" on what American miners threw away (Bowles 1869: 400) or working with "constant plodding and dogged perseverance" (Lloyd 1876: 244) put a shiny gloss on barefaced oppression.

Cultural factors also influenced the technologies that industry practitioners considered to be "progressive." Thad Van Bueren (2004: 14) notes a close correspondence in American mining between the general dismissal of Spanish mining techniques and the discrimination faced by Hispanic people. While Mexican miners experienced low wages, taxation, and outright exclusion, English-speaking whites enjoyed praise for their "naturally" industrious habits. Cornish surnames such as Elliott, Pearce, Martin, Tippett, and Trebilcock came to populate the higher-paid positions on mine payrolls (Rowe 1974: 173–74). Given this strong presence in mid- to upper-level management, it is not surprising that American underground mines during the mid- to late nineteenth century tended to follow Cornish ideas that Cornish methods represented the best way of doing things (see also Burt 2000, 2007).

One such device introduced to American mines by the Cornish happened to be the very same device that had broken Twain's resolve to make a living from mining. The gravity stamp crushed ore by the mechanical raising and dropping of a set of heavy rods into a box where ore was distributed. Gravity stamps processed high volumes of ore faster than other available crushing technologies. Within a couple of decades of the stamp mill's introduction, the din of falling stamps became more or less equated with the sounds of profits and progress.

The efficiency argument loses traction, however, when one considers that stamps required high startup costs and regular maintenance and that their early performance in American mining districts left much to be desired (Limbaugh and Fuller 2003: 44–45). Other crushing technologies such as the arrastra (introduced by the Spanish), which ground ore by dragging boulders around a circular trough, could be constructed from locally available materials and required minimal maintenance. In Mexico, arrastras remained a primary gold crushing and recovery technique in large-scale mills well into the early decades of the twentieth century.

In American mines, however, the arrastra retained favor only as a "poor man's mill" (Kelly and Kelly 1983; Van Bueren 2004: 13–14).

Anthropological studies of technology stress the importance of viewing technologies not simply as objects but as sets of coordinated activities or "operative chains" (Lemonnier 1986; Pfaffenberger 1998; Schiffer 2001). The fundamental concept here is that technologies require labor, and labor systems need to be learned. Mining universally involves digging material out of the ground, but the tasks to do this are organized in different ways. Thus, underground work involving the use of mechanized drills generally involved boring holes into a rock face, loading an explosive charge, cleaning up debris from the explosion, and removing rock from the mine. How these tasks were parsed out, however, was not a given. In a small mine, all tasks might be undertaken by the same worker. At a larger operation, tasks were more likely to be separated, assigned to drillers, who were responsible only for drilling the holes; muckers, who loaded the carts; and trammers, who hauled the material out of the mine. These divisions reflected a capitalist rationalization of underground work into differently paid skill sets. Ethnic traditions provided additional variety.

Cornish labor systems, for example, separated underground work into tribute and yardage contracts. Tribute miners bid competitively to excavate sections of an ore body. Yardage workers, by contrast, dug the shafts and crosscuts necessary for mine development (also termed "dead work"). While both tasks required that miners form teams to bid for contracts, tribute and yardage work calculated earnings differently. Pay for tribute miners ultimately hinged on the richness of the ore, whereas miners on yardage contracts received money for excavating a set distance (Rule 1998).

The Empire Mine (1850–1957), one of California's earliest and most productive lode gold mines, adopted the Cornish labor system wholesale (Wolf et al. 2008: 152–54), but local variations also existed. Work sheets for the Ely Mine in Vermont (1813–1958) indicate a dual labor system in which miners opted for either working under a tribute system or working for wages. At the New Almaden mercury mine in California (1846–1945), the Cornish system cleaved along racial lines. There, Cornish miners monopolized the yardage contracts, which generally provided a more reliable wage and also limited exposure to the health hazards of working with mercury ores. These dangers were faced instead by Mexican and Chilean miners, who took the tribute contracts, and by Chinese employees, who operated the reduction furnaces. The segregation of tasks mirrored segregation aboveground, for Cornish and Anglo-American employees resided in Englishtown, Mexican and Chilean miners in Spanishtown, and Chinese employees in Chinesetown (Johnston 2013: 171–80).

The payroll at New Almaden adhered to the Cornish system, but workplace infrastructure also incorporated Spanish mining practices. Leveled areas remaining today outside a few mine entrances were once sites of long sorting sheds, termed *planillas*, where tribute contractors graded ore under the watchful eye of supervisors. Wheelbarrow loads of the two richest categories, *gruesso* and *granza*, determined a team's earnings. Crews received no compensation for the third category, *tierra* (inferior-quality ore), although this material still entered the roasting furnaces for reduction (ibid.: 159n37).

The different mining systems at New Almaden also left signatures underground. Areas of the mine opened by yardage contractors revealed the application of principles of scientific management, with straight tunnels radiating out from shafts at regular depths. This contrasted with a veritable warren of excavations into the ore body where the Mexican and Chilean miners working tribute contracts adopted *el sistema del rato* (the system of the moment), which removed only as much surrounding rock as necessary. Following the twists and turns of veins certainly represented a logical choice for tribute miners, since they earned nothing for removing waste material and, during the early years of the operation, hauled out all excavated rock on their backs (ibid.: 138–52; Wells 1863: 31).

At New Almaden and elsewhere, systems of underground work also included appeals to spiritual protection—indeed, the unpredictability of one's fortunes underground encouraged it. A visitor touring New Almaden's labyrinthine workings in the 1860s remarked on the way Mexican tribute miners prostrated themselves before a statue of Our Lady of Guadalupe occupying a niche "hewn with more than ordinary care out of the solid rock" (Wells 1863: 41). The visitor's descriptions ended with the tribute miners, but Cornish miners, for their part, commonly attributed rockfalls, missing tools, strange noises underground, and the changing quality of ore veins to the actions of elf-like underground spirits called Tommyknockers. To ensure protection and good fortune, miners occasionally fashioned effigies from the clay used for mounting candles, positioning the figures at mine entrances and other needed places along with offerings of food and tallow (Hand 1942: 128; James 1992: 168).

The unique combination of work systems in mines like New Almaden complicates making any hard and fast definition of "American practice." Indeed, the dimensions of American mining are difficult to pinpoint in terms of specific technological devices—historian Roger Burt (2000, 2007) contends that Americans did not so much invent radically new technologies as modify existing traditions. Yet the term "American practice" had, by the turn of the twentieth century, increasingly peppered mining treatises and journals in regard to other national traditions. Without specific technologies to pin an American quality on, American practice was arguably better defined in terms of organizational parameters, including a penchant for American-made equipment and American managerial styles. The latter included schemes to incentivize individual achievement. We have already seen how American operators promoted the Chuquicamata Mine (chapter 3) as an American way of doing things—offering higher wages and instituting systems of reward for workers showing signs of self-improvement.

American managerial styles tended to favor any options that reduced an operation's dependence on labor. Thus, among the American alterations to the gravity stamp were automatic ore feeders that did away with the need for employing workers to shovel ore into the stamp mortar. Whether achieved through mechanization or through the restructuring of labor, such organizational modifications have also left traces in historical documents and materials.

American interests in mining rich coal seams on Spitsbergen (1906–16), an archipelago situated 500 miles north of Norway, faced several challenges in transforming an isolated set of prospects into a paying mine. Not least among the difficulties was convincing one hundred to three hundred men to spend a year on an island of ice, rock, and little else, where the temperature in the mines stayed below freezing and a 2–3-inch-thick crust of ice could form on the sides and bottoms of bunk beds because the accommodations were poorly insulated (Hartnell 2009: 124–25, 143, 165). Worker morale proved fleeting, and employee retention, elusive. A typical season ended with the Arctic Coal Company blacklisting one-third of the workforce and labeling another third as "no good" (ibid.: 123). Surviving correspondence indicates that recruiters had first hired unskilled Norwegian laborers from coastal towns and then looked farther afield after a series of labor strikes. Stereotypes of ethnic character strongly guided their selections. The company experimented next with a contingent of Finnish workers and then with a group of "whites" (British and American workers). Finding both sets to be equally as disgruntled as the original Norwegian workforce, managers entertained the notion of importing Chinese laborers but settled on recruiting Norwegians from rural areas, on the grounds that they were probably less experienced in union organizing. The presumption proved misguided (ibid.: 118–23; DePasqual 2009: 137).

Mining records indicate that the company also attempted underground solutions to the labor problem under the aegis of instituting "American practice." Between 1911 and 1916, the Arctic Coal Company replaced British foremen with American foremen, imported American machinery, and introduced a mining method widely practiced in American hard rock mines. The company had extracted coal initially by longwalling, a British technique that exposed an extensive section of a coal seam that miners then advanced as a working face. Two conditions reduced the effectiveness of the longwall system on Spitsbergen. First, a geological fault running diagonally through the deposit constricted the area suitable for setting up a longwall. The second obstinate problem concerned labor. Longwalling involved the coordination of more than one dozen men and the close sequencing of tasks. The company's hiring of unskilled labor from a range of ethnic groups meant that progress on the longwall was frequently arrested by communication problems and the need to train new groups of workers. Longwalling proceeded at the pace of the slowest worker, and this interdependence opened possibilities for disgruntled workers to intentionally slow production rates.

In 1912, the company experimented by opening the northern section of the mine with the room and pillar method (figure 5.2). This older mining method utilized smaller work teams (typically two to three miners per room) and also simplified the array of tasks. Payroll records indicate that a couple of men operated an excavation drill but most other miners were handed picks and shovels (DePasqual 2009: 153–59). Management promoted competition by paying teams by the tonnage excavated. Room-and-pillar miners in Mine No. 1 thus competed against teams working in other rooms and also against the miners working the longwall south of the mine entrance. In this case, Americanization underground was synonymous less with mechanization than with the application of time and motion studies and other scientific management principles that had come to be favored in American factories.

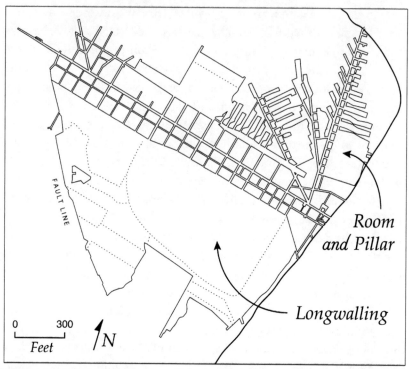

Figure 5.2. Underground map of the Arctic Coal Company's Mine No. 1, Spitsbergen, as it looked in September 1915. This mine was worked by two distinct mining systems—longwalling and room and pillar—as a means for testing labor efficiency. Dashed lines indicate blocks of ore removed by longwalling. Drawing by author.

Mapping Economies of Scale

American mining operations over the last century have generated arresting cultural landscapes. Driving through central Appalachia, one spots hillsides in the process of mountaintop removal and others undergoing "return to contour"—a technique using overburden to reconstruct hilly terrain after mining operations close, a more favored option than the previous use of this material to infill valleys. In northern Utah over the course of a century, the largest open-pit excavation in North America has turned a hill into a crater two and one-half miles across and deep enough to stack three Chrysler Buildings, base to antenna, with room to spare. Such landscapes are a far cry from the miner processing a few cubic yards of material each day in a rocker box. In lode mining, a single operator using dynamite and hand tools might hope to advance about a linear foot per day, a dramatic difference from the operator of a large shovel excavator, who removes many times this volume in a single grab.

The upshot is that historical mining landscapes range widely in scale from a smattering of prospect pits to work sites of truly daunting proportions. Calculating the area of a mine pit or waste pile provides a sense of the total amount of material moved (e.g., Coroneos 1995), but it is also apparent that mining enterprises draw in more-extensive landscapes of exploitation. Water supplied domestic needs and found essential uses also for excavation, dust control, equipment cooling, ore conveyance, metals recovery, and power generation. Water flumes, ditches, and pipelines could extend for considerable distances. Early twentieth-century ditches dramatically score tens of miles of treeless landscape north of Nome, Alaska. Along the Nome River drainage, three independent ditch systems—the Miocene, Seward, and Pioneer—cut across the same hillside at different elevations like widely spaced contour lines (Brooks 1908; Smith 1997). In Colorado, a spectacular 10-mile-long stretch of the Dolores and San Miguel Rivers includes sections of a nineteenth-century wooden flume still tethered to the canyon's sheer walls (Pfertsch 2005; Spivey et al. 2005). The archaeological analysis of ditch systems has identified unique construction styles and has drawn connections between ditch alignments and the politics involved in ensuring the best route (see Rhoades 2007), not dissimilar from the machinations involved in the competition for oil pipeline routes.

Timber served key uses as a construction material, as structural supports in underground workings, and as a fuel source. Mine smelters also required enormous volumes of charcoal to serve as both a fuel and flux in reducing ore to bullion. In Nevada, the dendrochronological analysis of tree stumps has revealed how woodcutting radiated out from mining centers and also that wooded pockets and thinned-out areas were exploited over longer time periods than often assumed (Hattori and Thompson 1987; Reno 1996). During the 1870s, the town of Eureka, Nevada, boasted more than a dozen smelters refining the area's silver-lead ores, prodigious enough to earn it acclaim as "the Pittsburgh of the West," the sooty exemplar of industrial busy-ness. Timber felling and charcoaling activities ranged gradually outward from Eureka. Charcoalers set their eyes on the juniper- and pinyon-studded Roberts Mountains, 20 miles distant from the town, as early as the 1860s. Operations continued for three decades until lowered regional processing costs ended smelting in Eureka. The area saw little subsequent industrial activity, and this has afforded archaeologists an uncommon glimpse into a well-preserved charcoaling landscape that encompasses several thousand acres.

Ronald Reno's (1996) survey of 10,000 acres in the Roberts Mountains identified thirty habitation sites related to charcoaling, close to four hundred charcoal pits, and numerous associated features such as watch shelters, corrals, and a forest of tree stumps beneath the regrowth. Principal camps tended to occupy the center of a valley, with smaller settlements found at higher and lower elevations. This suggests that charcoal burners worked within natural watersheds. The dendrochronology of cut stumps indicated that woodcutting occurred in multiple locations throughout a watershed in a given year. In other words, the lowest and most accessible woodlands were not simply the first trees to go. Reno (1996) suggests that this strategy may have helped secure against encroachment by rival companies, for the best way to show occupation of the land in this competitive industry was to use it. Cut dates also show broader movements over time. The earliest timber felling occurred in the northeastern section of the Roberts Mountains, and charcoaling over the course of a decade moved roughly clockwise through the range (Reno 1996: 270–73).

When it comes to sites of mineral extraction, however, the reworking of sites often obscures the ability to record historical phases. Nevertheless, archaeological typologies can at times distinguish mining processes to a high level of specificity from equipment and the wastes that they generated (Hovis 1992; Purdy 2007; Tordoff 2004; Twitty 2002). Judy Tordoff's (2004) and Sarah Purdy's (2007) investigations of placer tailings near, respectively, Folsom, California, and Elk City in north-central Idaho, for example, identify key differences between dredging methods. Floating dredges—the classic form of dredge in which the machine scoops up gravels by working in a pond—discarded material in undulating, arced ridges, each undulation formed by the machine's step-by-step advancement through the deposit and the arc formed by the dredge swiveling around its anchor point. Tailings from dragline dredging, by contrast, formed hummocks typically 15 feet apart. Power shovels left large single piles of tailings or reintroduced the tailings into excavated pits.

Because tailings often show horizontal stratigraphy, surface surveys can also document change over time. It is possible, for instance, to deduce the direction of a bucket dredge through the pay streak because the ridges of waste material form a concave arc in relation to the tailings stacker. Keith Baird's (2005) examination of dredging in Coal Creek, Alaska, noted the correspondence between the dredge's downstream progression and the shifting locations of company camps and associated domestic deposits. Archaeological surveys of the dredge piles revealed the use of the tailings area also for staging equipment overhauls. Dredge repair sites included piles of equipment parts such as bucket pieces, clutches, rubber hoses, rivets, riffles, and sorting screens. Workers piled like items together, converting the large expanse of tailings into a vast, open-air storage yard.

One reason to record the spatial extent of mining sites is that technologies often involved specific labor arrangements. The shift to mass-mining methods, for instance, rationalized mine production in ways that restructured and ultimately deskilled the labor force. The effects of this reorganization became widely apparent in the form of mining landscapes as well as in small changes to mining equipment.

A classic example is seen in the adoption of the machine drill. Prior to the 1890s, hard-rock mining mostly involved the use of hand steels and hammers to chisel holes into a rock face for packing explosives. Miners drove steels into the rock manually, substituting progressively longer drill steels as the hole deepened. Different steel lengths also corresponded to different hammering techniques. In single jacking, in which miners held the drill steel in one hand and a hammer in the other, the longest steel rarely exceeded 3 feet. An alternative method used drill steels as long as 6 feet and heftier hammers called double jacks to pound them home (Twitty 2002: 40). Owing to the heavier tools, "double jacking" required a team of two or three miners at the working face—one miner taking the unenviable position of holding the drill steel while his partner(s) walloped the end of it in near darkness.

The introduction of the rock drill in American mines beginning in the 1870s transformed the pace of underground mining. Rock drills mechanized the drilling process by attaching steels to a pneumatic hammer capable of striking three to four times faster than hand drilling at approximately the same cost per foot (Holman 1947: 9). Machine drills necessitated a larger capital outlay up front, but they did not require the same number of men at a given station. Historian Otis Young (1970: 206) estimates that a mine resupplied with machine drills could retire three-quarters of their double jack teams from the payroll. Worker resistance to machine drills in the Lake Superior copper mines led to the adoption of slower rock drills requiring two miners to operate, which allowed work to continue in teams (Lankton 1983: 34). Rock drills ultimately made it feasible at large-scale mines to abandon the excavation of ore veins in favor of extracting an ore body en masse. This shifting emphasis from quality to quantity contributed to the replacement of the jack-of-all-trades miner, versed in a wide range of mining tasks, by the task-specialized worker, adept at operating a particular machine (Hovis and Mouat 1996).

This gradual transformation also left a tangible record in the form of the drill steels. Hand drill steels sported a chisel-like cutting edge and a flattened striking platform. Machine drill steels, by contrast, typically used a more resilient star or cross pattern for the cutting edge (or attachable drill bits) and were fitted with a shank at the opposite end for slotting the steel into the drill's chuck. By the 1910s, most machine drill steels were also hollow in cross section. This enabled water and air to enter the shot hole during the course of drilling, cooling the steel and reducing the dust that rock drills generated in prodigious quantities (Holman 1947). Thus, an inventory of the type of drill steels—a common enough artifact found lying about mining sites—can offer a glimpse into the organization of underground work and, with it, a means for observing rates of mechanization.

An unusual opportunity along these lines presented itself in 1990, when blasting work by a gold mining operation near Virginia City, Nevada, exposed underground workings abandoned nearly a century earlier. A subsequent survey of the Gold Eagle Mine (White and James 1991)—among a handful of underground mine surveys conducted by archaeologists in the United States—inventoried activity areas and several dozen artifacts (figure 5.3). Equipment clusters indicated that miners had repurposed sections of the 800-foot-long main tunnel for general storage and that exploration had last focused on the end of a shorter drift. In this locale, miners had removed all the rock loosened by blasting and cleared the way for a new round of drilling, stashing hammers and drill steels nearby. Artifact dates indicate that the mine had been abandoned around 1900.

The presence of 4- and 8-pound hammers among the abandoned tools indicates that miners had worked individually and in pairs. The Comstock Lode had been among the first locations where rock drills were adopted, in the 1870s, yet miners at ventures such as the Gold Eagle clearly persisted in using older techniques. Miners competent in a variety of tasks and able to tell a single jack from a double jack remained the most

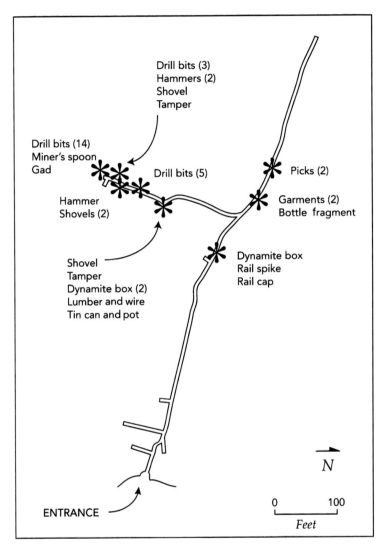

Figure 5.3. Clusters of mining equipment in a historic small-scale mine near Virginia City, Nevada. The active face is at the end of the offshoot tunnel to the left. The dangers of abandoned workings make studies of this sort rare. Drawing by author, adapted from White and James 1991.

desirable employees there. A set of initials on one of the double jacks also implies that some miners brought in their own equipment (White and James 1991: 29, 31).

These findings suggest that the mechanization of mine work occurred unevenly, but they also underscore how small-scale enterprises persisted decades after larger mines came to dominate production. Indeed, site for site, archaeologists encounter small-scale mines more frequently than the large-scale operations that dominated production statistics after the mineral stampedes. This is especially the case in the mining of precious metals because higher metal prices continued to create opportunities for realizing profits at multiple scales. Well-financed companies targeted low-grade ore reserves while smaller operators continued to rework old mines or explore pockets of ore too small to warrant larger interest.

A dramatic example of this persistence occurred at the so-called Binocular Prospect in south-central Alaska. Corporate interests in the outcrop's promising copper indications were dashed by its location midway up a 3,000-foot vertical cliff at the head of a remote glacial cirque. Mountain climbers funded by mining concerns had failed to reach the prospect, but smaller-scale efforts persisted. In 1929, prospector Martin Radovan reached the outcrop and staked a series of claims. Radovan continued to test the prospect for the next forty years, well into his eighties, reaching the outcrop by a combination of ladders and a trail—in places only a foot wide—that he had cut across the cliffs (Ringsmuth 2012). Although the outcrop never made him rich, his development of a way to access it and his construction of a cabin beside a nearby creek remain as testaments to his perseverance.

Small mines persisted also because some minerals never existed in great abundance. A case in point is the mining of saltpeter (potassium nitrate) during the eighteenth and nineteenth centuries. As a key ingredient in the manufacture of gunpowder, saltpeter offered Americans a coveted measure of independence from foreign imports during wartime. However, except for deposits found in the caves and rock-shelters of central Appalachia, the North American continent was essentially devoid of nitrates. Operations such as those at Mammoth Cave in Kentucky reached moderate proportions, but most saltpeter mining occurred at a reduced scale. Limited physical distribution thus made for low production levels, and because few operators left much in the way of written records, the archaeological record is often all that remains.

Dry cave conditions and comparative isolation have preserved evidence of several saltpeter operations. A typical saltpeter cave included extraction areas where miners scraped nitrate-rich sediments from the cave floor and processing locales for concentrating the nitrate. The analysis of cut marks on cave floors indicates excavation by mattocks, while the plotting of tally marks found inscribed into cave walls suggests that miners maintained a rough record of the sacks or cartloads of nitrates removed (Blankenship 2007). Processing areas often include leaching vats and water conduits, yet construction forms and overall arrangements tend to be unique to the locale (Duncan 1997: 93). Variations in the style of leaching vats may relate to different time periods or possibly to regional styles (Des Jean 1997; Duncan 1997; O'Dell and George 2014: 110–12). The dendrochronological analysis of vats in a Kentucky cave (Blankenship 2007) highlights how construction phases dovetailed with periods of increased demand for gunpowder. Vats dating to 1811 and the 1860s correspond closely with the War of 1812 (1812–15) and the Civil War (1861–65), respectively. A third vat constructed two years prior to the passage of the Guano Islands Act (1856)—in which legislators sought to destabilize a Peruvian monopoly on nitrates—again suggests that small and intermittent producers were nevertheless attuned to periods of escalating demand.

In sum, archaeological evidence supports the trend of increasing operative scale over time, but it also reveals the messier reality of mining districts populated by operators working with varied finances and employing different techniques. Most small-scale operations were underfinanced and short-lived, and such operations tended not to see more than a passing mention in industry journals. Indeed, the progress-minded mining engineer was more inclined to interpret the perseverance of small-scale industry as a sign of stasis or "backwardness." Small mines may not have reaped enormous profits, but success is ultimately a relative term. Smaller operators could still supply a working wage and a means of making a living while they lasted. As we will see, material evidence also indicates that operators, irrespective of scale, adjusted practices to meet changing circumstances at the mine.

Making the Mine Work

Developing a promising prospect into a profitable mine was easier said than done. Such a transformation required not only significant capital investment but also a good understanding of the peculiarities of an ore body and the best way to work it. Thumbing through any of the textbooks on mining practice that proliferated during the late nineteenth and early twentieth centuries reveals pages chock-full with technical detail. As expansive as works such as Robert Peele's *Mining Engineers' Handbook*

(1918) are, however, the diversity of technological practice becomes even more apparent in texts dedicated to exploring just one facet of mining, be it ore dressing (e.g., Richards and Locke 1940; Taggart 1927) or a subcomponent thereof such as cyanidation or flotation (e.g., Hamilton 1920; Megraw 1918). Such accounts remain invaluable as sources for historical and archaeological research because they indicate the state of knowledge at the time, explain variations in application, and detail select technical processes down to the level of components. It is sobering, nevertheless, to consider that these sources emphasized current practices and leading industry trends rather than the sorts of supplemented, jerry-rigged, and seemingly anachronistic arrangements one frequently encounters at mining sites.

Divergences between textbooks and practice inevitably occurred because no two ore bodies are alike in all respects. Miners learned this lesson the hard way during the mineral rushes when an ore's character was largely unknown. Historian Rodman Paul (1965: 131) noted that the early years of hard rock mining in California saw companies and corporations "formed by men who knew almost nothing about lode mining and less about the location, potentialities, and peculiarities of California veins. Elaborate and costly machinery, often of untested design, was shipped to California, there to be set up and operated by amateurs." Technological adjustments through trial and error continued because ore bodies frequently change over the course of exploration. Variations in chemical composition, hardness, and the nature of surrounding rock impacted the performance of equipment from drill bits to ore processing machines.

Milling facilities were common targets for adjustment because a mill's extractive efficiency—which translated directly to profits—was tied intimately to the character of an ore body. The gold recovery process of amalgamation, for instance, worked well for ores containing free gold (gold uncombined with other substances) but performed abysmally wherever sulfides were present, and this tended to occur as miners reached deeper underground. Mining engineers urged mill operators to experiment as a matter of course, and articles in mining journals drew attention to how even slight improvements in technical processes might resolve perplexing issues. Although finances conditioned the extent of modifications, operators commonly tweaked the performance of machinery and milling circuits. Mining companies could also anticipate change by locating mill

Figure 5.4. Variegated roofline of the Kennecott Mill, Alaska, reflecting a long history of adjustments and additions to the milling process. Photograph by Mark Schara, HAER AK-1-D-53.

sites in areas that allowed for future expansion as profits and prospects permitted.

Technological change is often evident in the jerry-rigged forms of milling structures. The hulking Kennecott copper concentrator in south-central Alaska (figure 5.4) began operative life in 1911 as a modestly sized facility but acquired its jumbled form through additions built on an as-needed basis. Progressive changes to the circuit—including the installa-tion of crushers, jigs, shaking tables, an ammonia leaching plant, and a flotation circuit—added new floors and widened the mill's lower levels

(Spude and Faulkner 1987). At its closure in 1938, the mill moved ore through fourteen levels. Internally, the flow from one floor to the next became increasingly convoluted as equipment became either reprioritized or stripped of function. Kennecott joined other aging plants of the nineteenth and early twentieth centuries in becoming a "timber maze through which pulp, operators, and superintendent seem[ed] to pursue each other in an endless chase" (Taggart 1947: 117).

The identification of milling equipment can reveal other sorts of changes occurring over time. Sand pumps installed at the New Standard Mill in Bodie, California (1899–1912), corresponded with company efforts to reprocess tailings after the richest veins had been worked out (Quivik 2003). HAER documentation of the Bald Mountain Gold Mill in South Dakota (1906–59) revealed a shift in the recovery circuit's emphasis from the working of sands to the processing of slimes (materials ground to silt size or smaller), while the addition of a roasting kiln indicates that operators also began encountering refractory ores (Eve 1992). Mill documentation also suggests how improvements to extractive efficiency could extend to worker surveillance. At the Shenandoah-Dives lead-zinc mine (1929–89) in southwestern Colorado, the discovery of gold ore led to changes in the milling facility. In addition to installing new machines, the company constructed a guardroom for controlling access into and out of the mill's gold recovery circuit (Bunyak and Lee 2007) (figure 5.5).

Even if companies did not invest in major alterations, the daily running of equipment still required upkeep. Components in devices such as gravity stamps wore out at different rates: stems and tappets (collars) lasted almost indefinitely, but the screens that crushed material passed through needed replacement every few months or less. The material record is replete with the signs of routine wear, as well as examples of the ingenuity, tinkering, and scrimping conducted to keep equipment in working order. At the Skidoo Mine (1906–17) in southern California, for example, small-scale operators kept gravity stamps in working order through the 1960s, decades after they had fallen out of fashion as a crushing device. An analysis of stamp components (White 2010) shows variation not explainable by routine wear. Differences among the cams used to lift each stem may have placed undue stress on the stamp battery, while stamp drop patterns differed across devices. The stamps remained functional, but differences among components and variations in drop sequences likely compromised crushing efficiency.

Figure 5.5. Surveillance room at the Shenandoah-Dives Mill, Silverton, Colorado. This room controlled access to the gold recovery circuit and, to limit the potential for collusion, was staffed by employees who resided outside the Silverton area. The board with numbered tags worked as an accounting system of who was on shift. Photograph by author.

Departures from textbook arrangements suggest that Skidoo's later operators encountered problems with finding proper replacement parts. Although suppliers of new parts had dwindled by the 1950s, junkyards and abandoned mills offered potential sources of supply. Stamp mills recorded near the Skidoo Mine show various states of salvage, suggesting that stamp components continued to circulate long after operations had folded (ibid.).

Remote locations especially encouraged the reuse and recycling of materials at hand, and technological pragmatism filtered down to many other aspects of mining operations. As at domestic sites (chapter 3), archaeological surveys of mining sites have documented various forms of adaptive reuse. Empty drums cut in half lengthwise found use as quenching tanks for blacksmiths, wheelbarrow beds, and ore cars. Flattened drums became ore chutes, roofing, and siding. Food cans found new life as lanterns. Pipes substituted for tram rails and launders, and drill steels functioned as fencing posts (see Greene 1981: 116; Sagstetter and Sagstetter 1998: 216–17). Cannibalizing parts and fashioning substitutions from materials on hand may have sacrificed technical efficiency. However, for operators with limited capital, being able to keep equipment running at little to no additional cost brought the more immediate benefit of staying solvent for another season.

Doubtful Prospects

Successful mines all share an obvious relationship with the natural environment: their location at a mineral outcropping rich enough to warrant its exploitation. However, knowing exactly where to dig and what minerals existed in profitable quantities were rarely obvious from the outset. The relationship is characterized best as a learning process (Hardesty 2003). Luck certainly remained a factor in finding worthwhile sites, but most prospectors located mineral outcrops through a combination of informed guesswork and systematic testing. Shallow prospect holes, test trenches, open cuts, cleared faces, and the ubiquitous claim marker frequently dot the hillsides of mining regions. The percentage of prospects that never panned out is difficult to calculate, in part because practitioners came to realize the worth of an endeavor at different stages. Some companies today boast ratios of one in five prospecting locations entering production as being outstanding. It follows that more holes, trenches, cuts, and faces relate to paltry mineral finds than to locations bringing high returns.

While the remoteness of many mineral regions and the inherently risky nature of mining endeavors presented undeniable challenges, these same factors also provided conditions ripe for deception. Masterworks ranged from the millions of dollars fleeced from investors during the Comstock rush to Reverend Prescott Jernegan's brazen scheme to recover gold from seawater on the Maine coast in the 1890s (Plazak 2006; see also Lingenfelter 1986, 2012). Scams and boosterism were especially rife during the western mineral rushes, reportedly prompting Mark Twain to define a mine as "a hole in the ground with a liar at the top." Yet the art of the mining scam neither originated nor ended with the nineteenth century. One of the biggest reported swindles to impact American investors occurred in the 1990s, when the Canadian company Bre-X doctored geological reports to indicate that its holdings in central Borneo sat atop 70 million ounces of gold (Goold and Willis 1997: 251–62). It follows that a fuller accounting of American mining practice must incorporate histories of both honest and dishonest mining endeavors.

Stings could deceive even the shrewdest expert, and while we know little about fleeces that were successfully executed, investors and mine inspectors cottoned on to some of the more obvious techniques. The majority of mining frauds were conducted on paper, but effective frauds usually involved well-placed ore samples or appeals to tangible evidence. Common techniques for "salting" a mine included adding choice specimens or coin filings surreptitiously to an inspector's sample bag or planting valuable minerals in the workings, such as by the inventive (and possibly fictitious) method of blasting gold dust into tunnel walls with a shotgun. Another tactic involved blocking passageways with rubble to prevent inspectors from venturing into less favorable parts of the mine or into areas already worked out (Rickard 1904: 9, 26–31; Young 1970: 40–52). Under deft hands, the trenches and cuts of abandoned workings became trussed up as signs of recent work. Likewise, the presence of older technologies such as arrastras could "prove" that a legendary mine had been discovered. Arizona's Spenazuma Mines scandal included the audacious claim that a nearby rock formation bore the profile of an Aztec prince, affirming that it had to be the locale of Montezuma's mine (Plazak 2006: 159–60).

Essential to any reassessment is a contextual reading of sources to identify inconsistencies between the geological information reported and the information knowable at the time, and between the work reported on the claims and the work actually conducted. But difficulties arise because historical mines leave a fragmentary and selective documentary trail that limits the ability to assess information from different angles. Moreover, material evidence was often intentionally made ambiguous. Such challenges are not always surmountable, but archaeological forays have been able to provide new insights into infamous scams as well as more-everyday forms of truth stretching.

Archaeological efforts along the first of these lines suggest that Martin Frobisher's expeditions to the Canadian Arctic during the 1570s constitute one of the earliest cases of mining fraud in North America. Frobisher's voyages are remembered mostly for being one more failed effort among many to find a navigable trade route between Europe and China around the top of the American continent. However, two of his three voyages to chart the Northwest Passage also included mining a "black ore" discovered on Countess of Warwick's Island (Kodlunarn Island) that Frobisher believed to be immensely rich in gold. Frobisher brought back twelve shiploads to England, but government assayers summarily dismissed the material as worthless. Though this incident has long been regarded as an honest failure—a rather expensive exercise in geological education—historical records also open the possibility of deceit. The account books of Frobisher's assayers, for instance, mysteriously fell out of the ship's porthole during a storm. Once back in England, possibly to save face from the allegations, Frobisher hired another assayer, who distributed a positively glowing report contradicting each one of the government's declarations. Réginald Auger (2000) has postulated further that these circumstances may also explain why Frobisher marooned several men on the island.

Investigations on Kodlunarn Island in the 1980s surveyed Frobisher's mineral prospects and assaying areas, the latter recognizable by scatters of slag, charcoal, anthracite, lead, and thousands of crucible fragments. Samples of the black ore were collected for analysis from trenches on the island, as well as from a shipwreck in Smerwick Harbor, Iceland, where an ore-laden vessel had foundered, and from Dartford, England, where the worthless material found use in boundary walls. Donald Hogarth's examination of more than sixty samples from these locations confirmed the presence of a gold-silver alloy, albeit at a concentration 1/26,000th of the quantity reported by Frobisher. Chemical testing of the lead globules found no gold or silver, ruling out the possibility that the high ore values mentioned by Frobisher were a consequence of accidental contamination (Auger 2000; Hogarth and Loop 1986). Frobisher, or at least his assayer, had to have been aware of the ore's negligible value.

Frauds such as Frobisher's made the headlines, yet far more prevalent forms of deception were promulgated by the generous provisions of nineteenth-century American resource laws. The General Mining Act (1866, 1872) had expedited the land claiming process by empowering U.S. citizens to stake unpatented mining claims themselves. Until a claimant chose to patent a claim, evaluations of mineral worth rested on the "prudent" judgment of the locator. Courts also permitted claimants to stake nonmineral lands as mill sites and to use water and timber for mining purposes within the boundaries of mining and mill site claims.

Such provisions aided mining operations immensely while at the same time opening ground for rampant speculation. The leniency of the General Mining Act's stipulations, the speed at which claims could be filed, and the impossibility of independently monitoring activities all created opportunities for abuse. Among them, the flexibility of what counted as proof of labor necessary for holding a claim meant that the Mining Act became an expedient way of acquiring land for nonmining purposes, including for building vacation homes and ski resorts in the Rockies and Sierras (Bakken 2008: 48–49, 128–30).

The misapplication of mining law ultimately deepened long-standing connections between the mining industry and Native American land dispossession. The consequences were severely felt in arid regions at the sites of reliable, potable water. Soon after the federal government opened the Papago Indian Reservation in Arizona to mining interests in 1934, the Tohono O'odham reported the construction of gas stations, residences, and whiskey stills on mining claims staked over water springs (U.S. Senate Committee on Indian Affairs 1934: 75–78). Similar developments occurred in Death Valley, California, where the Timbisha Shoshones, not afforded reservation status at the time, had recently been affected by the reclassification of much of their homeland in 1933 as a national monument "for the enjoyment of all." Mining claims staked over water springs in the area found uses for mining but also for commercial interests, such as gas stations, hoping to benefit from tourist traffic. At Triangle Spring in the heart of Death Valley, monument staff narrowly prevented the establishment of a brothel on a placer claim staked over what visitor maps identified as a rest stop (White 2008: 268–69).

Egregious instances of abuse can be expected to show marked discrepancies between written documents and material evidence. At Triangle Spring, miners had filed the appropriate forms at the country courthouse for a placer mining claim, but mining work did not transfer to the site. One finds instead a light timber scatter, a possible claim post, and the remnants of a shallow, triangular reservoir partially buried in sand. The architectural pun of a triangular pool at Triangle Spring seems less in keeping with mining concerns and more in line with the giant ducks and coffeepots and other novelty structures that were then proliferating along American highways to catch the attention and wallets of motorists (ibid.; Liebs 1995).

Direct connections between the General Mining Act and Native American land dispossession are evident farther south at Warm Spring, where claim markers indicate that mining law came head-to-head with federal Indian policy (figure 5.6). The dispute began in 1930 when a miner who had set up a camp at the spring to work claims in the area reneged on

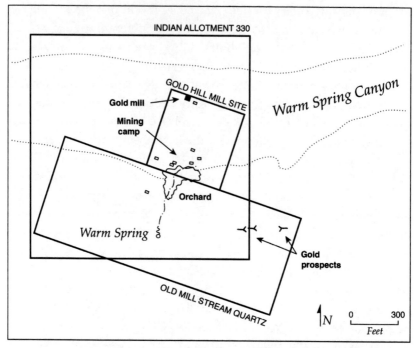

INDIAN ALLOTMENT 330

GOLD HILL MILL SITE

Warm Spring Canyon

Gold mill

**Mining
camp**

Orchard

Warm Spring

**Gold
prospects**

OLD MILL STREAM QUARTZ

N   0   300
        Feet

Figure 5.6. Conflicting land claims at Warm Spring in Death Valley, California, that pitted the General Mining Act against the Dawes Act. Drawing by author.

a verbal agreement to lease the water rights from Robert Thompson, a Timbisha Shoshone man who, if not born at Warm Spring, had lived there seasonally for many years. The miner, Louise Grantham, together with her associates, subsequently staked a mining claim over Warm Spring on the grounds of a gold discovery. Thompson responded in kind by applying for an Indian allotment under the Dawes Act to the same area.

When the water dispute eventually escalated to the courts, a geological appraisal found Grantham's mining claim to be of negligible worth. Recall, however, that court rulings did not require unpatented claims to have the same level of mineralogical proof. Grantham had dutifully filed paperwork each year as required by law, and the mining claim had also been staked earlier than the Indian allotment. These circumstances virtually guaranteed the court ruling in 1941 in favor of mining interests.

Today, clusters of fig trees and grapevines at Warm Spring rank among the few surviving remnants of historic Timbisha Shoshone land use.

While evidence of Grantham's mining of talc deposits along the canyon after the court trial abounds, archaeological examinations affirm that gold prospects near the spring never extended beyond a few short explorations and scrapings. Moreover, a technical analysis of the gold mill indicates ways that its capacity was exaggerated in court documents (White 2006). Above all, the positioning of Warm Spring near the center of the mining claim suggests that the claiming of water rights had always been the priority.

Documentary records also suggest that deeper entanglements occurred at Warm Spring than the pitting of one law against another. For instance, federal Indian agency and county land office records indicate that Thompson's Indian allotment represented the fourth attempt in as many decades by his family to claim ownership of the spring. Tribal elders recall Thompson as being something of a miner, and mining claim records list Thompson along with other Timbisha Shoshone individuals as having filed for mining claims and water appropriations throughout Death Valley, even before they were legally allowed to do so (ibid.). The Warm Spring dispute thus provides a case example of the complexities that historical and archeological analyses can draw out from even a small-scale mining landscape. Here, a mining workplace and a Shoshone winter camp occupied the same ground, a woman miner and a Native American miner vied for the control of water rights, and a large-scale process of land dispossession recurred again and again at the same place.

Recalibrating Technological Histories

The variability that archaeologists have identified at workplaces underscores a recurrent dichotomy in American mining practice between the ideal and the real. Textbooks charted the latest technological developments, but the continuing use of some technologies well after industry practitioners widely considered them "outmoded" demonstrates that adoption of the latest gizmos was far from universal practice. Archaeological evidence indicates that miners evaluated technologies not only in terms of economic efficiencies but also according to cultural preferences. Different labor systems could operate in the same mine simultaneously, and power inequalities aboveground often continued belowground, too. Cultural practices also established the parameters through which histories of litigation, fraud, and dispossession played out on mining landscapes. Archaeological attention to these facets highlights how technological practices are inherently social processes. Moreover, these sorts of legacies are very different from the themes monumented and memorialized in mining towns, in theme parks, and along America's roadsides, where we look next.

6

Mining *In Memoriam*

Historical mines are imbued with a mixed assortment of symbolism. The grizzled prospector panning for gold nuggets and protecting his claim remains one of the most iconic images, but hundreds of roadside markers memorialize mines, mining men, and mining disasters. John Park's (2000a, 2000b) two-volume guide of mining sites in the United States identifies more than 1,700 commemorative places and attractions, including ghost towns, railroads, trails, tailings piles, and historical parks, all classifiable better in terms of acreage. At theme parks, roller coasters careen tweeners through replicas of old mine workings, the sudden dips and turns akin to tracing an economic chart of mining boom-and-bust cycles. Venture into a state capitol building, and you have a one in five chance of seeing some mining-related appellation. Miners appear on four state flags (Idaho, West Virginia, Wisconsin, and Wyoming), and the pickax adorns another two (Oregon and Montana). Arizona's copper star acknowledges the continuing importance of the copper industry, as do the gold-colored stars on Alaska's flag in reference to gold mining and Montana's state motto, *Oro y plata*—gold and silver—words once emblazoned also on Nevada's state flag. The nicknames Golden, Silver, Copper, Gem, Granite, and Treasure States all pay homage to mining pasts and a mining present. Even the nickname Badger State had its origins in the term given to early nineteenth-century lead miners enduring Wisconsin winters in dugouts.

Weighty, sanguine, gaudy, there are clearly differing takes on how America's mining past is conveyed. The staid appearance of some memorials notwithstanding, commemoration is inherently an active process. Flags change and new monuments appear, while others become vandalized, replaced, destroyed, or forgotten. It is through memorialization, in other words, that the legacies of American mining are both mythologized and challenged. Such activities also have material traces and important stories to tell. Most notably, they draw attention to how Americans continue to engage with their mining past and shape public memory. It is fitting, then, that our survey of the American experience ends with a closer examination of memorialization and place-making processes.

This chapter explores commemoration through three lines of inquiry: how monuments erected to mining events fit historically within and against master narratives about the industry; how portrayals of mining in film and entertainment recapitulate enduring caricatures of the industry and how these processes leave material residues; and a look to environmental legacies, in which historical and archaeological perspectives highlight connections between changing environmental perceptions and landscape transformations. Topics such as museum displays here receive little treatment, but the intent is not to be exhaustive. Instead, this brief survey is intended to highlight the politics of representation and to provide a sense of how commemorative activities can be examined productively at different points in time and at multiple geographic scales.

Monuments Great and Small

In Cherry, Illinois, and in Ludlow, Colorado, one can observe nearly identical monuments erected by the United Mine Workers of America in memory of two very different mining tragedies (figure 6.1). The monument to the Cherry Mine disaster commemorates the deaths of 259 miners in an underground fire in 1909—the second-highest fatality on record at the time. The incident began when a kerosene lantern set a hay cart on fire. A series of increasingly desperate efforts to contain the flames failed spectacularly when the company attempted to blow out the fire by reversing the mine's ventilation fans. This action set the fan house ablaze and, with it, the wooden stairs and escape ladders leading out of the shaft. With the exception of 21 miners rescued after eight days underground, those miners unable to exit before the fan house caught fire asphyxiated from the gases (Tintori 2002).

Three states to the west, the Ludlow Memorial commemorates miners and their families killed four and a half years later during an assault of the Ludlow strike camp by the Colorado National Guard (chapter 4). The monument is sited beside the "death pit," where two women and eleven children hiding from the chaos in a root cellar had suffocated when the tent above them caught fire. Nine hundred miles separate the Cherry and

Figure 6.1. Memorials erected by the United Mine Workers of America to commemorate mining disasters at Cherry, Illinois (*left*), and Ludlow, Colorado (*right*). Photographs by author.

Ludlow monuments, but the similarities in form are striking. The shared design underscores an equivalence of suffering—that deaths from mining accidents and deaths from labor protests were both mining fatalities and that the deaths of miners underground and the deaths of miners and their families were of equal significance in mining communities. These connections offer a radically different perspective to industry statistics that list mining fatalities according to very restrictive definitions.

In *Hard Places*, Richard Francaviglia (1991: 4) argues that mining monuments "are one of the first indicators we have that man and nature, as well as labor and management, have traditionally been adversaries in mining country." The Cherry and Ludlow Memorials affirm this point, but they also highlight the importance of seeing memorialization as a performative action. The construction of these monuments sought to ensure that two disastrous events would be forever remembered, but it also inaugurated a role for the United Mine Workers of America in marking them as memorials. In these instances the conflict between capital and labor engaged in a war for the symbolic control of mining's master narrative.

Shauna Scott's (1995) account of a more recent project to commemorate the coal miners of Harlan, Kentucky, reveals how politics inherent to the industry created schisms over the memorial's design and dedication. Aims to list all county miners who died in the mines initially seemed unproblematic, but difficulties occurred in defining who a Harlan County miner was in the face of a highly transient workforce and in defining the conditions of a mining-related death: where to place, for instance, miners who died during labor disputes or from silicosis and other chronic work-related diseases. The paucity of funding, partly attributable to a local mining company's refusal to partake in the project, left the memorial in the shape of a broken cross incomplete. This situation ultimately seems to have influenced the memorial's later replacement with a less controversial design (ibid.).

Mining companies were not necessarily averse to contributing funds to miners' memorials, but they also invested in less somber events to display their achievements and aspirations. Well-financed operations contributed, for instance, to national and international exhibitions advertising America's mineral wealth. Eye-catching exhibits at turn-of-the-century expositions included displays of large ore specimens and simulations of coal dust explosions to demonstrate state-of-the-art mine rescue techniques (*Engineering and Mining Journal* 1904; *New York Times* 1891, 1900). Spectacles at the 1904 St. Louis World's Fair included a half-mile-long "mining gulch," complete with a working oil derrick, a coal mine, and a stamp mill that produced gold blocks in full view of spectators. Inside the nine-acre Palace of Mines and Metallurgy, Alabama's colossal cast-iron statue of the Roman god Vulcan drew large crowds (figure 6.2). Fifty-six feet high, and nude save for an apron and pair of sandals, the statue showcased iron as a key resource in the northern part of the state and, with it, entrepreneurial hopes that the city of Birmingham would become a premier iron and steelmaking center (Kierstead 2002).

Today, Vulcan overlooks Birmingham from atop Red Mountain and the ore seam from which its iron was mined. Although restored to its original

Figure 6.2. Vulcan Colossus on display at the 1904 St. Louis Exposition. Photograph by Jessie Tarbox Beals. Missouri History Museum, St Louis, N16471.

appearance, the first decades after its return from the 1904 exposition saw Vulcan's purpose change from being an envoy of Southern industry to an advertisement for fairground products. The hand that originally grasped a forging hammer at different times gripped a giant ice cream cone, a Coca-Cola bottle, and a pickle sign (Kierstead 2002: 68–69).

Like the Vulcan statue, some promotional mining exhibits took on longer public lives. Industrial machinery held by the Franklin Institute and the Smithsonian Museum (Hindle 1972: 208) and mineralogical collections at the Chicago Field Museum derive partly from displays gifted or abandoned after world's fairs and other expositions. An 18-foot-high statue of a silver queen flanked by cherubic figures holding cornucopias of gold and silver coins on show at the 1893 Columbian Exposition was publicly displayed for decades but "lost" en route to a museum in 1942. Montana's 9-foot-high silver effigy of Justice on display during the same exposition toured the country before being melted down in 1903 to settle a dispute between the two men who had contributed the silver. Justice nevertheless had already transferred to a more marketable form in 1895 when the Montgomery Ward department store offered differently sized replicas suitable for the fireplace mantel (Vendl and Vendl 2001: 33–36).

Mining companies also erected monuments on their own turf to company presidents and invested in landscaping. "Green engineering" softened the rough edges of mining towns and expressed a corporate generosity and commitment to social improvement. If the development of green space endeavored to reduce labor turnover and union activity, results along these lines generally proved disappointing (Malone 1998: 5). Landscapes and memorials in company towns nevertheless remain productive sites for examining the face of corporate paternalism.

The former company town of Calumet, Michigan, preserves sections of a century-old park commemorating the Calumet and Hecla Company's first president, Alexander Agassiz. By 1917, plans materialized to develop a park in an undeveloped area between the town proper and the industrial core where the mine's administrative offices, company-run school, and a mine entrance were situated. The 25-acre field had seen prior use for cattle grazing as well as a campground for several thousand Michigan militiamen during a miners' strike in 1913 (Alanen and Bjorkman 1998).

Warren Manning's design for Agassiz Park included several tree-lined promenades radiating out from the industrial core to different points of the town. A bronze statue of Agassiz in academic regalia occupied the convergence point. The pathways made for a practical use of the grounds by miners and children to access work and school. Words inscribed on the statue's base, that Agassiz was "a man of science who developed a great mine and wrought the welfare of its people," underscored the arterial connections for passersby between the company and their daily lives (figure 6.3). The park's symbolic power nevertheless waned with the company. As ore reserves dwindled in the 1960s, directors increasingly divested

Figure 6.3. Agassiz Park in Calumet, Michigan, in 1947. The pathways converged at a statue of the Calumet and Hecla Company's first president, with the mines and school beyond. Photograph by Wendell J. Kraft. Michigan Technological University Archives and Copper Country Historical Collections, Acc-06-088A-1136.

residential and town properties from company ownership. A few sections of the park were sold, and the Agassiz statue was relocated to another site (ibid.). Today, one's gaze along the tree-lined avenues converges on the garage doors of a state-subsidized housing complex—a reminder that the mines have closed and that corporate paternalism went with them.

The demise of a mining economy hardly closes the book on the potency of mining monuments. The Ludlow Memorial continues to serve today as a touchstone for union efforts, with a rally held each year on the anniversary of the massacre. Visitor logbooks record union and antiunion sentiments, and in 2003 vandals beheaded the statue of the miner and his wife. A locked fence around the recently restored Ludlow Memorial testifies to the past and present tensions of commemoration (Saitta 2007: 98). Even so, memorialization sites and markers for tragic historical events can readily slip from public memory. In 1897, an unarmed protest at Lattimer, Pennsylvania, for higher wages ended in tragedy when a sheriff-led posse fired into the protesters, killing nineteen foreign miners. Membership in the United Mine Workers of America swelled in response, but the site of the massacre remained unmarked for several decades. Paul Shackel and Michael Roller (2012) note that some locals today have no knowledge of the incident or recall the historical event in ways to advance positions for and against recent immigrants to the area. At Lattimer, as charged also at Ludlow, archaeological work has been framed in terms of a critical need to investigate sites that counter master narratives by revealing the widespread but often hidden histories of labor conflict and ethnic oppression in the United States. This need is framed provocatively as a means for archaeologists to engage more directly in social justice in the present (Little 2013; McGuire 2014; Roller 2015; Saitta 2007; Shackel 2014; Shackel and Roller 2012). The essential point is that the politics of memorialization are written into archaeological actions as much as in the monuments under study.

Simulacra: Mining and Entertainment

North Americans encounter the mining past ever more through re-creations, reenactments, replicas, and tongue-in-cheek caricatures. In theme parks especially, the simulation replaces the real entirely. Entertainment complexes with western mining themes have appeared in as historically unassociated places as Orlando, Florida. Jean Baudrillard contends in *Simulacra and Simulation* (1996) that distinctions between reality and representation have become increasingly blurred in the postmodern age. If we translate this argument to representations of mining, it follows that as Americans become more distant to mining (both through globalization of the industry and through increased mechanization), the mining simulation becomes ever more powerful in influencing public perceptions of the industry. Simulations also have reality, for even theme parks occupy physical space. Recognizing this material dimension offers archaeologists an opportunity to see how actual and simulated historical mining landscapes construct and reimagine the industry, and even to observe simulacra in places that at first appear about as authentic as one can get.

Bodie State Historic Park in Mono County, California, maintains one of America's best-preserved examples of a mining settlement occupied in the late nineteenth and early twentieth centuries. Originating with the discovery of gold in the Bodie Hills in the 1880s, the community grew to ten thousand residents. Approximately 170 buildings stand in arrested decay, including a stamp mill, a church, a union hall, and several hotels

Figure 6.4. Bodie, California. Photograph by Ronald Partridge.
HABS CAL, 26-BODI, 1-4.

and saloons. These structures represent less than 5 percent of the town's original size, but the view remains striking nonetheless (figure 6.4).

Since the park's creation in 1962, no fallen building has been restored, and no new buildings have been added to replace former structures. Building interiors remain largely untouched, as is evident in part by the thick patina of dust covering furniture and plates. These impressions aside, the town was never totally abandoned, and work crews make unobtrusive structural repairs and replacements. Preweathered wood and rusty nails replace fallen siding, irregular flat-pane glass replaces broken glass, and a clear coating on several buildings reduces fire risk. New roofing materials appear old following corrosive treatments with Coca-Cola (DeLyser 1999: 614). Structural repairs are added in ways that replicate the "hasty techniques of mining camp carpentry" (Toll 1972: 21). Even the dust accruing on artifacts reflects a deliberate intent to elicit a feeling that people just walked away.

The buildings left standing at Bodie are the ones that survived two town fires and decades of decay. This survival of the fittest also reflects processes of cultural selection. As Bodie's population declined, residents relocated to the sturdier and more spacious houses in the former middle-class part of town. Today's layout consequently evokes a greater sense of domesticity than existed in actuality. One sees the superintendent's residence, private residences, a church, hotels, and several other commercial establishments, but the town preserves neither tent frames nor the ramshackle dwellings constructed by poor and transient workers. The historical community presented is oddly similar to the profile of current park visitors—namely, white, middle-class suburbanites (DeLyser 1999: 608; Francaviglia 1991: 176).

A variety of historical parks employ costumed interpreters to enhance visitor experiences by "bringing the past to life." More than a few historic mining sites employ prospectors (real and actual) to showcase mining techniques and discuss frontier life. The fullest realization occurs in Nevada City, Montana, where today more than seventy costumed interpreters re-create daily life and actual events in a frontier mining town. Nevada City retains approximately one hundred historic structures dating from the 1860s through the early 1900s, of which fourteen are original to the townsite. The detailed interpretive program allows one to gab with a blacksmith, a saloonkeeper, a laundress, and prospectors, among other town residents. These opportunities are interspersed with reenactments of events drawn from local headlines, including the occasional hanging and shooting.

Calico State Park in southeastern California presents mining town life with even greater theatrical flair. The "new" Calico was founded in the early 1950s, when Walter Knott (founder of the Knott's Berry Farm amusement park) purchased this former mining town with the intention of restoring the place "to its original glory" (Archimede 2002: 195). Key here was not just the restoration of a town ravaged by two major fires but a restitution of the "lusty swaggering spirit that gave Calico its singular reputation" (ibid.). The vision was realized through the establishment of one of North America's first full-blown ghost town destinations, complete with staged gunfights occurring a few times each day (Archimede 2002: 193–96; Francaviglia 1991; Wolle 1953: 141–42).

The physical layout of Calico highlights the extent of Knott's vision. Only six of the thirty structures present on-site are originals. Buildings closely follow the original plan of the town in their arrangement along one primary thoroughfare. Building exteriors, paint, and enclosures conceal modern materials and equipment from view. Reconstructed buildings are intentionally dilapidated and shoddily repaired to suggest time's passage and conform to expectations of what an old western town should look like. One Knott-era structure uses charred timbers to suggest the presence of an upper story. Historic elements are blended with the modern necessities of pizza shops and popcorn stands, ATM machines, streetlights, and concrete paving down Main Street (Archimede 2002).

It is not a giant leap from these renditions of frontier life to the total fabrication of a mining community. To walk past the turnstile at Disneyland Park in Anaheim, California, is also—as Bodie, Calico, Deadwood, Nevada City, and Tombstone promise—to take a "walk back in time." As with the Victorian-era Main Street, U.S.A., Disney's vision of American mining is pigeonholed in time and space. Mining appears in Frontierland, a play land evoking the excitement and dangers of the Wild West. Riders on the Big Thunder Mountain Railroad speed by a southwestern landscape dotted with mining equipment on an "out of control" mine train. The ride culminates in passing beside a haphazard set of false-fronted buildings that includes a hotel, an assayer's office, and a saloon. One can encounter similar experiences at Disney resorts in Orlando, Tokyo, and Paris, at Knott's Berry Farm in Los Angeles, at Six Flags Over Texas, and on the Colorado Adventure in Phantasialand, Germany. The Mystery Mine in Dollywood, Tennessee, departs from the dominant western imagery in theme parks by centering instead on coal: the roller coaster runs through an artificial coal breaker and underground mine and narrowly avoids a simulated coal gas explosion.

Movies have strongly influenced public perception of what to expect in historic mining towns down to the setting, events, and personalities of town inhabitants. Cinematic depictions of the industry follow a limited selection of narratives. Films set in places where water is plentiful emphasize the adventure and the entrepreneurial spirit of discovery rushes, with plots pitting good against evil—*The Spoilers* (1942) and *Pale Rider* (1985) serving as two examples (Graebner 2003). Films set in arid environments focus on the darker side of human experience. Movies such as *The Treasure of the Sierra Madre* (1948), *Lust for Gold* (1949), and *Garden of Evil* (1954) play out themes of corruption, greed, and failure on a desolate canvas. The opening scene of *There Will Be Blood* (2007) cues the viewer early into the protagonist's eventual moral decline. William Graebner notes how "wet" and "dry" films have cycled in production, the former popular during the 1930s, '40s, and '60s, and the latter during the 1940s and 1950s as well as today (ibid.; see also Nordberg 2008).

Gold and coal are also the "most filmed" ores. Movies concerning gold mining are set in the West and those about coal in the East, a vision accurate only at the coarsest scale of resolution. Whereas films about gold generally fall into the theme of adventure, movies about coal emphasize labor struggles of the late nineteenth and early twentieth century. *The Molly Maguires* (1970), for instance, centers on the resistance of Irish coal miners in Pennsylvania during the 1870s. *Matewan* (1987) documents a violent exchange between West Virginia miners and company-hired guns during miners' attempts to unionize in the 1920s, and *Black Fury* (1935), a film banned for a time in several states, recounted labor conflict in Pennsylvania. Even a coal miner's psychotic rampage in *My Bloody Valentine* (1981)—later revamped into a 3-D gore spectacular (2009)—continues the theme of struggle while bringing coal mines soundly into the horror genre as well.

Consider for a moment the attributes that make up a "classic" western mining town. Our collective checklist no doubt includes a depot, a hotel/brothel with a second-story verandah, a saloon with chest-high swinging doors and counters long enough to hurl someone down during a bar fight, a sheriff's office, a town jail, and boardwalks, hitching posts, and barrels bordering a wide center street that sees its fair share of gunfights. One reason that the idealized western mining town coalesces around such sharpened imagery is that movies are often shot in a select number of prefabricated locations. Take one of the interstates north or northwest out of Los Angeles for about 30 minutes, and you can stop at a few western towns sure to prompt déjà vu experiences. Studio properties such as Melody Ranch (founded in 1915), Paramount Ranch (1927), and Disney's Golden Oak (1959), have served as backdrops for Hollywood productions for several decades. Paramount Studio's ranch, located just 30 miles from company headquarters, appeared in nearly one hundred movies in the span of two decades, among them films by Cecil B. DeMille and adaptations of Zane Grey novels. Now managed in part by the National Park Service, the property still serves as a film location.

The diverse landscape of film ranches enabled filmmakers to perfect the craft of illusion through carefully framed shots. The line of building fronts making up "Western Town" at Paramount Ranch have represented Tombstone, Arizona, in *Gunfight at the O.K. Corral* (1957) and a Colorado mining town in the TV drama *Dr. Quinn, Medicine Woman* (1993–98). Melody Ranch's false fronts have provided an authentic western backdrop to *Deadwood* (2004–6) and a gunfight sequence in *Django Unchained* (2012).

The layout of movie ranches echoes technical and cultural requirements of the industry (figure 6.5). Wide streets in early towns enabled horse teams to turn around. In western movie sets, wide streets ease the movement of film equipment and crew and also permit camera angles to include oblique and straight-on shots of buildings. Buildings arranged around a T-intersection enable filming under different lighting conditions and allow for an urban setting to fill the background if a larger town scene is required. Facades and fences disguise on-site sound stages and storage areas. Verandahs and false fronts evoke the Victorian era of classic mining town imagery and provide key hideaway spots for gunslingers. A two-story verandah for a corner building evokes the hotel at the center of town. A depot positioned at the end of Main Street imparts the importance of the railroad in connecting the frontier to the rest of the world. The jagged line of building fronts implies a town created overnight and a settlement adhering only loosely to a general design plan.

The physical separation between film sets and mining towns is not always so discrete. As Kevin Britz (1999) notes, dime novels and cinematic depictions of the Wild West during the early twentieth century generated considerable public interest in western landscapes. Western towns competed for attention by claiming historical connections to the famed figures of novels and Hollywood film. In Deadwood, South Dakota, the town's chamber of commerce marked several sites in 1930 that were considered to better secure the town's historical authenticity. This included identifying Saloon Number 10, where "Wild Bill" Hickok was murdered, the escape route of Hickok's assassin, Jack McCall, the Bella Union Saloon, and the Gem Theater (Britz 1999: 148)—all key aspects re-created in the HBO series *Deadwood*.

Mining towns such as Bodie, Deadwood, Nevada City, Tombstone, and Virginia City (Montana and Nevada) have staged their share of Westerns, and the arrival of moviemakers can also permanently alter appearances. The Pennsylvania coal town of Eckley preserves the remnants of a landscape formed doubly from coal mining and from the efforts of Hollywood craftsmen during the filming of *The Molly Maguires* (1970), starring Sean Connery. With operations only recently closed at the time of the shoot, film crews restored Eckley to a nineteenth-century appearance by laying

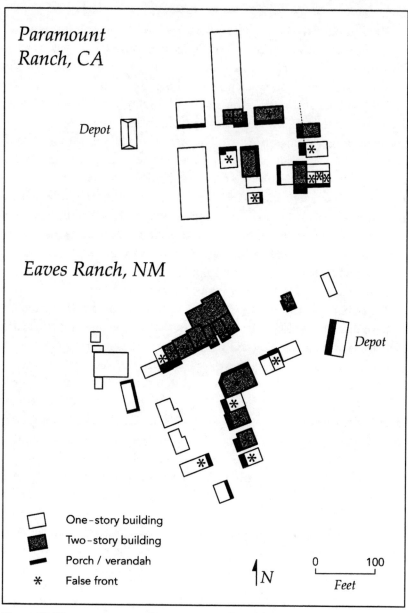

Figure 6.5. Western town sets of Paramount Ranch, California, and Eaves Ranch, New Mexico. Some one-wall props are here depicted as buildings. Drawing by author.

railroad tracks and constructing a company store. Most impressive of all is the coal breaker still looming over the town, an elaborate prop built to replace a metal-sided breaker considered too modern for the movie's nineteenth-century setting (Francaviglia 1991: 190–92). Connections between Hollywood and the Molly Maguires deepened with the unveiling of a memorial in Mahanoy City, half an hour's drive from Eckley. The sculpture depicts a hooded "Mollie" standing before the gallows, and an associated plaque lists Sir Sean Connery as the honorary chairman of the monument's advisory committee (da Costa Nunes 2008: 112–13).

The material traces of mining in the movies extend also into the realm of commodities. Beyond celluloid and film sets, the film industry produces DVD collections, soundtracks, movie posters, and other collectables. The release of *Toy Story 2* (1999) coincided with the marketing of several movie characters that included a curmudgeonly prospector named Stinky Pete. Sold variously as a plastic toy, a plush beanie, and a collector pin, this cartoon miner embodied the stereotype of a white-haired, grizzled, portly sourdough, with a pickax in hand, a hot temper, and a conniving demeanor to boot. At this writing, years after the merchandizing boom, a few Stinky Petes no doubt live up to their name in public landfills, decomposing slowly beside other small things forgotten.

The Spilled Environment

Seventy miles north of the James Marshall monument in Coloma, the Malakoff Diggins State Historic Park marks an altogether different mining legacy. The plaque for Landmark No. 852 begins familiarly enough by recognizing the North Bloomfield Mining and Gravel Company as a major mining concern, and one responsible for its share of engineering feats, but here the celebratory tone ends. The inscription goes on to state that the company "was the principal defendant in an anti-debris lawsuit settled by the Sawyer Decision in 1884. Judge Lorenzo Sawyer's famous decision created control that virtually ended hydraulic mining in California." Malakoff Diggins celebrates a landmark case in early U.S. conservation history by preserving a landscape of utter destruction. Hydraulic mining, which directed jets of pressurized water against gravel banks as a fast way to excavate material and recover gold, left in its wake stark and denuded landscapes even more than a century after operations closed. The main pit worked by the North Bloomfield Mining and Gravel Company measures

1.3 miles long and more than 0.5 miles wide, with the pit bottom more than 600 feet below the original ground surface.

Pound for pound, mining's by-products rather than its products are what constitute the bulk of what mining activity generates. The Environmental Protection Agency (EPA) estimates that mining operations in the United States discard 2 billion tons of material annually, accounting for up to 40 percent of the nation's solid waste (Hoye and Hubbard 1989: 4.48–49). Volume alone, however, is only a partial measure of a far more extensive environmental signature. Environmental characterization studies indicate how the weathering of sulfide minerals can entrain metals including iron, mercury, cadmium, and arsenic into solution and down watercourses. Abandoned metal mines have been identified in this way as a leading source of acid drainage—impacting to various extents the headwaters of about 40 percent of western watersheds and at least 3,000 miles of streams in Pennsylvania, Maryland, Ohio, and West Virginia. Hydrologists estimate that historical activities introduced 10 million pounds of mercury into California's water drainages, and gold mills topped this up with another 3 million pounds (Alpers et al. 2005: 3). A substantial portion of mercury remains sequestered in the environment in concentrations high enough to sustain health advisories against fishing in several rivers. The temporal and spatial dimensions of mining's environmental legacy are still being calculated.

It has been known for a long time that mining leaves a heavy footprint. In the 1500s, Georgius Agricola's treatise on European mining practice, *De Re Metallica*, reported how metal mining devastated fields, timber groves, and animal populations, to the extent that inhabitants of mining regions encountered "great difficulty in procuring the necessaries of life" (Agricola [1557] 1950: 8). Agricola, however, considered these to be acceptable costs, noting that miners "dig almost exclusively in mountains otherwise unproductive, and in valleys invested in gloom," that deforested lands could be sown with grain, and that "birds without number, edible beasts and fish can be purchased elsewhere" (ibid.: 14). American miners recapitulated this same attitude three centuries later during the discovery rushes of the mid-nineteenth century, but we should use the comparison with care. We have become used to framing development and environment as starkly oppositional terms, but a look to historical representations of the industry in artwork of the nineteenth and twentieth centuries indicates a varied interpretive palette. American painters portrayed coal tipples, smelters,

Figure 6.6. *Smelting Works at Denver, June 12th 1892*—a study in the technological sublime. Watercolor by Thomas Moran. Cleveland Museum of Art.

and factories as preying monsters, castles, and cathedrals, or simply as immense abstracts (see da Costa Nunes 2002: 24; Fahlman 2002). Artists also developed ways of framing industrial landscapes as expressions of harmony and progress (Marx 1964; Nye 1994). Initial efforts along these lines incorporated mining sites into bucolic settings. George Lafayette Clough's *Coal Mine on the Susquehanna* (1875), for example, depicts a classic idyll of two figures in the foreground walking along the bank of a meandering river with a dramatic mountain backdrop. The overall composition fits the industrial scene squarely into the Hudson River school repertoire—a mid-nineteenth-century movement of American landscape painters that emphasized romantic and naturalistic vistas and a harmonious balance existing between man and nature. The coal mine in Clough's composition is dwarfed by the surroundings, barely visible except for a wisp of smoke (see da Costa Nunes 2002: 14).

A shift in the conventions that artists used to depict a "technological sublime" is evident early, as in Thomas Moran's *Smelting Works at Denver* (1892) (figure 6.6). Unlike Clough's depiction of the machine in the garden, Moran placed industry center stage and employed an industrial palette of blacks, grays, and umbers. His watercolor blurs distinctions between the yellow-brown hues of a sunset and the sulfurous haze of smelter emissions—a provocative turn for an artist better known for his naturalistic depictions of western landscapes. Moran nevertheless seems to have painted the smelter not with a dystopia in mind but with an eye to creating an industrial aesthetic (Hine and Faragher 2000: 492–3).

However artistic views of industry played out on canvas, few nineteenth-century rushers seem to have entertained serious concerns about the detrimental and long-term impacts of their activities upon the land. The term *environment* was not common parlance, and environmental problems were conceptualized instead in terms of specific components: air, water, and soil (Smith 1987: 3). The repercussions of water pollution, outside of "muddy water," were rarely comprehended. To the contrary, the orange streams and the reds, yellows, and grays of mine dumps embodied the colors of work and the promise of money.

What makes this of archaeological interest is that perceptions influence actions. Thus, attitudes about the environment can be expected to have some connection to mining practices, particularly the treatment of wastes. During the nineteenth century, and continuing in remote districts well into the twentieth century, engineers preferred to site milling facilities next to watercourses because streams provided an efficient way to remove wastes. Such practices resolved problems at the mine but clearly pushed problems downstream for considerable distances. One example is the bare patches of tailings at the Grant-Kohrs Ranch National Historic Site in Montana, deposited in the early 1900s when a flood carried copper milling waste down 40 miles of the Clark Fork River (Quivik 2000). Sedimentation and contamination problems worsened with the processing of lower-grade metal ores. The mining of lower grades not only meant higher waste-to-product ratios but also tended to increase the presence of sulfide minerals.

Lawsuits and legislation impacted waste dumping practices. By the late nineteenth century, resource laws increasingly required that companies treat their wastes on-site. Operators reintroduced waste rock into underground workings or constructed storage dams to allow the reprocessing of tailings if ore prices warranted. Mining companies sold solid wastes as fertilizer, concrete aggregate, and road and railroad gravel. Smelter slag found use as railroad ballast, road gravel, and roofing materials, and when cast into blocks as a material for building retaining walls (Quivik 2000; White 2003).

Managers found air pollution a more vexing problem to solve. Metal smelters and ore roasters produced sulfur in prodigious quantities sufficient to kill off vegetation and poison animals dozens of miles distant. Prior to the development of sulfuric acid plants, most fixes emphasized increasing atmospheric dispersal. Nineteenth-century copper smelters included multiple stacks, but the smog and lawsuits these generated ultimately directed expedient solutions toward consolidating emissions into a single stack positioned on higher terrain. Flues constructed between smelter furnaces and emission stacks increased the opportunity for smelter gases to cool and precipitate heavy metals. The masonry stack at Anaconda, Montana—standing 585 feet tall, with an internal diameter tapering from 75 feet at the base to 60 feet at the top—epitomizes efforts to build larger and taller. Constructed between 1917 and 1919, the Anaconda Stack had six times the carrying capacity of the 300-foot-tall stack it replaced. A sobering indicator of the volume of material it handled is that the earlier chimney had expelled 1,700 tons of sulfur and 40 tons of arsenic into the atmosphere each day (Anaconda Mining Company 1920: 43; MacMillan 2000: 233–34).

In places such as Butte and Anaconda where mines were the primary employer, companies had significant political sway in framing environmental costs as an acceptable consequence of the industry. The downplaying of environmental impacts at times required creative flair. William Clark, one of Montana's copper kings, argued that the sulfurous smoke benefited the health of Butte's citizens by killing harmful microbes. The ladies, he added, were also fond of Butte "because there [was] just enough arsenic there to give them a beautiful complexion" (Clark quoted in Smith 1987: 45). Extensive litigation did occur between area farmers and the mining concerns in Butte and Anaconda. Although farmers won victories, the legal cases were drawn-out and costly and the compensations comparatively meager (Curtis 2013: 163–210; Quivik 1998).

All told, regulatory efforts to limit the environmental impacts of mining did not so much end the problem of waste as shift it to new forms. Tailings impoundments offer a prime example, for not only are they significant point sources of acid drainage but also their structural failure can bring catastrophe. A nightmare scenario occurred in 1972 when the collapse of an impoundment dam on Buffalo Creek in West Virginia sent a tidal wave of coal sludge down a narrow valley, ripping through sixteen towns and killing 125 people, injuring more than 1,000, and leaving 4,000 people homeless (Stern 2008). Seven years later, the breach of a tailings dam at Church Rock, New Mexico, released 1,100 tons of uranium milling waste and 12 million cubic feet of radioactive water down 70 miles of the Rio Puerco—the largest spill of radioactive materials in the United States to date. These disasters are two of more than eighty tailings dam failures that have occurred in the United States since the mid-twentieth century (International Commission on Large Dams 2001: 84–97). The millions of gallons of mine waste accidentally released into Colorado's Animas River during environmental cleanup work in August 2015 indicates that the problems are far from over (Finley and McGhee 2015).

Such circumstances justifiably have drawn attention to the broader threats to public health and safety that present-day and past mining operations cause and raise the question of what to do with abandoned properties. Over the past few decades, U.S. federal and state-based initiatives to remediate hazards at abandoned mines have increased notably. The Environmental Protection Agency's Superfund program—the most recognized of all government initiatives—targets the gravest cases of mine waste contamination. Remediation work is conducted also by agencies operating under the Department of the Interior's Abandoned Mine Lands program, which focuses especially on the issue of acid rock drainage. A sense of the overall scale can be gleaned from initiatives by the Bureau of Land Management (BLM), which administers one-eighth of the nation's land area and has actively worked on inventorying and remediating abandoned mine hazards for twenty-five years. As of 2011, the BLM has assessed twenty-eight thousand abandoned mines on its holdings and remediated hazards at one-quarter of them, some during the process of inventory (US BLM 2013: 6–9).

The expansion of remediation programs is both a cause for celebration and a source of concern. During cleanup work, little attention has typically been paid to historic preservation concerns beyond the Section 106 process—and problems occur here as well (Hardesty 2001; Quivik 2001). Few would debate the need to mitigate sites posing immediate threats to human life, but it is important to recognize that hazard classifications are often subjective. How deep does a prospect pit need to be in order to present a safety hazard? Does fencing an open shaft constitute a satisfactory or unsatisfactory fix? Is an abandoned mill building an "attractive nuisance" or a "heritage resource"? In short, evaluations are undergirded by the notion of acceptable risk, and acceptable risk is influenced heavily by disciplinary value systems.

Most characterization studies do not consider mining wastes to be valuable repositories of historical information. The permeability and reactivity of overburden, ore dumps, tailings, and other mining sediments—the characteristics making them environmental problems to begin with—certainly make wastes problematic storehouses. Even so, archaeological studies of tailings and other wastes distributed throughout processing facilities have identified telltale signatures of recovery processes such as amalgamation through the presence of mercury (Barnes 2002; Trinkley 1986, 1988; White 2003). Soils sampled from a nineteenth-century borax works in Death Valley, California, revealed the relative efficiency of different stages—namely, that the first steps of the recovery process were the most successful in extracting borax (Teague and Shenk 1977). Elemental analysis of milling sediments has also helped identify the source of ores last run through an abandoned milling plant (White 2003), and environmental characterization has also identified differences in tailings indicative of a facility's operation as a custom mill (Baltzer 1991). At the very least, research potential exists for a closer integration of environmental characterization and archaeological testing regimens.

But environmental problems have also confounded the ability of former mining communities to tap into heritage tourism. Whereas the marketing of heritage has given many western mining towns a new lease on life, fate has been much less kind to places associated with large-scale extraction and environmental contamination. The well-preserved mining landscape of Butte, Montana, includes mining head frames, a historic downtown, a mining school (now incorporated into Montana Tech), and the gaping Berkeley Pit, an abandoned open-pit operation that catapulted to public attention in 1995 when a migrating flock of snow geese took respite in the pit's acidic waters and promptly died (Dobb 1996). *Travel and Leisure* had already deemed Butte "the ugliest spot in Montana," and the city continues to face an image problem despite historic preservation efforts. In 2008, Butte received a listing as one of the world's "must-miss" vacation spots (Morin 2009: 257).

Yet even for the most contaminated sites, imaginative takes exist for repurposing mining landscapes. In 1997, the fourteen-year-long, multimillion-dollar environmental remediation of the copper smelting works in neighboring Anaconda ended on a celebratory note with the opening of a Jack Nicklaus–designed golf course. Built entirely atop remediated ground, the Old Works Golf Course incorporates views of smelter flues, ore roasters, and the Anaconda stack. Pulverized slag borders the fairways and finds additional use for sand traps. Reporting on the opening, the *Butte Montana Standard* waxed eloquent: "Where the yellowish mounds of arsenic tainted dirt sat, grassy fairways flourish. . . . And where copper ore was refined, cool lakes provide a drink for deer and marmots" (quoted in Shovers 2004: 64). The Old Works Golf Course injected a measure of economic revival into Anaconda, but it remains an environmental and economic experiment (ibid.: 70) and an experiment also in the presentation of industrial heritage.

Historical Perspectives, in Historical Perspective

A complex and reciprocal relationship has long existed in the ways that Americans have elected to memorialize the mining industry. A historical perspective identifies not only that forms of commemoration have ranged widely in intent and scale but also how these different projections continue to inform one another. Theme parks and movies caricature select aspects of America's mining heritage that both influence and affirm our notions of authenticity, and in some western mining towns, the lines between historical events and creative interpretations based on Hollywood imagery have arguably become irrevocably blurred. The marking of celebratory and tragic aspects of America's mining past by way of monuments and memorials also set in concrete contested views about the value of the industry, which remain in flux. Of particular note, the growing awareness of mining's long-lasting environmental impacts has come to raise new, fundamental issues for industrial heritage. Questions remain as to whether unmitigated waste piles retain interpretive value as integral components of mining landscapes (Hardesty 2001). Are some material aspects of toxic legacies worth preserving as reminders of the costs of human endeavors? Do remediated mine sites, where barren tailings piles become reshaped and seeded with grass, detrimentally sanitize one's understanding of past mining endeavors or suggest that environmental problems have somehow gone away? How possible is it to address heritage concerns while also improving public health and aiding the economic revitalization of former mining communities? These questions challenge us to consider the role that mining has played in the American experience and the ways in which archaeology can reveal the inconvenient truths about the consequences of this industry.

Conclusion

Scaling Up and Out

I have been to the mountaintop, but it wasn't there.
If it wasn't grown, it had to be mined.
Earth first. We'll strip mine the other planets later.
West Virginia—Almost Level.

Chances are that if you live in an active mining region, you will have spotted stickers with one of these slogans adorning the backs of Priuses and pickups. The polarizing dialogue is an apt reflection of mining's conflicting legacy as a supplier of key resources and employer of more than 300,000 people (NIOSH 2013) and as an industry connected directly to long-term and large-scale environmental ruin. A recent survey sponsored by the World Bank (GlobeScan 2013; World Bank Institute 2014) contends that extractive industries are perceived positively, but Oxfam counters that the survey polled only those with Internet access and avoided communities directly affected by mining (Gary 2014). Other polls suggest that mining enterprises in the United States and worldwide have gained a greater reputation for their undesirable consequences than for their beneficial products (Prager 1997).

The controversies surrounding mineral extraction are heated because so much is at stake. Most minerals are classified as nonrenewable resources, which means that arguments for and against mining weigh benefits and costs across different time scales. Notwithstanding the investment and inventiveness behind neologisms such as "clean coal" and "sustainable mining," the industry will always be blunt in the presentation of its economic underpinnings. Mining raises hard questions. After all, the mineral industry supplies the petroleum, plastics, and metals that undergird much of what we have become accustomed to in American society.

But is this level of consumption sustainable for future generations? What standard of living do we consider to be a right? More pointedly, who gets to enjoy it, and whose lives and futures become compromised for "the greater good"? Adding to the complexity of positions on the issue is that among the lives compromised by mining are miners themselves. The pay is generally good, but mining remains a dangerous job.

A historical perspective shows that conflicts of value have long underwritten the American experience of mining. Desires for mineral wealth fueled an early and competitive interest among European nations to claim the continent. Subsequent mineral discoveries transformed the United States into an industrial power and stepped up the pace of Native American land dispossession. Mineral development also sparked property and resource disputes between different land users. Changes in the organization of mining endeavors prompted violent confrontations between capital and labor. The conflicts that surround mining are varied, deeply felt, and difficult to resolve because mining goes about its business with little room for subtlety.

One of the leading values of archaeological research is the ability to contextualize disputes within broader historical frames, yet archaeological investigations of mining sites also take place within the fray. Miners have asked whether I am pro-mining or anti-mining or inquire more circumspectly about whether I am interested in mining or mining history. Environmental practitioners question the need to preserve places they frankly consider to be abominations, and I have been asked, at times facetiously, to calculate the heritage value of features ranging from a couple of rusted drums to a heap of tailings. These inquiries all seek clarification as to what the documentation of historical mining features is really in aid of. The concerns are well-founded, for we increasingly operate in a litigious environment in which survey findings might result in the levying of restrictions, fines, and lawsuits.

Archaeologists have an important role to play here because we are intimately involved in the memory business. Part of the legacy of mining involves the intentional setting aside of places considered significant to American history. The earliest archaeological excavations of mining sites occurred as part of this process, and archaeological fieldwork continues to contribute along these lines. Each year, archaeologists generate the data by which mining sites and districts are nominated for listing in the National Register of Historic Places. Archaeological investigation evaluates the integrity of sites—it develops and tests frameworks by which those tailings might be considered significant, unique, representative, or just another heap of crushed rock. Above all, we document what is there because material evidence provides a different perspective into the past and because a site nearly always has a story to tell.

Let us delve further into this issue. James Deetz's illustrious career in historical archaeology alit only briefly upon mining sites, but he nevertheless honed in on a central contribution. Remarking on his reasons for investigating a historic coal mine in Somersville, California, Deetz explained,

> It struck me that it would be a marvelous place to conduct some of the kind of historical archaeology that I think we need so much of. To get some sense of what life was in fact like for miners coming into this country working fourteen hours a day. What the day-to-day life was like, beyond what the records tell us. Here we know the men, and by the way only the men, that voted. We know that they paid their taxes, and we know that they built houses. We have photographs. But somehow there's a missing texture there, which archaeology can in fact provide. You look at the pictures, and it must have been an amazing place. It must have been an awful place. (Deetz 1980)

The texture that archaeology is so good at recording concerns the human scale of experience, for it is in the items used and discarded every day that we glimpse how people went about their lives. Material evidence reveals meaningful patterns in the humdrum aspects of life, and it also highlights everyday forms of creativity that few bothered to record. We gain insight into local adaptations, from the ingenuity required to make a system work to the ingenuity inherent to daily life in frontier communities. Archaeology tracks the inventive ways that miners repurposed materials on hand at the workplace, formed new social identities, and recapitulated others. Above all, we get a sense of who these people were and an appreciation for what they accomplished. Material evidence also reveals hardships of the mining life that tend to go undocumented, whether in the litany of failed endeavors dotting mining districts, in the structured exclusions built into racialized townscapes, or in the sites of violent labor struggle. What the material record reveals consistently is the existence of an immense amount of local variation in the historical experience of mining. Archaeology provides avenues for charting and assessing this diversity.

We are still in the process of understanding these legacies, and perhaps the greatest challenge for archaeological work still concerns this matter of recording the human scale. Not long ago, I signed up for a tour of a gold mine blasting its way into a hillside in interior Alaska. Although the mine was small by industry standards, the magnitude of operations was mesmerizing. Operators had quarried half a mile into the Earth in less than two decades, creating a pit a mile long by half a mile wide and growing. A line of mine trucks, each carrying more than 200 tons of rock, dumped their payloads into the maw of a giant crusher every five minutes. The milling plant processed thousands of tons of material a day, vastly exceeding the capacity of a historic stamp mill that a small field crew and I had spent the previous few weeks recording in detail. A few decades earlier, that historic mill ranked as the largest gold producer in the district. The cavernous facility at the open-pit mine, however, met the entire production record of the historic operation every day and a half, while staffed by only a handful of workers.

The most lasting impression is not that this particular open-pit constitutes the biggest this-or-that in the state—pending approvals at other properties, it will not be. Rather, the point is that this scale of mining is increasingly the norm, and it defies the methodologies that we have developed thus far for recording mining sites. Ground reconnaissance is more likely to record the treads of enormous earthmoving machines than the footprints of miners. Satellite imagery can capture the physical extent of an operation, but it likewise falls short of capturing the lived experience. Such landscapes confound our senses. But open-pits and strip mines are still experienced; they remain cultural, they remain peopled, and they also have histories. If findings at smaller mines are anything to go by, mines at any scale are not created the same, and closer inspection will likely reveal localized and at times unique adaptations, fixes, and corner cutting that have always attended American mining practice.

This need to grapple with scale also extends beyond the single mining site to connections between geographically distant sites. The industry's global connections range from the flippant to the profound. An elegant mirror in the lobby of the Palace Hotel in Kalgoorlie, Australia, was gifted by Herbert Hoover (later the thirty-first president of the United States) in remembrance of a barmaid he had fancied when stationed there as a mining engineer. Nineteenth-century emigration of Welsh coal miners is why there is not only Cardiff, Wales, on the map but also Cardiffs in Alabama, U.S.A., and Alberta, Canada, among other locations. The Cornish pasty, a savory pastry that served as a staple miners' lunch, has outlived the Cornish immigrants of Grass Valley, California, Michigan's Upper Peninsula, and the silver mining district of Pachuca, Mexico.

Consider also that, today, the industry quip that "it takes a mine to run a mine" has never been more apt. Mining companies advertise property portfolios that include operations in widely dispersed locales. Giants such as Rio Tinto administer mines on six continents, working minerals from diamonds to salt. This diversification is strategic rather than coincidental. Janet Finn's (1998) historical and anthropological examination of the Anaconda Company's interests in Butte, Montana, and Chuquicamata, Chile, notes how the stockpiling of ores, among other strategies, afforded Anaconda flexibility in weathering fluctuations in mineral prices and even a measure of control in setting them. The ability to ramp up or decrease production at different mines enabled the company to play one location against another, ushering in a highly effective strategy for breaking labor unions. At the human scale, miners in different parts of the globe live closely interconnected lives even though they will never meet.

The legacy of American mining is still being written because mines continue to operate in this country and because we still have much left to investigate. It should be apparent not only that archaeology is making substantive inroads into assessing the material legacies of mining but also that ample opportunities exist for expanding its scope. Archaeological findings to date have conditioned and challenged some of the romanticized views of American mining. Numerous prospects exist to balance out the current attention to select minerals, regions, and time periods. Further work along these lines offers an ability to depart meaningfully from the caricatures that have dominated depictions of the industry. With this will come a fuller reckoning of the historical trajectories that led us here and an improved vantage point for seeing the legacies that we need to consciously preserve.

REFERENCES

Adams, William Hampton, Peter Bowers, and Robin Mills. 2001. Commodity Flow and National Market Access: A Case Study from Interior Alaska. *Historical Archaeology* 35 (2): 73–105.

Agricola, Georgius. (1557) 1950. *De Re Metallica*. Translated by Herbert Clark Hoover and Lou Henry Hoover. New York: Dover.

Alanen, Arnold R., and Lynn Bjorkman. 1998. Plats, Parks, Playgrounds, and Plants: Warren H. Manning's Landscape Designs for the Mining Districts of Michigan's Upper Peninsula, 1899–1932. *IA: Journal of the Society for Industrial Archeology* 24 (1): 41–60.

Ali, Saleem. 2003. *Mining, the Environment, and Indigenous Development Conflicts*. Tucson: University of Arizona Press.

Allen, James B. 1966. *The Company Town in the American West*. Norman: University of Oklahoma Press.

Alpers, Charles N., Michael P. Hunerlach, Jason T. May, and Roger L. Hothem. 2005. *Mercury Contamination from Historical Gold Mining in California*. U.S. Geological Survey Fact Sheet 2005—3014 version 1.1. http://pubs.usgs.gov/fs/2005/3014/.

Amundson, Michael. 2004. *Yellowcake Towns: Uranium Mining Communities in the American West*. Boulder: University of Colorado Press.

Anaconda Mining Company. 1920. *The Anaconda Reduction Works, July 1920*. Anaconda, Mont.: Anaconda Mining Company.

Andrews, David. 1994. Written in Rock and Rust. *Common Ground* 7 (2). www.nps.gov/archeology/cg/fd_vol7_num2/index.htm.

Archimede, Gianfranco. 2002. Assessing Value in the Historic Mining Landscape of the Mojave Desert and the Industrial Archaeology of the Keane Wonder Mining Company, Death Valley National Park, California. MA thesis, Michigan Technological University.

Auger, Réginald. 2000. Frobisher the Fraud. *British Archaeology* 53 (June). www.britarch.ac.uk/BA/ba53/ba53feat.html.

Axsom, Jessica. 2009. Yeong Wo Mercantile on the Comstock. MA thesis, University of Nevada, Reno.

Baird, Keith P. 2005. Archaeological Investigation of the Transformation of the Coal Creek Mining Landscape, Yukon-Charley Rivers National Preserve, Alaska. MA thesis, Michigan Technological University.

Baker, Steven D. 1978. Historical Archaeology for Colorado and the Victorian Mining Frontier: Review, Discussion, and Suggestions. *Conference on Historic Sites Archaeology Papers 1977* 12: 1–31.

Bakken, Gordon Morris. 2008. *The Mining Law of 1872: Past, Politics, and Prospects.* Albuquerque: University of New Mexico Press.

Ballard, Chris, and Glenn Banks. 2003. Resource Wars: The Anthropology of Mining. *Annual Review of Anthropology* 32: 287–313.

Baltzer, Charles V. 1991. *Developing Mineral Waste Sampling Plans for Reprocessing Studies.* Hazardous Materials Control Research Institute, Monograph Series: Sampling and Monitoring 1. Silver Spring, Md.: Hazardous Materials Control Research Institute.

Banks, Chelsea N. 2011. Keeping Up Appearances: Cosmetics in Sulphur, Nevada. MA thesis, University of Nevada, Reno.

Barker, Leo R., and Ann E. Huston, eds. 1990. *Death Valley to Deadwood: Kennecott to Cripple Creek; Proceedings of the Historic Mining Conference, January 23–27, Death Valley National Monument.* San Francisco: National Park Service.

Barna, Benjamin T. 2008. A Material Culture of Making Do: Adapting to the Great Depression in the Rabbithole Mining District. MA thesis, University of Nevada, Reno.

Barnes, James J. 2002. The Life of Reilly: The Archaeology of an 1880s Silver Mine in Panamint Valley, California. MS thesis, Sonoma State University.

Barth, Gunther. 1988. *Instant Cities: Urbanization and the Rise of San Francisco and Denver.* Albuquerque: University of New Mexico Press.

Baudrillard, Jean. 1996. *Simulacra and Simulation.* Translated by Sheila Glaser. Ann Arbor: University of Michigan Press.

Beaudry, Mary C. 2005. Concluding Comments: Revolutionizing Industrial Archaeology? In *Industrial Archaeology: Future Directions,* edited by Eleanor Conlin Casella and James Symonds, 301–14. New York: Springer.

Becker, Roberta L. 1981. Mining Communities: How to Interpret a Blue Goose. MA thesis, University of Nevada, Las Vegas.

Blankenship, Sarah. 2007. Archaeological and Dendrochronological Investigations at Cagle Saltpetre Cave, Van Buren County, Tennessee. MA thesis, University of Tennessee, Knoxville.

Blustain, Jonah S. 2013. "You Could Bomb It into Oblivion and Never Notice the Difference": An Archaeological Research Design for Nevada's Uranium Mining Industry, 1951–1968. MA thesis, University of Nevada, Reno.

Bowden, Ellen P. 1999. An Investigation of Faunal Material from Four Virginiatown Loci: Areas D, B, B1, C. MA thesis, California State University, Sacramento.

Bowles, Oliver. 1947. Seventy-Five Years of Progress in the Nonmetallics. In Parsons, *Seventy-Five Years of Progress,* 303–57.

Bowles, Samuel. 1869. *Our New West: Records of Travel between the Mississippi River and the Pacific Ocean.* Hartford, Conn.: Hartford Publishing.

Branch, Edgar Marquess, Michael B. Frank, and Kenneth M. Sanderson, eds. 1987. *Mark Twain's Letters.* Vol. 1, *1853–1866.* Berkeley: University of California Press.

Brighton, Stephen A. 2004. Symbols, Myth-Making, and Identity: The Red Hand of Ulster in Late Nineteenth-Century Paterson, New Jersey. *International Journal of Historical Archaeology* 8 (2): 149–64.

Brinsmade, Robert B. 1907. Italians as Mine Workers. *Engineering and Mining Journal* 83 (18): 842.

Britz, Kevin M. 1999. Long May Their Legend Survive: Memory and Authenticity in Deadwood, South Dakota; Tombstone, Arizona; and Dodge City, Kansas. PhD dissertation, University of Arizona.

Brooks, Alfred H. 1908. Development of the Mining Industry. In *The Gold Placers of Parts of Seward Peninsula, Alaska*, by Arthur J. Collier, Frank L. Hess, Philip S. Smith, and Alfred H. Brooks, 10–39. U.S. Geological Survey Bulletin 328. Washington, D.C.: Government Printing Office.

Brooks, Allyson. 1995. Anticipating Mobility: How Cognitive Processes Influenced the Historic Mining Landscape in White Pine, Nevada, and the Black Hills of South Dakota. MS thesis, University of Nevada, Reno.

Brown, Ronald C. 1979. *Hard Rock Miners: The Intermountain West, 1860–1920*. College Station: Texas A&M University Press.

Buchanan, R. Angus. 2000. The Origins of Industrial Archaeology. In *Perspectives on Industrial Archaeology*, edited by Neil Cossons, 18–38. London: Science Museum.

Buechler, Jeffrey. 1987. *Proceedings of the Workshop on Historic Mining Resources: Defining the Research Questions for Evaluation and Preservation*. Vermillion, S.Dak.: State Historic Preservation Center.

Bunyak, Dawn, and J. Lawrence Lee. 2007. *Shenandoah-Dives Mill*. HAER No. CO-91. Washington, D.C.: U.S. Department of the Interior, National Park Service.

Burnette, Richard T. 2014. Masculinity in a Nineteenth Century Western Mining Town: Gendered Relations of Power in a Red-Light District, the Vanoli Sporting Complex (5or30), Ouray, Colorado. MA thesis, Colorado State University.

Burnston, Sharon Ann, and Ronald A. Thomas. 1981. Archaeological Data Recovery at Catoctin Furnace Cemetery, Frederick County, Maryland. Report submitted to Maryland Department of Transportation. On file at Western Maryland Regional Preservation Center, Frostburg State College.

Burt, Roger. 2000. Innovation or Imitation? Technological Dependency in the American Non-ferrous Mining Industry. *Technology and Culture* 41 (2): 321–47.

———. 2007. Technological Backwardness in the Western American Mining Industry in the Nineteenth Century. *Mining History Journal* 14: 23–39.

Chan, Sucheng. 2000. A People of Exceptional Character: Ethnic Diversity, Nativism, and Racism in the California Gold Rush. In *Rooted in Barbarous Soil: People, Culture, and Community in Gold Rush California*, edited by Kevin Starr and Richard J. Orsi, 44–85. Berkeley: University of California Press.

Chung, Sue Fawn, and Priscilla Wegars, eds. 2005. *Chinese American Death Rituals: Respecting the Ancestors*. Walnut Creek, Calif.: AltaMira.

Comp, T. Allen. 1975. The Tooele Copper and Lead Smelter. *IA: The Journal of the Society for Industrial Archeology* 1 (1): 29–46.

Conlin, Joseph R. 1986. *Bacon, Beans, and Galantines: Food and Foodways on the Western Mining Frontier*. Reno: University of Nevada Press.

Conrotto, Eugene L. 1973. *Miwok Means People: The Life and Fate of the Inhabitants of the California Gold Rush Country*. Fresno, Calif.: Valley Publishers.

Coroneos, Cosmos. 1995. Why Is That Hole So Big? An Analysis of Expenditure versus Gain in Alluvial Gold Mining. *Australasian Historical Archaeology* 13: 24–30.

Costello, Julia G. 1981. Gold Rush Archaeology: Excavating the Mother Lode. *Archaeology* 34 (2): 18–26.

Costello, Julia G., Rand F. Herbert, and Mark D. Selverston. 2007. Mining Sites: Historic Context and Archaeological Research Design. Report prepared for Cultural and Community Studies Office, Division of Environmental Analysis, California Department of Transportation, Sacramento.

Couch, Samuel L. 1996. Topophilia and Chinese Miners: Place Attachment in North Central Idaho. PhD dissertation, University of Idaho.

Cowan, Ruth Schwartz. 1983. *More Work for Mother: The Ironies of Household Technology from the Open Hearth to the Microwave*. New York: Basic Books.

Cowie, Sarah E. 2011. *The Plurality of Power: An Archaeology of Industrial Capitalism*. New York: Springer.

Cranstone, David. 2005. After Industrial Archaeology? In *Industrial Archaeology: Future Directions*, edited by Eleanor Conlin Casella and James Symonds, 77–92. New York: Springer.

Crawford, Margaret. 1995. *Building the Workingman's Paradise: The Design of American Company Towns*. London: Verso.

Culver, William, and Thomas Greaves, eds. 1985. *Mines and Mining in the Americas*. Manchester: Manchester University Press.

Cunningham, Judith. 1990. Survey and Mitigation at Royal/Mountain King Mines, Calaveras County, California. In Barker and Huston, *Death Valley to Deadwood*, 151–56.

Curran, Daniel J. 1993. *Dead Laws for Dead Men: The Politics of Federal Coal Mine Health and Safety Legislation*. Pittsburgh: University of Pittsburgh Press.

Curtis, Kent. 2013. *Gambling on Ore: The Nature of Metal Mining in the United States, 1860–1910*. Boulder: University of Colorado Press.

da Costa Nunes, Jadviga M. 2002. Pennsylvania's Anthracite Mines and Miners: A Portrait of the Industry in American Art, c. 1860–1940. *IA: Journal of the Society for Industrial Archeology* 28 (1): 11–32.

———. 2008. From Monuments to Memory Sites: Representing Pennsylvania's Anthracite Industry in Public Sculpture, 1855–2010. *IA: Journal of the Society for Industrial Archeology* 34 (1–2): 101–16.

Dale, Emily S. 2011. Archaeology on Spring Street: Discrimination, Ordinance 32, and the Overseas Chinese in Aurora, Nevada. MA thesis, University of Nevada, Reno.

Da Ponte, T. S. 1920. Books in Coal and Metal Mining Towns. *Engineering and Mining Journal* 110 (5): 211–13.

Deetz, James. 1980. Interview in *Other People's Garbage*, directed by Ann Peck and Claire Andrade-Watkins. Documentary film, PBS Odyssey Series.

———. (1977) 1996. *In Small Things Forgotten: An Archaeology of Early American Life*. New York: Anchor Books.

DeGolyer, Everette Lee. 1947. Seventy-Five Years of Progress in Petroleum. In Parsons, *Seventy-Five Years of Progress*, 270–302.

Delgado, James P. 2009. *Gold Rush Port: The Maritime Archaeology of San Francisco's Waterfront*. Berkeley: University of California Press.

DeLony, Eric. 1999. HAER and the Recording of Technological Heritage: Reflections on 30 Years' Work. *IA: Journal of the Society for Industrial Archeology* 25 (1): 5–28.

DeLyser, Dydia. 1999. Authenticity on the Ground: Engaging the Past in a California Ghost Town. *Annals of the Association of American Geographers* 89 (4): 602–32.

DePasqual, Seth. 2009. Winning Coal at 78° North: Mining, Contingency, and the *Chaîne Opératoire* in Old Longyear City. MS thesis, Michigan Technological University.

Des Jean, Tom. 1997. Niter Mining in the Area of the Big South Fork of the Cumberland River. *Tennessee Anthropologist* 22 (2): 225–39.

Dinius, Oliver J., and Angela Vergara. 2011. Introduction. In *Company Towns in the Americas: Landscape, Power, and Working-Class Communities*, edited by Oliver J. Dinius and Angela Vergara, 1–20. Athens: University of Georgia Press.

Dixon, Kelly J. 2005. *Boomtown Saloons: Archaeology and History in Virginia City*. Reno: University of Nevada Press.

———. 2006. Sidling up to the Archaeology of Western Saloons: Historical Archaeology Takes on the Wild of the West. *World Archaeology* 38 (4): 576–85.

Dobb, Edwin. 1996. Pennies from Hell: In Montana, the Bill for America's Copper Comes Due. *Harper's Magazine* 293: 39–54.

Dollar, Clyde. 1968. Some Thoughts on Theory and Method in Historical Archaeology. *Conference on Historic Site Archaeology Papers 1967* 2 (2): 3–30.

Duncan, M. Susan. 1997. Examining Early Nineteenth Century Saltpeter Caves: An Archaeological Perspective. *Journal of Cave and Karst Studies* 59 (2): 91–94.

Elwes, Hugh G. 1910. Points about Mexican Labor. *Engineering and Mining Journal* 90 (14): 662.

Engineering and Mining Journal. 1904. Notes from the Louisiana Purchase Exposition. 77 (1): 12–23.

Estes, J. Worth. 1988. The Pharmacology of Nineteenth-Century Patent Medicines. *Pharmacy in History* 30 (1): 3–18.

Evans, Cadwallader, Jr. 1947. Seventy-Five Years of Progress in the Anthracite Industry. In Parsons, *Seventy-Five Years of Progress*, 247–69.

Eve, David. 1992. *Bald Mountain Gold Mill*. HAER No. SD-2. Washington, D.C.: U.S. Department of the Interior, National Park Service.

Fahlman, Betsy. 2002. Introduction: The Art of American Industry. *IA: Journal of the Society for Industrial Archeology* 28 (1): 5–10.

Faulkner, Charles T., Sarah E. Cowie, Patrick E. Martin, Susan R. Martin, C. Shane Mayes, and Sharon Patton. 2000. Archaeological Evidence of Parasitic Infection from the 19th Century Company Town of Fayette, Michigan. *Journal of Parasitology* 86 (4): 846–49.

Fay, Albert. 1916. *Coal-Mine Fatalities in the United States, 1870–1914*. U.S. Bureau of Mines Bulletin 115. Washington, D.C.: Government Printing Office.

Feierabend, Carey. 1990. Historic Mine Lands as Cultural Landscapes. In Barker and Huston, *Death Valley to Deadwood*, 24–27.

Fenenga, Franklin. 1947. Artifacts from the Excavation of Sutter's Sawmill, 1947. In *California Gold Discovery: Centennial Papers on the Time, Site and Artifacts*, 54–56. San Francisco: California Historical Society.

———. 1967. Post-1800 Mining Camps. *Historical Archaeology* 1: 80–82.

Fenske, Gail. 2013. A Brief History of the Twentieth-Century Skyscraper. In *The Tall Buildings Reference Book*, edited by Dave Parker and Antony Wood, 13–32. London: Routledge.

Ferris, Dawna E. 1991. The Best of Times, the Worst of Times: A Bio-cultural Analysis of the Ferguson District, 1892–1909. MA thesis, University of Nevada, Las Vegas.

Finley, Bruce, and Tom McGhee. 2015. Animas Mine Disaster: Arsenic, Cadmium, Lead Broke Water Limits. *Denver Post*, August 11. www.denverpost.com/environment/ci_28614946/epa-taking-damage-claims-toxic-spill-animas-river.

Finn, Janet L. 1998. *Tracing the Veins: Of Copper, Culture, and Community from Butte to Chuquicamata*. Berkeley: University of California Press.

Fisher, Charles L., Karl J. Reinhard, Matthew Kirk, and Justin DiVirgilio. 2007. Privies and Parasites: The Archaeology of Health Conditions in Albany, New York. *Historical Archaeology* 41 (4): 172–97.

Flink, James J. 1993. *The Automobile Age*. Cambridge, Mass.: MIT Press.

Foley, Vincent P. 1968. On the Meaning of Industrial Archaeology. *Historical Archaeology* 2: 66–72.

———. 1969. Reply to Vogel. *Historical Archaeology* 3: 93–4.

Ford, Ben. 2011. Worker Housing in the Vermont Copper Belt: Improving Life and Industry through Paternalism and Resistance. *International Journal of Historical Archaeology* 15: 725–50.

Foster, Michael S., John M. Lindly, and Ronald F. Ryden. 2005. The Soiled Doves of South Granite Street: The History and Archaeology of a Prescott, Arizona, Brothel. *Kiva* 70 (4): 349–74.

Fowler, Don D. 2006. J. C. Harrington Medal in Historical Archaeology: Donald L. Hardesty. *Historical Archaeology* 40 (2): 1–5.

Francaviglia, Richard V. 1991. *Hard Places: Reading the Landscape of America's Historic Mining Districts*. Iowa City: University of Iowa Press.

Gartman, David. 1994. *Auto Opium: A Social History of American Automobile Design*. London: Routledge.

Gary, Ian. 2014. Bizarre Methodology Skews World Bank Survey on Oil, Mining "Perceptions." Oxfam America, *Politics of Poverty*, April 16. http://politicsofpoverty.oxfamamerica.org/2014/04/bizarre-methodology-skews-world-bank-survey-on-oil-mining-public-perceptions/.

Gedicks, Al. 1993. *The New Resource Wars: Native and Environmental Struggles against Multinational Corporations*. Boston: South End Press.

Gier, Jaclyn J., and Laurie Mercier, eds. 2006. *Mining Women: Gender in the Development of a Global Industry, 1670 to the Present*. New York: Palgrave Macmillan.

Gillespie, William B., and Mary M. Farrell. 2002. Work Camp Settlement Patterns: Landscape-Scale Comparisons of Two Mining Camps in Southeastern Arizona. *Historical Archaeology* 36 (3): 59–68.

Globescan. 2013. CSR Reputation Mining Industry. www.globescan.com/component/ed ocman/?view=document&id=141&Itemid=591.

Goddard, Richard A. 2002. Nothing But Tar Paper Shacks. *Historical Archaeology* 36 (3): 85–93.

Godoy, Ricardo A. 1985. Mining: Anthropological Perspectives. *Annual Review of Anthropology* 14: 199–217.

Goebel, Ted, Michael R. Waters, and Dennis H. O'Rourke. 2008. The Late Pleistocene Dispersal of Modern Humans in the Americas. *Science* 319: 1497–502.

Goin, Peter, and C. Elizabeth Raymond. 2004. *Changing Mines in America*. Santa Fe, N.Mex.: Center for American Places.

Goold, Douglas, and Andrew Willis. 1997. *The Bre-X Fraud*. Toronto: McClelland and Stewart.

Gordon, Robert B. 1996. *American Iron, 1607–1900*. Baltimore, Md.: Johns Hopkins University Press.

Gordon, Robert B., and Patrick M. Malone. 1994. *The Texture of Industry: An Archaeological View of the Industrialization of North America*. New York: Oxford University Press.

Gradwohl, David M., and Nancy M. Osbourn. 1984. *Exploring Buried Buxton: Archaeology of an Abandoned Iowa Coal Mining Town with a Large Black Population*. Iowa City: University of Iowa Press.

Graebner, William. 2003. Prospecting for Cultural Gold: The Western Mining Film, 1935–1960. *Mining History Journal* 10: 47–70.

Graton, L. C. 1947. Seventy-Five Years of Progress in Mining Geology. In Parsons, *Seventy-Five Years of Progress*, 1–39.

Green, Archie. 1972. *Only a Miner: Studies in Recorded Coal-Mining Songs*. Urbana: University of Illinois Press.

Green, Hardy. 2010. *The Company Town: The Industrial Edens and Satanic Mills That Shaped the American Economy*. New York: Basic Books.

Greene, Linda. 1981. *Historic Resource Study: A History of Mining in Death Valley National Monument*. Vol. 1. Denver: National Park Service.

Greenwood, Roberta S. 1992. Testing the Myths of the Gold Rush. In *Historical Archaeology of Nineteenth-Century California: Papers Presented at a Clark Library Seminar*, edited by Jay D. Frierman and Roberta S. Greenwood, 55–79. Los Angeles: William Andrews Clark Memorial Library at the University of California, Los Angeles.

Greever, William S. 1963. *The Bonanza West: The Story of the Western Mining Rushes, 1848–1900*. Norman: University of Oklahoma Press.

Griffin, Eve, and Karl Gurcke. 2011. An Overview of Chilkoot Trail Archaeology. In *Eldorado! The Archaeology of Gold Mining in the Far North*, edited by Catherine Holder Spude, Robin O. Mills, Karl Gurcke, and Roderick Sprague, 145–63. Lincoln: University of Nebraska Press.

Guggenheim, Harry F. 1920. Building Mining Cities in South America. *Engineering and Mining Journal* 110 (5): 204–10.

Guilmartin, Lore A. 2002. Textiles from the Steamboat *Bertrand*: Clothing and Gender on the Montana Mining Frontier. PhD dissertation, Texas A&M University.

Gust, Sherri M. 1993. Animal Bones from Historic Urban Chinese Sites: A Comparison of Sacramento, Woodland, Tucson, Ventura, and Lovelock. In Wegars, *Hidden Heritage*, 177–212.

Gutman, Herbert G. 1976. *Work, Culture, and Society in Industrializing America*. New York: Alfred A. Knopf.

Hall, Daniel S. 1997. Historical Archaeology and the Garnet Mining Camp, 1865–1912. In *The Historical Archaeology of Garnet Mining Town*, by Daniel S. Hall, Garren J. Meyer, Tammy Howser, and Jennifer K. Spencer, 1–94. Contributions to Anthropology 10. Missoula: Department of Anthropology, University of Montana.

Hall, Daniel S., Garren J. Meyer, Tammy Howser, and Jennifer K. Spencer. 1997. *The Historical Archaeology of Garnet Mining Town*. Contributions to Anthropology 10. Missoula: Department of Anthropology, University of Montana.

Hamilton, E. M. 1920. *Manual of Cyanidation*. New York: McGraw-Hill.

Hand, Waland D. 1942. California Miners' Folklore: Below Ground. *California Folklore Quarterly* 1 (2): 127–53.

Hanson, Todd A. 2016. *The Archaeology of the Cold War*. Gainesville: University Press of Florida.

Hardesty, Donald L. 1986. Industrial Archaeology on the American Mining Frontier: Suggestions for a Future Research Agenda. *Journal of New World Archaeology* 1 (4): 47–56.

———. 1988. *The Archaeology of Mining and Miners: A View from the Silver State*. Special Publications Series 6. Pleasant Hill, Calif: Society for Historical Archaeology.

———. 1991. Toward an Historical Archaeology of the Intermountain West. *Historical Archaeology* 25 (3): 29–35.

———. 1994. Class, Gender Strategies, and Material Culture in the Mining West. In *Those of Little Note: Gender, Race, and Class in Historical Archaeology*, edited by Elizabeth M Scott, 129–45. Tucson: University of Arizona Press.

———. 1998. Power and the Industrial Mining Community in the American West. In *Social Approaches to an Industrial Past: The Archaeology and Anthropology of Mining*, edited by A. Bernard Knapp, Vincent C. Pigott, and Eugenia W. Herbert, 81–96. London: Routledge.

———. 2001. Issues in Preserving Toxic Wastes as Heritage Sites. *Public Historian* 23 (2): 19–28.

———. 2003. Mining Rushes and Landscape Learning in the Modern World. In *Colonization of Unfamiliar Landscapes: The Archaeology of Adaptation*, edited by Marcy Rockman and James Steele, 81–95. London: Routledge.

———. 2010. *Mining Archaeology in the American West: A View from the Silver State*. Lincoln: University of Nebraska Press and Society for Historical Archaeology.

Hardesty, Donald, and Barbara Little. 2000. *Assessing Site Significance: A Guide for Archaeologists and Historians*. Walnut Creek, Calif.: AltaMira.

Harrod, Ryan P., Jennifer L. Thompson, and Debra L. Martin. 2012. Hard Labor and Hostile Encounters: What Human Remains Reveal about Institutional Violence and

Chinese Immigrants Living in Carlin, Nevada (1885–1923). *Historical Archaeology* 46 (4): 85–111.

Hartnell, Cameron C. 2009. Arctic Network Builders: The Arctic Coal Company's Operations on Spitsbergen and Its Relationship with the Environment. PhD dissertation, Michigan Technological University.

Hattori, Eugene M. 1975. *Northern Paiutes on the Comstock: Archaeology and Ethnohistory of an American Indian Population in Virginia City, Nevada.* Occasional Papers 2. Carson City: Nevada State Museum.

———. 1998. "And Some of Them Swear Like Pirates": Acculturation of American Indian Women in Nineteenth-Century Virginia City. In *Comstock Women: The Making of a Mining Community*, edited by Ronald James and C. Elizabeth Raymond, 229–45. Reno: University of Nevada Press.

Hattori, Eugene M., and Jerre L. Kosta. 1990. Packed Pork and Other Foodstuffs from the California Gold Rush. In Pastron and Hattori, *Hoff Store Site*, 82–93.

Hattori, Eugene M., and Marna A. Thompson. 1987. Using Dendrochronology for Historical Reconstruction in the Cortez Mining District, North Central Nevada. *Historical Archaeology* 21 (2): 60–73.

Heath, Kingston William. 1989. False-Front Architecture on Montana's Urban Frontier. *Perspectives in Vernacular Architecture* 3: 199–213.

Heffner, Sarah C. 2012. Investigating the Intersection of Chinese and Euro-American Healthcare Practices in Nevada from 1860–1930. PhD dissertation, University of Nevada, Reno.

Heizer, Robert F. 1947. Archaeological Investigation of Sutter Sawmill Site in 1947. In *California Gold Discovery: Centennial Papers on the Time, Site and Artifacts*, 28–53. San Francisco: California Historical Society.

Heizer, Robert F., and Franklin Fenenga. 1948. Survey of Building Structures of the Sierran Gold Belt, 1848–70. In *Geologic Guidebook along Highway 49—Sierran Gold Belt: The Mother Lode Country*, prepared by Olaf P. Jenkins, 91–165. Bulletin 141. San Francisco: Division of Mines.

Herod, Andrew. 2011. Social Engineering through Spatial Engineering: Company Towns and the Geographic Imagination. In *Company Towns in the Americas: Landscape, Power, and Working-Class Communities*, edited by Oliver J. Dinius and Angela Vergara, 21–44. Athens: University of Georgia Press.

Higgs, Andrew S., and Robert A. Sattler. 2011. Cabin Comforts: The Archaeology of Bachelor Cabins on Fish Creek, Alaska. In *Eldorado! The Archaeology of Gold Mining in the Far North*, edited by Catherine Holder Spude, Robin O. Mills, Karl Gurcke, and Roderick Sprague, 288–308. Lincoln: University of Nebraska Press.

Hindle, Brooke. 1972. Museum Treatment of Industrialization: History, Problems, Opportunities. *Curator* 15 (3): 206–19.

Hine, Robert V., and John Mack Faragher. 2000. *The American West: A New Interpretive History.* New Haven, Conn.: Yale University Press.

Hoagland, Alison K. 2010. *Mine Towns: Buildings for Workers in Michigan's Copper Country.* Minneapolis: University of Minnesota Press.

Hogarth, Donald D., and John Loop. 1986. Precious Metals in Martin Frobisher's "Black

Ores" from Frobisher Bay, Northwest Territories. *Canadian Mineralogist* 24 (2): 259–63.

Hollister, Ovando J. 1867. *The Mines of Colorado*. Springfield, Mass.: Samuel Bowles.

Holman, Tamara. 2016. Social Construction of Technology in the Workplace: Lode Mining in the Fairbanks Mining District, Alaska, 1902–1942. MA thesis, University of Alaska Anchorage.

Holman, Treve. 1947. Historical Relationship of Mining, Silicosis, and Rock Removal. *British Journal of Industrial Medicine* 4: 1–29.

Horn, Claire Helen. 2009. Well Enough to Work: Health and Class in South Colorado Coal Mining Towns, 1900–1930. PhD dissertation, State University of New York, Binghamton.

Horobik, Heather. 2011. Finding Privacy in the Red-Light District: An Analysis of Victorian Era Medicine Bottles from the Vanoli Site (5OR30) in Ouray, Colorado. MA thesis, Colorado State University.

Hovis, Logan W. 1992. Historic Mining Sites: A Typology for the Alaskan National Parks. Manuscript on file at National Park Service, Alaska Regional Office, Anchorage.

Hovis, Logan W., and Jeremy Mouat. 1996. Miners, Engineers, and the Transformation of Work in the Western Mining Industry, 1880–1930. *Technology and Culture* 37 (3): 429–56.

Hovis, Logan W., and Mike Shields. 1999. Abandoned Explosives: An Orientation. Handouts provided at Hazard Safety Training, Wrangell–St. Elias National Park and Preserve, Alaska.

Howard, Robert A. 1975. Black Powder Manufacture. *IA: The Journal of the Society for Industrial Archeology* 1 (1): 13–28.

Hoye, Robert L., and S. Jackson Hubbard. 1989. Mining Wastes. In *Standard Handbook of Hazardous Waste Treatment and Disposal*, edited by Harry M. Freeman, 4.48–49. New York: McGraw-Hill.

Hudson, Kenneth. 1963. *Industrial Archaeology: An Introduction*. Methuen: London.

Humphrey, H. B. 1960. *Historical Summary of Coal-Mine Explosions in the United States, 1810–1958*. Bureau of Mines Bulletin 586. Washington, D.C.: Government Printing Office.

Hunt, Charles B. 1959. Dating Mining Camps with Tin Cans and Bottles. *Geotimes* 3 (8): 10, 34.

Hurtado, Albert L. 1988. *Indian Survival on the California Frontier*. New Haven, Conn.: Yale University Press.

Hyde, Charles K. 1986. Undercover and Underground: Labor Spies and Mine Management in the Early Twentieth Century. *Business History Review* 60 (1): 1–27.

———. 1990. Documenting a Copper Mine: The Quincy Mine Recording Project, Summer of 1978. In Barker and Huston, *Death Valley to Deadwood*, 91–92.

———. 1991. The Birth of the SIA and Reminiscences by Some of Its Founders. *IA: Journal of the Society for Industrial Archeology* 17 (1): 3–16.

International Commission on Large Dams. 2001. *Tailings Dams Risk of Dangerous Occurrences: Lessons Learnt from Practical Experiences*. Paris: Commission Internationale des Grandes Barrages.

James, Ronald L. 1995. *Ruins of a World: Chinese Gold Mining at the Mon-Tung Site in the Snake River Canyon.* Idaho Cultural Resource Series 4. Washington, D.C.: Bureau of Land Management.

James, Ronald M. 1992. Knockers, Knackers, and Ghosts: Immigrant Folklore in the Western Mines. *Western Folklore* 51 (2): 153–77.

———. 2012. *Virginia City: Secrets of a Western Past.* Lincoln: University of Nebraska Press.

Jameson, Elizabeth. 1998. *All That Glitters: Class, Conflict, and Community in Cripple Creek.* Urbana: University of Illinois Press.

Janson, Lone. 1981. *Mudhole Smith: Alaskan Flier.* Anchorage: Alaska Northwest Publishing.

Johnson, Matthew. 2010. *Archaeological Theory: An Introduction.* 2nd ed. Malden, Mass.: Wiley-Blackwell.

Johnston, Andrew Scott. 2013. *Mercury and the Making of California: Mining, Landscape, and Race, 1840–1890.* Boulder: University Press of Colorado.

Kelly, Roger E., and Marsha C. S. Kelly. 1983. Arrastras: Unique Western Historic Mining Sites. *Historical Archaeology* 17 (1): 85–95.

Kenyon, William M. 1919. The Town Site of New Cornelia Copper Co., Ajo, Arizona. *Architecture: The Professional Architectural Monthly* 39 (1): 7–10, plates XI–XV.

Kerber, Jordan E., ed. 1994. *Cultural Resource Management: Archaeological Research, Preservation Planning, and Public Education in the Northeastern United States.* Westport, Conn.: Bergin and Garvey.

Kierstead, Matthew A. 2002. Vulcan: Birmingham's Industrial Colossus. *IA: Journal of the Society for Industrial Archeology* 28 (1): 59–74.

Kirsch, Stuart. 2014. *Mining Capitalism: The Relationship between Corporations and Their Critics.* Berkeley: University of California Press.

Knapp, A. Bernard, Vincent C. Pigott, and Eugenia W. Herbert, eds. 1998. *Social Approaches to an Industrial Past: The Archaeology and Anthropology of Mining.* London: Routledge.

Knee, Alexis Ryan. 2012. Material Culture, Social Networks and the Chinese of Ouray, Colorado, 1880–1920. MA thesis, Colorado State University.

Kotlensky, T. Arron. 2009. From Forest and Mine to Foundry and Cannons: An Archaeological Study of the Blast Furnace at the West Point Foundry. *IA: Journal of the Society for Industrial Archeology* 35 (1–2): 49–72.

Krause, David J. 1992. *The Making of a Mining District: Keweenaw Native Copper, 1500–1870.* Detroit, Mich.: Wayne State University Press.

LaLande, Jeffrey M. 1981. Sojourners in the Oregon Siskiyous: Adaptation and Acculturation of the Chinese Miners in the Applegate Valley, ca. 1855–1900. MA thesis, Oregon State University.

———. 1985. Sojourners in Search of Gold: Hydraulic Mining Techniques of the Chinese on the Oregon Frontier. *IA: Journal of the Society for Industrial Archeology* 11 (1): 29–52.

Landon, David B., and Timothy A. Tumberg. 1996. Archeological Perspectives on the

Diffusion of Technology: An Example from the Ohio Trap Rock Mine Site. *IA: Journal of the Society for Industrial Archeology* 22 (2): 40–57.

Langa, Helena. 2002. Deep Tunnels and Burning Flues: The Unexpected Political Drama in 1930s Industrial Production Prints. *IA: Journal of the Society for Industrial Archeology* 28 (1): 43–58.

Langenwalter, Paul E. 1980. The Archaeology of 19th Century Chinese Subsistence at the Lower China Store, Madera County, California. In *Archaeological Perspectives on Ethnicity in America: Afro-American and Asian American Culture History*, edited by Robert L. Schuyler, 102–12. Farmingdale, N.Y.: Baywood Publishing.

Lankton, Larry D. 1983. The Machine under the Garden: Rock Drills Arrive at the Lake Superior Copper Mines, 1868–1883. *Technology and Culture* 24 (1): 1–37.

———. 1991. *Cradle to Grave: Life, Work, and Death at the Lake Superior Copper Mines*. New York: Oxford University Press.

Lankton, Larry D., and Charles K. Hyde. 1982. *Old Reliable: An Illustrated History of the Quincy Mining Company*. Hancock, Mich.: Quincy Mine Hoist Association.

Larkin, Karin, and Randall H. McGuire, eds. 2009. *The Archaeology of Class War: The Colorado Coalfield Strike of 1913–1914*. Boulder: University Press of Colorado.

Lawrence, Susan. 1998. Gender and Community Structure on Australian Colonial Goldfields. In *Social Approaches to an Industrial Past: The Archaeology and Anthropology of Mining*, edited by A. Bernard Knapp, Vincent C. Pigott, and Eugenia W. Herbert, 39–58. London: Routledge.

Layton, Thomas. 2002. *Gifts from the Celestial Kingdom: A Shipwrecked Cargo for Gold Rush California*. Stanford: Stanford University Press.

LeDuc, Stephen D. 2005. The Ethnic Composition of Underground Labor in a Michigan Copper Township: A Quantitative Portrait, 1870–1920. *Mining History Journal* 12: 81–98.

Lemonnier, Pierre. 1986. The Study of Material Culture Today: Toward an Anthropology of Technical Systems. *Journal of Anthropological Archaeology* 5: 147–86.

Leone, Mark P., and Parker B. Potter Jr., eds. 1999. *Historical Archaeologies of Capitalism*. New York: Kluwer Academic/Plenum Publishers.

Lewis, Kenneth. 1984. *The American Frontier: An Archaeological Study of Settlement Pattern and Process*. Orlando, Fla.: Academic Press.

Liebs, Chester H. 1995. *Main Street to Miracle Mile: American Roadside Architecture*. Baltimore, Md.: Johns Hopkins University Press.

Lightfoot, Kent G. 1995. Culture Contact Studies: Redefining the Relationship between Prehistoric and Historic Archaeology. *American Antiquity* 60 (2): 199–217.

Limbaugh, Ronald H. 1999. Making Old Tools Work Better: Pragmatic Adaptation and Innovation in Gold-Rush Technology. In *A Golden State: Mining and Economic Development in Gold Rush California*, edited by James Rawls and Richard Orsi, 24–51. Berkeley: University of California Press.

Limbaugh, Ronald H., and Willard P. Fuller. 2003. *Calaveras Gold: The Impact of Mining on a Mother Lode County*. Reno: University of Nevada Press.

Limerick, Patricia Nelson. 1987. *The Legacy of Conquest: The Unbroken Past of the American West*. New York: W. W. Norton.

——. 1998. The Gold Rush and the Shaping of the American West. *California History* 77 (1): 30–41.

Lindley, Curtis H. 1903. *A Treatise on the American Law Relating to Mines and Mineral Lands within the Public Lands States and Territories: And Governing the Acquisition and Enjoyment of Mining Rights in Lands of the Public Domain.* 2nd ed. San Francisco: Bancroft-Whitney.

Lingenfelter, Richard E. 1974. *Hard Rock Miners: A History of the Mining Labor Movement in the American West, 1863–1893.* Berkeley: University of California Press.

——. 1986. *Death Valley and the Amargosa: A Land of Illusion.* Berkeley: University of California Press.

——. 2012. *Bonanzas and Borrascas: Gold Lust and Silver Sharks, 1848–1884.* Western Lands and Waters Series 26. Norman, Okla.: Arthur H. Clark.

Little, Barbara. 2013. Reversing the Narrative from Violence to Peace: Some Thoughts from an Archaeologist. *Historical Archaeology* 47 (3): 124–29.

Lloyd, B. E. 1876. *Lights and Shades in San Francisco.* San Francisco: A. L. Bancroft and Company.

Long, Priscilla. 1989. *Where the Sun Never Shines: A History of America's Bloody Coal Industry.* New York: Paragon House.

Longenecker, Julia G., and Darby Stapp. 1993. The Study of Faunal Remains from an Overseas Chinese Mining Camp in Northern Idaho. In Wegars, *Hidden Heritage,* 97–122.

Lovejoy, Owen R. 1906. Child Labor in the Coal Mines. *Annals of the American Academy of Political and Social Science* 27 (2): 35–41.

——. 1907. Child Labor in the Soft Coal Mines. *Annals of the American Academy of Political and Social Science* 29 (1): 26–34.

Lukas, J. Anthony. 1997. *Big Trouble: A Murder in a Small Western Town Sets Off a Struggle for the Soul of America.* New York: Simon and Schuster.

Lynch, Martin. 2002. *Mining in World History.* London: Reaktion Books.

Lyon, James S., Thomas J. Hilliard, and Thomas N. Bethell. 1993. *Burden of Gilt: The Legacy of Environmental Damage from Abandoned Mines and What America Should Do about It.* Washington, D.C.: Mineral Policy Center.

MacMillan, Donald. 2000. *Smoke Wars: Anaconda Copper, Montana Air Pollution, and the Courts, 1890–1924.* Helena: Montana Historical Society Press.

Malone, Michael P. 1981. *The Battle for Butte: Mining and Politics on the Northern Frontier, 1864–1906.* Helena: Montana Historical Society Press.

Malone, Patrick. 1998. Introduction to Green Engineering. *IA: Journal of the Society for Industrial Archeology* 24 (1): 5–8.

Marshall, Daniel P. 1996. Rickard Revisited: Native "Participation" in the Gold Discoveries of British Columbia. *Native Studies Review* 11 (1): 91–108.

Martin, Patrick E. 1992. An Archaeological Perspective on Nineteenth Century Copper Mining Communities in Upper Michigan, USA. In *Towards a Social History of Mining in the Nineteenth and Twentieth Centuries,* edited by Klaus Tenfelde, 197–212. Munich: C. H. Beck.

————. 1998. Industrial Archaeology and Historic Mining Studies at Michigan Tech. *CRM* 21 (7): 4–7.

————. 2009. Industrial Archaeology. In *International Handbook of Historical Archaeology*, edited by Teresita Majewski and David Gaimster, 285–97. New York: Springer.

Martin, Susan R. 2004. Evidence for Indigenous Hardrock Mining of Copper in Ancient North America. *Journal of the West* 43 (1): 8–13.

Marx, Karl. 1967. *Capital: A Critique of Political Economy*. New York: Vintage.

Marx, Leo. 1964. *The Machine in the Garden: Technology and the Pastoral Ideal in America*. New York: Oxford University Press.

Mason, Richard B. 1848. Correspondence to Brigadier-General R. Jones, August 17. In *Letters Received by the Office of the Adjutant General, Main Series M1432*. National Archives Microfilm Publication M567, roll 386. Record Group 94. National Archives Building, Washington, D.C.

Matthews, Christopher N. 2010. *The Archaeology of American Capitalism*. Gainesville: University Press of Florida.

McDonnell, Janet A. 1991. *The Dispossession of the American Indian, 1887–1934*. Bloomington: Indiana University Press.

McDougall, Dennis P. 1990. The Bottles of the Hoff Store Site. In Pastron and Hattori, *Hoff Store Site*, 58–74.

McEvoy, Arthur F. 1986. *The Fisherman's Problem: Ecology and Law in the California Fisheries, 1850–1980*. New York: Cambridge University Press.

McGowan, Barry. 1996. The Typology and Techniques of Alluvial Mining: The Example of the Shoalhaven and Mongarlowe Goldfields in Southern New South Wales. *Australasian Historical Archaeology* 14: 34–45.

McGuire, Randall H. 2014. Won with Blood: Archaeology and Labor's Struggle. *International Journal of Historical Archaeology* 18 (2): 259–71.

McGuire, Randall H., and Paul Reckner. 2009. Building a Working Class Archaeology: The Colorado Coal Field War Project. In *The Archaeology of Class War: The Colorado Coalfield Strike of 1913–1914*, edited by Karin Larkin and Randall H. McGuire, 217–41. Boulder: University Press of Colorado.

McMurry, Sean Elisabeth. 2007. A View of the West: Community and Visual Landscape in Depression-Era Rabbithole Springs Mining District, Pershing County, Nevada. MA thesis, University of Nevada, Reno.

Meeks, Eric V. 2003. The Tohono O'odham, Wage Labor, and Resistant Adaptation, 1900–1930. *Western Historical Quarterly* 34 (4): 468–89.

Megraw, Herbert A. 1918. *The Flotation Process*. 2nd ed. New York: McGraw-Hill.

Meltzer, David J. 2009. *First Peoples in a New World: Colonizing Ice Age America*. Berkeley: University of California Press.

Merritt, Christopher W. 2010. "The Coming Man from Canton": Chinese Experience in Montana (1862–1943). PhD dissertation, University of Montana.

Metheny, Karen Bescherer. 2006. *From the Miners' Doublehouse: Archaeology and Landscape in a Pennsylvania Coal Company Town*. Knoxville: University of Tennessee Press.

Meyer, A., and M. Steyn. 2015. Chinese Indentured Mine Labour and the Dangers Associated with Early 20th Century Deep-Level Mining on the Witwatersrand Gold Mines, South Africa. *International Journal of Osteoarchaeology.* DOI 10.1002/oa.2455.

Miller, Charles W. 1998. *The Automobile Gold Rushes and Depression Era Mining.* Moscow: University of Idaho Press.

Mills, Robin O. 1998. Historical Archaeology of Alaskan Placer Gold Mining Settlements: Evaluating Process-Pattern Relationships. PhD dissertation, University of Alaska Fairbanks.

Miner, H. Craig. 1976. *The Corporation and the Indian: Tribal Sovereignty and Industrial Civilization in Indian Territory, 1865–1907.* Norman: University of Oklahoma Press.

Moore, Marat. 1996. *Women in the Mines: Stories of Life and Work.* New York: Twayne Publishers.

Morin, Bode J. 2009. Reflection, Refraction, and Rejection: Copper Smelting Heritage and the Execution of Environmental Policy. PhD dissertation, Michigan Technological University.

Morse, Kathryn. 2003. *The Nature of Gold: An Environmental History of the Klondike Rush.* Seattle: University of Washington Press.

Mulholland, James A. 1981. *A History of Metals in Colonial America.* Tuscaloosa: University of Alabama Press.

Mumford, Lewis. 1963. *Technics and Civilization.* 2nd ed. New York: Harcourt, Brace, and World.

Murphy, Lucy Eldersveld. 2000. *A Gathering of Rivers: Indians, Métis, and Mining in the Western Great Lakes, 1737–1832.* Lincoln: University of Nebraska Press.

Murray, Jeffrey S., and Jennifer F. A. Hamilton. 1986. Cultural Resource Inventory, Proposed Chilkoot Trail National Historic Park: Summary of 1984 Archaeological Survey. Microfiche Report Series 349. Ottawa, Ont.: Parks Canada.

Murray, W. F. 1907. Italians as Coal Miners. *Engineering and Mining Journal* 83 (22): 1059–60.

Nash, June. 1993. *We Eat the Mines and the Mines Eat Us: Dependency and Exploitation in Bolivian Tin Mines.* Rev. ed. New York: Columbia University Press.

Neasham, Aubrey. 1947. Sutter's Sawmill. *California Historical Society Quarterly* 26 (2): 109–33.

New York Times. 1891. The Coming Charleston Exposition. September 8, magazine supp. 14.

———. 1900. American Coal Exhibit. April 29.

NIOSH (National Institute for Occupational Safety and Health). 2013. Mining Facts—2013. www.cdc.gov/niosh/mining/works/statistics/factsheets/miningfacts2013.html.

Noble, Bruce J. 1990. Evaluating Historic Mining Resources: A National Register Perspective. In Barker and Huston, *Death Valley to Deadwood,* 28–30.

Noble, Bruce J., Jr., and Robert Spude. 1997. *Guidelines for Identifying, Evaluating, and Registering Historic Mining Sites.* National Register Bulletin 42. Rev. ed. Washington, D.C.: National Park Service. www.nps.gov/nr/publications/bulletins/nrb42/.

Nordberg, Erik. 2008. Mining in the Movies. Paper presented at 19th Annual Mining History Conference, Mining History Association, Chisholm, Minn., June 13.

Norman, William. 2012. Tradewinds and Traditions: Exploring the Archaeology of German Gulch. MA thesis, University of Montana.

Nye, David E. 1994. *American Technological Sublime*. Cambridge, Mass.: MIT Press.

Nystrom, Eric. 2014. *Seeing Underground: Maps, Models, and Mining Engineering in America*. Reno: University of Nevada Press.

Obenauer, Marie L. 1925. Living Conditions in the Anthracite Region and the Composition of the Mining Population. In U.S. Coal Commission, *Report of the United States Coal Commission*, part 2: *Anthracite—Detailed Studies*, 527–72. Washington, D.C.: Government Printing Office.

Obermayr, Erich, and Robert W. McQueen. 2016. *Historical Archaeology in the Cortez Mining District: Under the Nevada Giant*. Reno: University of Nevada Press.

O'Dell, Gary A., and Angelo I. George. 2014. Rock-Shelter Saltpeter Mines of Eastern Kentucky. *Historical Archaeology* 48 (2): 91–121.

Ogborne, Jennifer Honora. 2013. "Setting the Best Table in the Country": Food and Labor at the Coloma Gold Mining Town. PhD dissertation, College of William and Mary.

Ohio Mining Commission. 1872. *Report of the Mining Commission, Appointed under the Joint Resolution of the General Assembly of the State of Ohio, Passed May 2d, 1871*. Columbus: Nevins and Myers State Printers.

Olien, Diana Davids, and Roger M. Olien. 2002. *Oil in Texas: The Gusher Age, 1895–1945*. Austin: University of Texas Press.

Orser, Charles E., Jr. 1996. *A Historical Archaeology of the Modern World*. New York: Plenum Press.

———. 2004. *Historical Archaeology*. 2nd ed. Upper Saddle River, N.J.: Pearson Prentice Hall.

———. 2007. *The Archaeology of Race and Racialization in Historic America*. Gainesville: University Press of Florida.

Ostrogorsky, Michael. 1982. An Idaho Model of Frontier Settlement. *North American Archaeologist* 3 (1): 85–92.

Owens, Kenneth N., ed. 2002. *Riches for All: The California Gold Rush and the World*. Lincoln: University of Nebraska Press.

Paine, Albert Bigelow. 1924. *Mark Twain's Autobiography*. Vol. 2. New York: P. F. Collier and Son.

Park, John R. 2000a. *A Guidebook to Mining in America*. Vol. 1, *West*. Miami, Fla.: Stonerose Publishing.

———. 2000b. *A Guidebook to Mining in America*. Vol. 2, *East*. Miami, Fla.: Stonerose Publishing.

Parsons, A. B., ed. *Seventy-Five Years of Progress in the Mineral Industry, 1871–1946*. New York: American Institute of Mining and Metallurgical Engineers.

Pastron, Allen G. 1990. The Hoff Store Site: An Introduction. In Pastron and Hattori, *Hoff Store Site*, 1–3.

Pastron, Allen G., and Eugene M. Hattori, eds. 1990. *The Hoff Store Site and Gold Rush Merchandise from San Francisco, California*. Special Publication Series 7. Ann Arbor, Mich.: Society for Historical Archaeology.

Paul, Rodman W. 1947. *California Gold: The Beginning of Mining in the Far West*. Cambridge, Mass.: Harvard University Press.

———. 1963. *Mining Frontiers of the Far West, 1848–1880*. New York: Holt, Rinehart, and Winston.

Paynter, Robert. 2000. Historical Archaeology and the Post-Columbian World of North America. *Journal of Archaeological Research* 8 (3): 169–217.

Peele, Robert, ed. 1918. *Mining Engineers' Handbook*. New York: John Wiley and Sons.

Pehrson, Elmer W. 1947. Seventy-Five Years of Progress in Mineral Production. In Parsons, *Seventy-Five Years of Progress*, 358–75.

Peterson, Richard H. 1977. *The Bonanza Kings: The Social Origins and Business Behavior of the Western Mining Entrepreneurs, 1870–1900*. Norman: University of Oklahoma Press.

Petsche, Jerome E. 1974. *The Steamboat* Bertrand: *History, Excavation, and Architecture*. Washington, D.C.: National Park Service.

Pfaffenberger, Bryan. 1988. Fetishised Objects and Humanised Nature: Towards an Anthropology of Technology. *Man*, n.s., 23 (2): 236–52.

———. 1998. Mining Communities, *Chaînes Opératoires*, and Sociotechnical Systems. In *Social Approaches to an Industrial Past: The Archaeology and Anthropology of Mining*, edited by A. Bernard Knapp, Vincent C. Pigott, and Eugenia W. Herbert, 291–300. London: Routledge.

Pfertsch, Jack. 2005. History and Background of the Hanging Flume. http:// hanging-flume.org/wp-content/uploads/2013/12/History-and-Background-of-the-Hanging-Flume.pdf.

Pisani, Donald J. 1999. "I Am Resolved Not to Interfere, But Permit All to Work Freely": The Gold Rush and American Resource Law. In *A Golden State: Mining and Economic Development in Gold Rush California*, edited by James Rawls and Richard Orsi, 123–48. Berkeley: University of California Press.

Plazak, Dan. 2006. *A Hole in the Ground with a Liar at the Top: Fraud and Deceit in the Golden Age of American Mining*. Salt Lake City: University of Utah Press.

Poirier, David A., and Mary G. Harper. 1998. Newgate Prison and Copper Mine. *CRM* 21 (7): 15–16.

Pollard, Gordon C., and Haagen D. Klaus. 2004. A Large Business: The Clintonville Site, Resources, and Scale at Adirondack Bloomery Forges. *IA: Journal of the Society for Industrial Archeology* 30 (1): 19–46.

Portelli, Alessandro. 2011. *They Say in Harlan County: An Oral History*. New York: Oxford University Press.

Prager, Sharon. 1997. Changing North America's Mind-Set about Mining. *Engineering and Mining Journal* 198 (2): 36–44.

Prucha, Francis Paul, ed. 1973. *Americanizing the American Indians: Writings by the "Friends of the Indian," 1880–1900*. Cambridge, Mass.: Harvard University Press.

Purdy, Sarah E. 2007. Analysis of Dredge Tailings Pile Patterns: Applications for Historical Archaeological Research. MA thesis, Oregon State University.

Purser, Margaret. 1999. Ex Occidente Lux? An Archaeology of Later Capitalism in the

Nineteenth-Century West. In *Historical Archaeologies of Capitalism*, edited by Mark Leone and Parker Potter, 115–41. New York: Plenum Press.

Queen, Rolla L. 1987. Historical Archaeology and Historic Preservation at Candelaria and Metallic City, Nevada. MA thesis, University of Nevada, Reno.

Quivik, Fredric L. 1998. Smoke and Tailings: An Environmental History of Copper Smelting Technologies in Montana, 1880–1930. PhD dissertation, University of Pennsylvania.

———. 2000. Landscapes as Industrial Artifacts: Lessons from Environmental History. *IA: Journal of the Society for Industrial Archeology* 26 (2): 55–64.

———. 2001. Integrating the Preservation of Cultural Resources with Remediation of Hazardous Materials: An Assessment of Superfund's Record. *Public Historian* 23 (2): 47–61.

———. 2003. Gold and Tailings: The Standard Mill at Bodie, California. *IA: Journal of the Society for Industrial Archeology* 29 (2): 5–27.

Rautman, Alison E., and Todd E. Fenton. 2005. A Case of Historic Cannibalism in the American West: Implications for Southwestern Archaeology. *American Antiquity* 70 (2): 321–41.

Rawls, James J. 1976. Gold Diggers: Indian Miners in the California Gold Rush. *California Historical Quarterly* 55 (1): 28–45.

———. 1984. *Indians of California: The Changing Image*. Norman: University of Oklahoma Press.

Reckner, Paul E. 2004. Home Rulers, Red Hands, and Radical Journalists: Clay Pipes and the Negotiation of Working-Class Irish/Irish-American Identity in Late-Nineteenth-Century Paterson, New Jersey. In *Smoking and Culture: The Archaeology of Tobacco Pipes in Eastern North America*, edited by Sean Rafferty and Rob Man, 241–72. Knoxville: University of Tennessee Press.

———. 2009. Social Difference, Community-Building, and Material Social Practice: Solidarity and Diversity at the Ludlow Tent Colony, 1913–14. PhD dissertation, State University of New York, Binghamton.

Reinhard, Karl J. 1994. Sanitation and Parasitism at Harpers Ferry, West Virginia. *Historical Archaeology* 28 (4): 62–67.

Reinhard, Karl J., and A. Mohamad Ghazi. 1992. Evaluation of Lead Concentrations in 18th-Century Omaha Indian Skeletons Using ICP-MS. *American Journal of Physical Anthropology* 89: 183–95.

Reno, Ronald L. 1996. Fuel for the Frontier: Industrial Archaeology of Charcoal Production in the Eureka Mining District, Nevada 1869–1891. PhD dissertation, University of Nevada, Reno.

Reno, Ronald L., Stephen R. Bloyd, and Donald L. Hardesty. 2001. Chemical Soup: Archaeological Hazards at Western Ore Processing Sites. In *Dangerous Places: Health, Safety, and Archaeology*, edited by David A. Poirier and Kenneth L. Feder, 205–19. Westport, Conn.: Bergin and Garvey.

Reps, John W. 1975. Bonanza Towns: Urban Planning on the Western Mining Frontier. In *Pattern and Process: Research in Historical Geography*, edited by Ralph E. Ehrenberg, 271–86. Washington, D.C.: Howard University Press.

Rhoades, Ruth M. 2007. Rush for Gold, Rush for Water: A Historical Archaeology of Late Gold Rush Era Water Conveyance Systems near Oroville, California. MA thesis, Sonoma State University.

Richards, Robert H., and Charles E. Locke. 1940. *Textbook of Ore Dressing*. 3rd ed. New York: McGraw-Hill.

Rickard, T. A. 1904. *The Sampling and Estimation of Ore in a Mine*. New York: Engineering and Mining Journal.

———. 1932. *A History of American Mining*. New York: McGraw-Hill.

———. 1938. Indian Participation in the Gold Discoveries. *British Columbia Historical Quarterly* 2 (1): 3–18.

———. 1941. The Use of Meteoric Iron. *Journal of the Royal Anthropological Institute of Great Britain and Ireland* 71 (1–2): 55–66.

Riddell, Francis. 1997. Franklin Fenenga, 1917–1994. *Society for American Archaeology Bulletin* 15 (3). www.saa.org/Portals/0/SAA/publications/SAAbulletin/15-3/SAA24. html.

Ringsmuth, Katherine. 2012. *Tunnel Vision: The Life of a Copper Prospector in the Nizina River Country*. Washington, D.C.: Government Printing Office.

Ritchie, Neville A. 1986. Archaeology and History of the Chinese in Southern New Zealand during the Nineteenth Century: A Study of Acculturation, Adaptation, and Change. PhD dissertation, University of Otago, New Zealand.

———. 1993. Form and Adaptation: Nineteenth Century Chinese Miners' Dwellings in Southern New Zealand. In Wegars, *Hidden Heritage*, 335–73.

Robbins, William G. 1994. *Colony and Empire: The Capitalist Transformation of the American West*. Lawrence: University of Kansas Press.

Rockman, Marcia Helen. 1995. Investigation of Faunal Remains and Social Perspectives on Natural Resource Use in an 1867 Wyoming Gold Mining Town. MA thesis, University of Arizona.

Rohe, Randall E. 1984. The Geography and Material Culture of the Western Mining Town. *Material Culture* 16 (3): 99–120.

———. 1985. Hydraulicking in the American West: The Development and Diffusion of a Mining Technique. *Montana Historical Society* 35 (2): 18–35.

Rolando, Victor R. 1992. *200 Years of Soot and Sweat: The History and Archaeology of Vermont's Iron, Charcoal, and Lime Industries*. Burlington: Vermont Archaeological Society.

Roller, Michael P. 2015. Migration, Modernity and Memory: The Archaeology of the Twentieth Century in a Northeast Pennsylvania Coal Company Town, 1897–2014. PhD dissertation, University of Maryland, College Park.

Roth, Leland M. 1992. Company Towns in the Western United States. In *The Company Town: Architecture and Society in the Early Industrial Age*, edited by John S. Garner, 173–206. New York: Oxford University Press.

Rothschild, Nan A., and Diana diZerega Wall. 2014. *The Archaeology of American Cities*. Gainesville: University Press of Florida.

Rouse, Wendy L. 2005. Archaeological Excavations at Virginiatown's Chinese Cemeteries. In *Chinese American Death Rituals: Respecting the Ancestors*, edited by Sue Fawn Chung and Priscilla Wegars, 81–106. Lanham, Md.: AltaMira.

Rowe, John. 1974. *The Hard-Rock Men: Cornish Immigrants and the North American Mining Frontier*. London: Harper and Row.

Rule, John. 1998. A Risky Business: Death, Injury, and Religion in Cornish Mining, c. 1780–1870. In *Social Approaches to an Industrial Past: The Archaeology and Anthropology of Mining*, edited by A. Bernard Knapp, Vincent C. Pigott, and Eugenia W. Herbert, 155–73. London: Routledge.

Russell, Jane. 1991. An Ethnohistorical and Archaeological Examination of the Chew Kee (Store), Fiddletown, California. MA thesis, California State University, Sacramento.

Ryzewski, Krysta. 2008. Archaeology of a Colonial Industry: Domestic Ironworking and Industrial Evolution in Rhode Island, 1642–1800. PhD dissertation, Brown University.

Sagstetter, Beth, and Bill Sagstetter. 1998. *The Mining Camps Speak: A New Way to Explore the Ghost Towns of the American West*. Denver: Benchmark Publishing.

Saitta, Dean J. 2007. *The Archaeology of Collective Action*. Gainesville: University Press of Florida.

Saleeby, Becky M. 2011. *Beneath the Surface: Thirty Years of Historical Archaeology in Skagway, Alaska*. Anchorage: National Park Service, Alaska Regional Office.

Schablitsky, Julie Marie. 2002. The Other Side of the Tracks: Archaeology and History of a Virginia City, Nevada, Neighborhood. PhD dissertation, Portland State University.

Schiffer, Michael B., ed. 2001. *Anthropological Perspectives on Technology*. Albuquerque: University of New Mexico Press.

Schlatter, Evelyn A. 1997. Drag's a Life: Women, Gender, and Cross-Dressing in the Nineteenth-Century West. In *Writing the Range: Race, Class, and Culture in the Women's West*, edited by Elizabeth Jameson and Susan Armitage, 334–48. Norman: University of Oklahoma Press.

Schmitt, Dave N., and Charles D. Zeier. 1993. Not by Bones Alone: Exploring Household Composition and Socioeconomic Status in an Isolated Historic Mining Community. *Historical Archaeology* 27 (4): 20–38.

Schruers, Eric J. 2002. John Willard Raught, Corwin Knapp Linson, and Stephen Crane: Picturing the Pennsylvania Coal Industry in Word and Image. *IA: Journal of the Society for Industrial Archeology* 28 (1): 33–42.

Scott, Shauna. 1995. *Two Sides to Everything: The Cultural Construction of Class Consciousness in Harlan, Kentucky*. Albany, N.Y.: State University of New York Press.

Seely, Bruce E., and Patrick E. Martin. 2006. A Doctoral Program in Industrial Heritage and Archeology at Michigan Tech. *CRM: The Journal of Heritage Stewardship* 3 (1): 24–35.

Selso, Karen A., Richard R. Burky, Donna L. Kirner, Judith E. Thomas, John R. Southon, and R. E. Taylor. 2000. Late Prehistoric Petroleum Collection in Pennsylvania: Radiocarbon Evidence. *American Antiquity* 65 (4): 749–55.

Shackel, Paul A. 2004. Labor's Heritage: Remembering the American Industrial Landscape. *Historical Archaeology* 38 (4): 44–58.

———. 2009. *The Archaeology of American Labor and Working-Class Life*. Gainesville: University Press of Florida.

———. 2013. Changing the Past for the Present and the Future. *Historical Archaeology* 47 (3): 1–11.

Shackel, Paul A., and Michael Roller. 2012. The Gilded Age Wasn't So Gilded in the Anthracite Region of Pennsylvania. *International Journal of Historical Archaeology* 16 (4): 761–75.

Shelley, Percy Bysshe. 1819. "Sonnet: Ozymandias." In *Rosalind and Helen, A Modern Eclogue; with Other Poems*. London: C. and J. Ollier.

Shinn, Charles H. 1885. *Mining Camps: A Study in American Frontier Government*. New York: Charles Scribner's Sons.

Shipley, Rosalind. 2008. The Town That Photography Built: Images from the Consolidated Coal Company Photograph Collection, 1911–1946. *IA: Journal of the Society for Industrial Archeology* 34 (1–2): 87–100.

Shovers, Brian. 2004. The Old Works Golf Course, Anaconda, Montana. *Montana: The Magazine of Western History* 54 (3): 64–70.

Simmons, Alexy. 1989. *Red Light Ladies: Settlement Patterns and Material Culture on the Mining Frontier*. Anthropology Northwest 4. Corvallis: Oregon State University.

Sisson, David A. 1993. Archaeological Evidence of Chinese Use along the Lower Salmon River, Idaho. In Wegars, *Hidden Heritage*, 33–63.

Skaggs, Jimmy M. 1994. *The Great Guano Rush: Entrepreneurs and American Overseas Expansion*. New York: St. Martin's Press.

Smith, Duane. 1967. *Rocky Mountain Mining Camps: The Urban Frontier*. Boulder: University Press of Colorado.

———. 1987. *Mining America: The Industry and the Environment, 1800–1980*. Lawrence: University Press of Kansas.

Smith, Howard L. 1997. *Nome River Water Control Structures*. BLM-Alaska Open File Report 62. Anchorage: U.S. Department of the Interior, Bureau of Land Management.

Smith, Jessica L. K. 2006. A Land of Plenty: Depression-Era Mining and Landscape Capital in the Mojave Desert, California. PhD dissertation, University of Nevada, Reno.

Snipp, Matthew. 1986a. The Changing Political and Economic Status of American Indians: From Captive Nations to Internal Colonies. *American Journal of Economics and Sociology* 45 (2): 142–57.

———. 1986b. American Indians and Natural Resource Development: Indigenous Peoples' Land, Now Sought After, Has Produced New Indian-White Problems. *American Journal of Economics and Sociology* 45 (4): 457–74.

South, Stanley. 1977. *Method and Theory in Historical Archaeology*. New York: Academic Press.

Spence, Clark C. 1958. *British Investments and the American Mining Frontier, 1860–1901*. Ithaca, N.Y.: Cornell University Press.

———. 1970. *Mining Engineers and the American West: The Lace Boot Brigade*. New Haven, Conn.: Yale University Press.

Spencer, Jennifer Kathleen. 1994. Site Abandonment Behavior for the Mining Town of Garnet, Montana. MA thesis, University of Montana.

Spivey, Justin M., Helena Merryman, Kent Diebolt, and Ronald W. Anthony. 2005. Investigation of the Construction of a 19th Century Wooden Flume Suspended on a Cliff. In *Conservation of Historic Wooden Structures: Proceedings of the International Conference (Florence 22–27 February, 2005)*, edited by Gennaro Tampone, 229–36. Tuscany: Alter Ego Ing Arch.

Sportman, Sarah P. 2011. Halcyon Days: The Historical Archaeology of Community and Identity at Hammondville, New York, 1870–1900. PhD dissertation, University of Connecticut.

Spude, Catherine. 2005. Brothels and Saloons: An Archaeology of Gender in the American West. *Historical Archaeology* 39 (1): 89–106.

Spude, Catherine Holder, Robin O. Mills, Karl Gurcke, and Roderick Sprague, eds. 2011. *Eldorado! The Archaeology of Gold Mining in the Far North*. Lincoln: University of Nebraska Press.

Spude, Robert L. S. 1990a. Introduction. In Barker and Huston, *Death Valley to Deadwood*, 3–7.

———. 1990b. Mining Technology and the National Register. In Barker and Huston, *Death Valley to Deadwood*, 31–38.

———. 2005. The Arizona Photographic Company and the Mine Promotion Game. *Mining History Journal* 12: 52–66.

———. 2011. An Overview History of the Alaska-Yukon Gold Rushes, 1880–1918. In *Eldorado! The Archaeology of Gold Mining in the Far North*, edited by Catherine Holder Spude, Robin O. Mills, Karl Gurcke, and Roderick Sprague, 9–24. Lincoln: University of Nebraska Press.

Spude, Robert L. S., and Sandra McDermott Faulkner. 1987. *Kennecott, Alaska*. Anchorage: National Park Service, Alaska Region.

Stapp, Darby C. 1990. The Historic Ethnography of a Chinese Mining Community in Idaho. PhD dissertation, University of Pennsylvania.

Staski, Edward. 1993. The Overseas Chinese in El Paso: Changing Goals, Changing Realities. In Wegars, *Hidden Heritage*, 125–49.

Staudenmaier, John M. 1985. *Technology's Storytellers: Reweaving the Human Fabric*. Cambridge, Mass.: MIT Press.

Steeves, Laban Richard. 1984. Chinese Gold Miners of Northeastern Oregon, 1862–1900. MS thesis, University of Oregon.

Steffen, Jerome O. 1980. *Comparative Frontiers: A Proposal for Studying the American West*. Norman: University of Oklahoma Press.

Stern, Gerald M. 2008. *The Buffalo Creek Disaster*. New York: Vintage Books.

Stevenson, Marc G. 1982. Toward an Understanding of Site Abandonment Behavior: Evidence from Historic Mining Camps in the Southwest Yukon. *Journal of Anthropological Archaeology* 1: 237–65.

———. 1989. Sourdoughs and Cheechakoos: The Formation of Identity Signaling Social Groups. *Journal of Anthropological Archaeology* 8: 270–312.

Street, Franklin. 1851. *California in 1850, Compared with What It Was in 1849, with a Glimpse at Its Future Destiny*. Cincinnati: R. E. Edwards and Company.

Sweitz, Sam R. 2012. Consumer Strategy and Household Consumption in the Cripple

Creek Mining District, Colorado, USA. *International Journal of Historical Archaeology* 16: 227–66.

Switzer, Ronald R. 2013. *The Steamboat* Bertrand *and Missouri River Commerce.* Norman, Okla.: Arthur H. Clark.

Taggart, Arthur F. 1927. *Handbook of Ore Dressing.* New York: John Wiley and Sons.

———. 1947. Seventy-Five Years of Progress in Ore Dressing. In Parsons, *Seventy-Five Years of Progress,* 82–125.

Taussig, Michael T. 1980. *The Devil and Commodity Fetishism in South America.* Chapel Hill: University of North Carolina Press.

Tays, E. A. H. 1907. Present Labor Conditions in Mexico. *Engineering and Mining Journal* 84 (14): 621–24.

Teague, George A. 1987. The Archaeology of Industry in North America. PhD dissertation, University of Arizona.

Teague, George A., and Lynette O. Shenk. 1977. *Excavations at Harmony Borax Works.* Western Archaeological Center Publications in Anthropology 6. Washington, D.C.: National Park Service.

Terry, Paula B., and Allen G. Pastron. 1990. Chinese Export Porcelain in Gold Rush San Francisco. In Pastron and Hattori, *Hoff Store Site and Gold Rush Merchandise,* 75–81.

Thompson, Judy Ann. 1992. Historical Archaeology in Virginia City, Nevada: A Case Study of the 90-H Block. MA thesis, University of Nevada, Reno.

Thrush, Paul, and U.S. Bureau of Mines Staff, ed. 1968. *A Dictionary of Mining, Mineral, and Related Terms.* Washington, D.C.: Government Printing Office.

Thurlo, Margaret Anne. 2010. Masculine Domesticity in the Mining West: An Archaeological Investigation at Coloma Ghost Town. MA thesis, University of Montana.

Tintori, Karen. 2002. *Trapped: The 1909 Cherry Mine Disaster.* New York: Atria Books.

Toll, David W. 1972. In the Matter of Certain Ghost Towns. *Westways* (April): 18–74.

Tordoff, Judy. 2004. *The Evolution of California's Placer Mining Landscape: A View from Prairie City.* Sacramento: California Department of Transport.

Toulouse, Julian. 1970. High off the Hawg: Or How the Western Miner Lived, as Told by the Bottles He Left Behind. *Historical Archaeology* 4: 59–69.

Trennert, Robert A. 2001. *Riding the High Wire: Aerial Mine Tramways in the West.* Boulder: University of Colorado Press.

Trigger, Bruce G. 1993. Marxism in Contemporary Western Archaeology. *Archaeological Method and Theory* 5: 159–200.

Trinkley, Michael. 1986. *Archaeological Investigations at the Reed Gold Mine Engine Mill House (31CA18**1), Reed Gold Mine State Historic Site, Cabarrus County, North Carolina.* Research Series 6. Columbia, S.C.: Chicora Foundation.

———. 1988. *Additional Investigations at the Reed Gold Mine Engine Mill House, Reed Gold Mine State Historic Site, Cabarrus County, North Carolina, 31CA18**1.* Research Series 12. Columbia, S.C.: Chicora Foundation.

Turnbaugh, Sarah Peabody. 1983. 17th and 18th Century Lead-Glazed Redwares in the Massachusetts Bay Colony. *Historical Archaeology* 17 (1): 3–17.

Twain, Mark. (1872) 1996. *Roughing It.* New York: Oxford University Press.

Twitty, Eric Roy. 2001. *Blown to Bits in the Mine: A History of Mining and Explosives in the United States*. Ouray, Colo.: Western Reflections Publishing.

———. 2002. *Riches to Rust: A Guide to Mining in the Old West*. Montrose, Colo.: Western Reflections Publishing.

U.S. BLM (Bureau of Land Management). 2013. *Abandoned Mine Lands: "A New Legacy."* www.blm.gov/wo/st/en/prog/more/Abandoned_Mine_Lands/AML_Publications.html.

U.S. Bureau of the Census. 1872. *The Statistics of the Wealth and Industry of the United States Embracing the Tables of Wealth, Taxation, and Public Indebtedness: of Agriculture; Manufacturers; Mining; and the Fisheries*. Ninth Census, vol. 3. Washington, D.C.: Government Printing Office.

U.S. Coal Commission. 1925. *Report of the United States Coal Commission*. 5 vols. Washington, D.C.: Government Printing Office.

U.S. EPA (U.S. Environmental Protection Agency, Abandoned Mine Lands Team). 2004. *Reference Notebook*. www.epa.gov/aml/tech/amlref.pdf.

U.S.G.S. (U.S. Geological Survey). 2005. *Mineral Resource Data System*. Edition 20120127. Reston, Va.: U.S. Geological Survey.

U.S. National Park Service. 1938. *Death Valley Guide*. Brochures, D36865, Death Valley National Park Archives, Death Valley, Calif.

U.S. Senate Committee on Indian Affairs. 1934. *Hearing Before the Committee on Indian Affairs, United States Senate, 73rd Congress, 2nd Session on S. J. Res. 95: A Joint Resolution Restoring Lands of the Papago Indian Reservation in Arizona to Exploration and Location under the Public Land Mining Laws, April 24, 1934*. Washington, D.C.: Government Printing Office.

Valentine, David W. 1999. Historical and Archaeological Investigations at 26PE2137: American Canyon, Pershing County, Nevada. MA thesis, University of Nevada, Las Vegas.

———. 2002. Chinese Placer Mining in the United States: An Example from American Canyon, Nevada. In *The Chinese in America: A History from Gold Mountain to the New Millennium*, edited by Susie Lan Cassel, 37–53. Walnut Creek, Calif.: AltaMira.

———. 2003. Blue Goose Conundrums. *In-Situ: Newsletter of the Nevada Archaeological Association* 7 (2): 8–12.

Van Bueren, Thad M. 2004. The Poor Man's Mill: A Rich Vernacular Legacy. *IA: Journal of the Society for Industrial Archeology* 30 (2): 5–23.

Van Der Merwe, A. E., M. Steyn, and E. N. L'Abbé. 2010a. Trauma and Amputations in 19th Century Miners from Kimberley, South Africa. *International Journal of Osteoarchaeology* 20: 291–306.

Van Der Merwe, A. E., M. Steyn, and G. J. R. Maat. 2010b. Adult Scurvy in Skeletal Remains of Late 19th Century Mineworkers in Kimberley, South Africa. *International Journal of Osteoarchaeology* 20: 307–16.

———. 2011. Dental Health of 19th Century Migrant Mineworkers from Kimberley, South Africa. *International Journal of Osteoarchaeology* 21: 379–90.

Vendl, Karen, and Mark Vendl. 2001. The Mines and Mining Building of the World's Columbian Exposition, 1893: A Photographic Essay. *Mining History Journal* 8: 30–41.

Vermeer, Andrea C. 2006. Making the West: Approaches to the Archaeology of Prostitution on the 19th-Century Mining Frontier. PhD dissertation, University of Arizona.

Vogel, Robert M. 1969. On the *Real* Meaning of Industrial Archaeology. *Historical Archaeology* 3: 87–93.

Voss, Barbara L., and Rebecca Allen. 2008. Overseas Chinese Archaeology: Historical Foundations, Current Reflections, and New Directions. *Historical Archaeology* 42 (3) 5–28.

Walker, Mark. 2003. The Ludlow Massacre: Class, Warfare, and Historical Memory in Southern Colorado. *Historical Archaeology* 37 (3): 66–80.

Wallace, William J. 1999. Franklin Fenenga and California Archaeology (1917–1994). *Journal of California and Great Basin Anthropology* 21 (1): 2–5.

Wallerstein, Immanuel M. 1974. *The Modern World System*. New York: Academic Press.

Warshall, Peter. 2002. Tilth and Technology: The Industrial Redesign of Our Nation's Soils. In *The Fatal Harvest Reader: The Tragedy of Industrial Agriculture*, edited by Andrew Kimbrell, 167–80. Washington, D.C.: Island Press.

Wegars, Priscilla. 1991. The History and Archaeology of the Chinese in Northern Idaho, 1880 through 1910. PhD dissertation, University of Idaho.

———, ed. 1993. *Hidden Heritage: Historical Archaeology of the Overseas Chinese*. Amityville, N.Y.: Baywood.

Weigand, Phil C., and Garman Harbottle. 1993. The Role of Turquoises in the Ancient Mesoamerican Trade Structure. In *The American Southwest and Mesoamerica: Systems of Prehistoric Exchange*, edited by Jonathon E. Ericson and Timothy G. Baugh, 159–78. New York: Plenum Press.

Wells, William V. 1863. The Quicksilver Mines of New Almaden, California. *Harper's Magazine* 27 (157): 25–41.

West, Elliott. 1979. *The Saloon on the Rocky Mountain Mining Frontier*. Lincoln: University of Nebraska Press.

———. 1982. Five Idaho Mining Towns: A Computer Profile. *Pacific Northwesterly Quarterly* 73 (3): 108–20.

Wheeler, Candace. 2008. The Comstock Cemeteries: Changing Landscapes of Death. MA thesis, University of Nevada, Reno.

White, Paul J. 2003. Heads, Tails, and Decisions In-Between: The Archaeology of Mining Wastes. *IA: Journal of the Society for Industrial Archeology* 29 (2): 47–66.

———. 2006. Troubled Waters: Timbisha Shoshone, Miners, and Dispossession at Warm Spring. *IA: Journal of the Society for Industrial Archeology* 32 (1): 4–24.

———. 2008. Chuckwalla and the Belligerent Burro: Timbisha Shoshone, Miners, and the Footprints of Dispossession in the Panamints. PhD dissertation, Brown University.

———. 2010. The Rise and Fall of the California Stamp: Historical and Archaeological Perspectives on the Aging of a Technology. *IA: Journal of the Society for Industrial Archeology* 36 (1): 64–83.

———. 2016. The Archaeology of Underground Mining Landscapes. *Historical Archaeology* 50 (1): 154–68.

White, Richard. 1991. *"It's Your Misfortune and None of My Own": A New History of the American West*. Norman: University of Oklahoma Press.

White, William G., and Ronald M. James. 1991. Little Rathole on the Big Bonanza: Historical and Archaeological Assessment of an Underground Resource. Report submitted to Nevada State Historic Preservation Office, Carson City, Nevada.

Williams, Harold D. 1993. *The Georgia Gold Rush: Twenty-Niners, Cherokees, and Gold Fever*. Columbia: University of South Carolina Press.

Wolf, Frederick, Bruce Finnie, and Linda Gibson. 2008. Cornish Miners in California: 150 Years of a Unique Sociotechnical System. *Journal of Management History* 14 (2): 144–60.

Wolle, Muriel S. 1953. *The Bonanza Trail: Ghost Towns and Mining Camps of the West*. Bloomington: Indiana University Press.

Wood, Margaret C. 2002. "Fighting for Our Homes": An Archaeology of Women's Domestic Labor and Social Change in a Working-Class, Coal Mining Community, 1900–1930. PhD dissertation, Syracuse University.

Woods, Daniel B. 1851. *Sixteen Months at the Gold Diggings*. New York: Harper and Brothers.

Woods, Josephine Hoeppner. 1935. *High Spots in the Andes: Peruvian Letters of a Mining Engineer's Wife*. New York: G. P. Putnam's Sons.

World Bank Institute, GEI Program. 2014. Public Perceptions Survey on Extractive Industries. www.surveyextractives.com/extractives/gei-extractives-summary-findings.pdf.

Wurst, LouAnn. 2006. A Class All Its Own: Explorations of Class Formation and Conflict. In *Historical Archaeology*, edited by Martin Hall and Stephen W. Silliman, 190–208. Oxford, U.K.: Blackwell.

Wylie, Jerry, and Richard E. Fike. 1993. Chinese Opium Smoking Techniques and Paraphernalia. In Wegars, *Hidden Heritage*, 255–303.

Wyman, Mark. 1979. *Hard Rock Epic: Western Miners and the Industrial Revolution, 1860–1910*. Berkeley: University of California Press.

Yergin, Daniel. 1991. *The Prize: The Epic Quest for Oil, Money, and Power*. New York: Simon and Schuster.

Young, Otis E. 1970. *Western Mining: An Informal Account of Precious-Metals Prospecting, Placering, Lode Mining, and Milling on the American Frontier from Spanish Times to 1893*. Norman: University of Oklahoma Press.

Zanjani, Sally S. 1990. To Die in Goldfield: Mortality in the Last Boomtown on the Mining Frontier. *Western Historical Quarterly* 21 (1): 47–69.

———. 1997. *A Mine of Her Own: Women Prospectors in the American West, 1850–1950*. Lincoln: University of Nebraska Press.

INDEX

PAUL J. WHITE is associate professor of anthropology at the University of Alaska Anchorage. He is the author of several publications, including articles in *Historical Archaeology* and *IA: Journal of the Society for Industrial Archeology*.

CPSIA information can be obtained
at www.ICGtesting.com
Printed in the USA
LVOW07*0405040817
543787LV00008B/174/P